INFORMATION
LITERACY
SOURCEBOOKS

Information Literacy Collaborations that Work

Edited by Trudi E. Jacobson *and* Thomas P. Mackey

Neal-Schuman Publishers, Inc.

New York   London

The New Library Series

1. Finding Common Ground: Creating the Library of the Future Without Diminishing the Library of the Past
2. Recreating the Academic Library: Breaking Virtual Ground
3. Becoming a Library Teacher
4. Teaching the New Library to Today's Users: Reaching International, Minority, Senior Citizens, Gay/Lesbian, First Generation College, At-Risk, Graduate and Returning Students, and Distance Learners
5. Designing, Building, and Teaching in the Electronic Library Classroom
6. Digital Reference Service in the New Millenium: Planning, Management, and Evaluation
7. Developing Web-Based Instruction: Planning, Designing, Managing, and Evaluating for Results
8. Motivating Students in Information Literacy Classes

Information Literacy Sourcebooks

1. Information Literacy Instruction: Theory and Practice
2. Learning to Lead and Manage Information Literacy Instruction
3. Information Literacy Instruction That Works: A Guide to Teaching by Discipline and Student Population
4. Information Literacy Collaborations that Work

Published by Neal-Schuman Publishers, Inc.
100 William Street, Suite 2004
New York, NY 10038–4512

Printed and bound in the United States of America.

The paper used in this publication meets the minimum requirements of American National Standard for Information Sciences – Permanence of Paper for Printed Library Materials, ANSI Z39.48-1992.

ISBN-13: 978-1-55570-579-4
ISBN-10: 1-55570-579-0

Library of Congress Cataloging-in-Publication Data

Information literacy collaborations that work / edited by Trudi E. Jacobson and Thomas P. Mackey.
     p. cm. — (The new library series)
    Includes index.
    ISBN 1-55570-579-0 (alk. paper)
    1. Information literacy—Study and teaching (Higher) 2. Electronic information resource literacy—Study and teaching (Higher) 3. Academic libraries—Relations with faculty and curriculum. 4. Research—Methodology—Study and teaching (Higher) 5. Library orientation for college students. I. Jacobson, Trudi. II. Mackey, Thomas P.
ZA3075.I533 2007
028.7071'1—dc22
                                                  2006035095

Dedication

The authors would like to collectively dedicate this book to their students, who have taught us so very much about teaching. They make what we do challenging, exciting, and a sheer pleasure.

To my parents, for their love of learning and their incredible patience in teaching. They have been wonderful role models. And also to John, an amazing teacher in his own right.
—Trudi Jacobson

To family and friends, for providing so many learning opportunities and life lessons in collaboration, especially to my mother for her valuable insights and ongoing encouragement, also to Steven, Dawn and Karre, Jane Ann, Mary, Jane, Jen, Dennis and John, Murphy, Bowie, Jasper, Jose, and to James for his sense of humor, optimism, and support. Also to my father for teaching us the importance of enjoying one's work.
—Tom Mackey

Contents

List of Figures

List of Appendices

Chapter 14

Series Editor's Foreword

Ask anyone working with students what their concerns are about the quality of research being done, and their answers will probably include some of the following: "Google," "random," "plagiarism," "Wikipedia," "blogging," "MySpace," "online-only," "electronic-only," and "what's easy, quick, and gotten-off-the-Web." Improved technology—and that does include Google—enables researchers to increase both the depth and breadth of their research, and therefore, presumably, the quality of that research. Ironically, some students skim the foam off the top of the oceans of materials available to them by doing a quick search of the Web rather than fully exploring richer research options. Maybe this is simply human nature; taking the path of least resistance is what many opt to do. Perhaps the many digital distractions in today's culture—cell phones, Blackberries, iPods, and the like—make it more difficult to concentrate on what's really important. But what's most alarming is the widespread number of students who are following this strategy throughout their undergraduate and graduate careers. Based on our work with students and faculty, we get the sense these numbers are growing.

If you've read this far I'm sure you already identify with these concerns because you're sufficiently interested in the issue to have picked up this book (or read an excerpt on Amazon.com). But that's precisely why all of us interested in the quality of student research need to read *Information Literacy Collaborations that Work*. Trudi Jacobson and

Thomas Mackey have identified certain basic truths (they do exist—I believe this) about research instruction and edited a book to help the rest of us work with them.

I have been excited about *Information Literacy Collaborations that Work* ever since Trudi and Tom originally proposed it because of the underlying truth defined by its premise: working closely with faculty to teach students research methods is the real key to successful library instruction and the optimal means of preparing students to become lifelong learners. Whether that means co-developing curricula and team-teaching classes or finding imaginative, collaborative ways for students to present their research or combining courses, the best teaching involves active participation by librarians and faculty members—and Trudi, Tom, and the other authors represented here obviously know this very well.

These authors have succeeded in building alliances to prepare their students for the real world, with its potential distractions as well as serendipitous discoveries. They provide just enough theory and plenty of practical advice for the rest of us to take their examples, adapt and develop them, and put them to work for us. The bottom line? We all need to read this book.

Cheryl LaGuardia
Editor, The New Library Series
and Research Librarian
Harvard University
Cambridge, Massachusetts

Foreword

As one long concerned with the practice and advancement of information literacy, I always feel joy in seeing our professional thinking evolve to higher levels of accomplishment. Nowhere is this more evident than in our move from perceiving information literacy as a library issue to our understanding of it as an educational issue that requires ongoing interaction among teachers and librarians.

It is not a new issue, but it is a crucial one. *Information Literacy Collaborations that Work* now takes its place among other important works on this important topic. One of the first, published in 2000, was *The Collaborative Imperative: Librarians and Faculty Working Together in the Information Universe* by Richard Raspa (Professor of English) and Dane Ward (Librarian). They shared a history of working together to ensure students' mastery of research skills years before collaborating on their book. Such alliances are so important to students' mastery of lifelong learning skills that they were also highlighted in a major work published in 2003 by an agency outside of librarianship, The Middle States Commission on Higher Education.

Yet, as important as the topic has always been to successful library instruction programs, the growing focus on student learning outcomes by campuses (in response to the accrediting agencies' increased demands in this area) makes such alliances of even greater importance. Moving from library instruction programs (what we teach students) to information literacy (what students can do) necessitates the integration of such learning within the learning objectives of programs and courses.

Fortunately, in the more than six years since the Raspa-Ward publication, significant progress has been made in building such alliances, and Trudi Jacobson and Tom Mackey have done an excellent job of capturing the breadth and depth of such partnerships to share with readers. The entire book practices what it preaches!

Each chapter shares the results of collaborations on the part of the authors, who offer up their experiences with enough detail to provide practical value to other faculty-librarian teams seeking to enhance their efforts to date. The editors begin each major part with a thoughtful overview providing readers with a context for each chapter. This allows, among other things, clues as to points-of-interest to readers even when there is not a direct match on type of academic program or subject. For the faculty and librarians wishing to think more deeply to advance their understanding of the important underpinnings of information literacy programs, the thoughtful "key strategies" at the end of the overview sections will be particularly helpful.

Information Literacy Collaborations that Work can be an important tool for strengthening existing faculty and librarian information literacy efforts and for promoting new alliances. Our profession has always excelled at presenting and emulating best practices, as indeed, this book facilitates. However, as important as the collective examples are, the book offers much more to those faculty and librarians who take time to be serious readers of it.

Patricia Senn Breivik
Vice President
Nehemiah Communications and
Chair Emeritus
The National Forum on Information Literacy

Preface

Collaboration is an essential dynamic in preparing students to become information literate. Librarians have known for quite some time that it is difficult, if not impossible, to advance meaningful initiatives for lifelong learning entirely on their own. They do not have enough time with students during the traditional library sessions, and despite the close connections librarians often make with students through research support in the library or by teaching in classes, they seldom can assess the outcome of their work. Information literacy encompasses so much more than just the specific skills needed to complete assignments that a full picture of student learning is not always clear.

Faculty members may be teaching their students some aspects of information literacy although they may not use this term. Some may be required to incorporate information literacy into their courses for the first time as part of a departmental or campus-wide initiative, or perhaps in response to an assessment strategy or an accreditation process. While some faculty members have an appreciation for the contribution of librarians and the valuable resources offered by libraries, they may not have had the opportunity to work in partnership with librarians, especially in co-teaching situations. It may be difficult to envision how partnerships focused on information proficiency complement a specific disciplinary perspective or how these connections motivate student learning beyond a particular course. When faculty members and librarians learn to rely on one another, the process of learning itself will be transformed. *Information Literacy Collaborations that Work* offers frontline reports of some of the most innovative ideas that are leading the way to proven programs encouraging superior student performance.

The American Library Association's (ALA) *Presidential Report on Information Literacy: Final Report (1989)* envisioned a central role for collaboration in higher education in which "teachers would work consistently with librarians, media resource people, and instructional designers . . . to ensure that student projects and explorations are challenging, interesting, and productive learning experiences . . . ." This vision involves several partnerships on campus beyond the library and ultimately influences how information literacy is defined and integrated into instructional efforts. Given the ongoing changes in technology and the evolving modes of information access and media production, these relationships are more important than ever.

All of the regional accrediting agencies have committed to focusing their assessment efforts on student learning outcomes and some of them have specifically included information literacy among the needed outcomes. For example, the Middle States Commission on Higher Education emphasizes "collaboration between professional library staff and faculty in teaching and fostering information literacy skills relevant to the curriculum" (*Characteristics of Excellence in Higher Education*, 2002). In their publication *Developing Research & Communication Skills: Guidelines for Information Literacy in the Curriculum* (2003), six key proficiencies are detailed, with the responsibility for teaching students shared between faculty members and librarians.

As Breivik (1998) points out, "The shift in focus from teaching to learning makes librarians and other information providers and instructional specialists important and necessary contributors to the learning environment" (p. 31). Partnerships enhance the ability of educators to integrate information literacy with the curriculum and to prepare institutions for successful accreditation and assessment. At the same time, students benefit from an approach that challenges them to apply information knowledge throughout their academic careers and to ultimately understand information literacy as a continuing practice of lifelong learning.

Librarians frequently make connections with faculty members to develop assignments, individual sessions, and even classes that teach students how to improve their understanding of information. They work with faculty to reinforce and build on the information literacy competencies students already possess. Faculty members also reach out to librarians for instructional support and expertise. There are many forms that such collaborations can take. While these partnerships face many challenges, we have found in the process of editing this book that a great deal of innovative work is taking place through such alliances.

Information literacy efforts are most effective when they are institutionalized, a required piece of the educational fabric. It is critical to envision information literacy instruction as an integral part of the undergraduate experience, and it is ideal to provide opportunities for graduate students to be successful at finding, using, and evaluating information. Institutionalizing information literacy also provides an incentive for faculty and librarians to work together on common goals and objectives. The successful partnerships represented in the chapters that follow will reinforce the need for cooperation and collaboration at all levels. The success of these models, along with a deep concern for institutional support and a willingness to fight for it, encourages change.

Information Literacy Collaborations that Work presents fourteen successful models from a variety of types of institutions and disciplines. The chapters are written by the key members of the collaboration: both librarians and faculty members. Each team faced different impediments and it is instructive to learn from their experiences.

While no two institutions are alike, and the situations in which librarians and faculty members find themselves differ in the details, many of the overall issues and problems are universal. We have found the collaborative models described in these chapters to be eye-opening and inventive. We have shared chapters with our colleagues who are in the disciplines (either as faculty or as subject specialist/bibliographer) and we plan to use the ideas proposed, either as is or with a bit of fine-tuning for our situation, in our own work.

We hope that you will be similarly inspired.

Book Organization

The book is divided into three parts, each tackling a different area. The first addresses information literacy in different types of academic programs: undergraduates university-wide at a research institution, first-year students in a writing program, and graduate students. The second part examines information literacy in a variety of disciplines, either in individual courses, in a major, or in a program. The third part focuses on the integration of technology into information literacy courses and programs. Each chapter gives an overview of the collaborators' goals; a literature review for those who would like to delve further into the writings in that particular area or discipline; a sense of the institutional context, and where applicable, the disciplinary perspective; a detailed description of the information literacy collaborative venture and its innovations; and an assessment of the initiative.

Part I

Part I, "Higher Education and Information Literacy Collaboration: Fostering Connections in Undergraduate Programs and Graduate Education," begins with a discussion of an expansive information literacy program to advance undergraduate research. The University of California, Berkeley, received a Mellon Foundation grant that enabled them to address the needs of undergraduates and to initiate collaborative opportunities among faculty and librarians focused on an inquiry-based learning experience for students. This program led to the redesign of over thirty courses at the undergraduate level, re-emphasizing critical thinking and student-centered research, opening dialogue among faculty and librarians as well as administrators, and re-energizing the role of the library on campus.

The next chapter explores the integration of information literacy and rhetoric/composition in a first year composition course at York College of Pennsylvania that encourages students to be informed citizens. The outcome of this interdisciplinary approach allowed students to make connections between research and writing toward the larger goal of civic engagement.

While the emphasis of information literacy is often centered on undergraduate education, the faculty-librarian team at Ursuline College reminds us that graduate students also have a pressing need for information literacy instruction. This model for collaboration led to the development of credit-bearing course for a Master Apprentice Program (MAP) on student-centered research resulting in a significant and quantifiable increase in graduate student knowledge.

Part II

Part II, "The Disciplines and Information Literacy Collaboration: Building Partnerships with the Humanities, Social Sciences, and Sciences," reviews the impact of information literacy collaboration on student learning in the disciplines represented by English literature, linguistics, Chicano and Latino studies, political science, general education science, biology, environmental studies, information studies, and education.

Authors from Kansas State University describe a collaborative triangle in a literature course, composed of faculty, librarians, and students engaged in an interconnected and collaborative process that advances and supports information literacy within a particular disciplinary context. This work resulted in improved student essays produced for the Web, enhanced student research skills that allowed for a better appreciation of library resources, and a shared vision for lifelong learning among faculty and librarians.

A Coastal Carolina initiative developed for an introductory linguistics course and now also used in a first year composition course implements an in-depth word inquiry as the vehicle to teach information literacy. This model encourages students to follow the linguistic thread of a word to gain insights about the word itself, as well as language, academic research, the world in which students live and their individual identities, in preparation for future investigations and lifelong learning.

At California State, Long Beach, a librarian and a member of the Chicano and Latino Studies Department developed an information literacy training program for faculty, with the goal that those involved in the grant-funded project would eventually enable the instructors to teach these skills on their own. This inventive approach enabled the faculty-librarian team to embed information literacy into the curriculum and to teach students a progressive and integrative approach to research and writing from the perspective of a particular discipline.

An initiative at Dickinson College explored ways to combine coursework, research, and writing for undergraduate education students. Through collaboration, the instructors incorporated a reflective dimension to a research paper assignment that provided students with insights about the research process within a specific disciplinary framework. This method increased student interest and involvement in their own learning, enhanced their awareness about the research process, and ultimately improved the quality of their research papers.

A political science professor and a librarian at the University of West Georgia worked together in an effort to integrate information literacy into a sequence of political science courses. This collaborative venture improved the information literacy competency of their students and supported the authors' hypotheses that this form of instruction is needed throughout higher education and that these proficiencies increase with experience.

At Lock Haven University a semester-long poster project was the impetus for learning a systematic approach to research methods in a biology course. This faculty-librarian team developed this model to teach students scientific concepts along with information-seeking skills. Students gained an enthusiasm for the material and for the learning process itself which led to improved problem-solving abilities and confidence in conducting research.

Students in a general education science course at Moravian College were given the opportunity to develop information literacy competencies through an innovative team-taught interdisciplinary course about pseudoscience. This course required students to maintain a journal, develop an annotated bibliography, and prepare for a final presentation. Students expanded their information and critical thinking skills and gained a better appreciation for scientific reasoning that will benefit them throughout their lives.

The information literacy collaboration at the University of Vermont involved the entire environmental studies core curriculum, including introductory, intermediate, and advanced courses. This led to the redesign of core courses and the integration of information literacy concepts into the curriculum, which increased student competencies within an interdisciplinary context.

Part III

Part III, "Technology and Information Literacy Collaboration: Creating Links through the Web, Video, Wireless, and Blogging," shifts to the influence of technology on information literacy initiatives. At Lafayette College, for example, a team of librarian-faculty authors describe measures developed within a first year experience course that challenged students' reliance on the Web for research. This approach had a significant impact on how students view the Web, providing them with a new understanding of this technology as a somewhat limited medium for academic research. It also enhanced their understanding of library resources and provided them with the critical thinking skills to analyze and evaluate information.

In a first-year writing course at York College of Pennsylvania, developmental students at William Paterson University of New Jersey had the opportunity to learn information literacy skills through a role playing assignment that was ultimately videotaped. This unique approach broadens the scope of instructional technology beyond the Web to include video presentation to motivate student learning, and to enhance their confidence as competent researchers, writers, and performers.

The editors of this book, in conjunction with another University at Albany librarian, describe collaborative sessions in an undergraduate information studies course that meets the university's information literacy general education requirement. In this closing chapter we explore the implementation of current technologies such as Web logs and wireless access to the Internet to encourage collaboration and critical thinking among students.

Adapting Ideas for Your Institution

The chapter authors are very willing to answer questions. You will find an e-mail address at the end of each biographical statement.

We hope that you will find a multitude of ideas in this volume that you might be able to launch at your institution—perhaps with students at the undergraduate or graduate level or with students in different disciplines. Our goal is that the contents of *Information Literacy Collaborations that Work* will spark an idea [0]that would be ideal for your setting. Ultimately, the varied and distinctive approaches to information literacy illustrated in this book may lead to a dialogue among faculty, librarians, and administrators about the transformative impact of collaboration on student learning.

References

American Library Association. 1989. "Presidential Committee on Information Literacy: Final Report." Retrieved May 27, 2006, from http://www.ala.org/ala/acrl/acrlpubs/whitepapers/presidential.htm.

Breivik, Patricia 1998. *Student Learning in the Information Age.* Phoenix, AZ: The Oryx Press.

Middle States Commission on Higher Education. 2002. "Characteristics of Excellence in Higher Education: Eligibility Requirements and Standards for Accreditation." Philadelphia: MSCHE.

———. 2003. "Developing Research & Communication Skills: Guidelines for Information Literacy in the Curriculum." Philadelphia: MSCHE.

Acknowledgments

We would like to thank all the faculty and librarian authors who contributed to this project. We learned so much from working with you, in conversation, through e-mail, and in editing your collaborative essays. We value your innovative approaches to teaching information literacy as well as your remarkable commitment to students and student learning.

We would also like to thank our colleagues at the University at Albany for ongoing conversations about the progress of the book. In addition, we are grateful to the University Libraries for providing such excellent resources.

We thank Michael Kelley of Neal-Schuman for his guidance through the book-publishing process and Christine O'Connor, Production Editor.

We appreciate the contribution of Cheryl LaGuardia for writing a series editor preface that situates this book within a larger framework of *The New Library Series*.

We are also grateful to Patricia Senn Breivik for providing us with such a wonderful foreword as well as such thoughtful feedback as the final draft of our preface developed.

Part I
Higher Education and Information Literacy Collaboration: Fostering Connections in Undergraduate Programs and Graduate Education

Every college and university makes its own choices about information literacy instruction and the venues through which it will offer such instruction to students. On some campuses, this decision is thoroughly discussed among key players, and the result is logical and planned. On other campuses, such an inclusive discussion has not yet taken place, and the teaching of information literacy concepts and skills occurs when librarians and faculty members work with each other on a course-by-course basis. And some institutions fall between these two categories, where instruction has found a home within particular departments or curricula, such as first-year experience programs. On a number of campuses, composition courses host units that teach information literacy skills. These courses may be required or may enroll a large percentage of first-year students, making this connection a sound one.

Frequently, information literacy initiatives, such as those just mentioned, have focused on teaching undergraduates. Graduate students are expected to enter their programs possessing these critical skills, which they learned in their undergraduate major. Sometimes it is believed that assuming graduate students need such instruction would be insulting. Both faculty and librarians have come to realize, however, that many graduate students do need to learn about the latest research tools and methods for conducting intensive research. The resources available to students in the library and online change frequently, so knowledge gained even two or three years ago will be in need of updating. Also, many graduate students fall into the category of returning students. Libraries and their offerings, as well as the methods for gathering and evaluating information, have changed dramatically since these individuals were last in school.

The three chapters in this section examine approaches for information literacy in the role of undergraduate education, both across the curriculum and in conjunction with writing, and also within graduate education.

It is often difficult to find a locus for the teaching of information literacy for undergraduates, particularly at large research universities. The University of California, Berkeley, is the site of an initiative to infuse information literacy instruction throughout the undergraduate experience as a part of a Mellon Library and Faculty Fellowship for Undergraduate Research, funded by a four-year grant. Elizabeth A. Dupuis, Christina Maslach, Cynthia D. Schrager, and Sarah McDaniel describe their efforts at Berkeley to "provide the opportunity for the campus community to meet this challenge [of integrating research skills into the curriculum] by redesigning courses across disciplines, re-energizing large enrollment courses, and enabling students to develop their information literacy and critical thinking abilities within and outside of the formal classroom." The authors provide analyses of two courses, biology and sociology, that have participated in this program.

Dominic DelliCarpini, Joel Burkholder, and Susan Campbell of York College of Pennsylvania developed a collaboration that paired information literacy and first-year writing in order to help meet the goal of producing students who are informed citizens. Through this dynamic combination, students learned how to use, interpret, and evaluate information not only in the academic area but in the civic one as well. Their partnership extends beyond the traditional model of including one or two information literacy class periods within the scope of the entire course. They linked the information literacy and the first-year writing courses in a prototype that has begun to have an impact on the general education program at the college and upon the teaching of literacies other than information.

Alice Crosetto, Polly Wilkenfeld, and Dianne Runnestrand of Ursuline College noted that many of their graduate students seemed unprepared for the requirements of research. They developed a credit-bearing course within the Master Apprenticeship Program (MAP) of the master of arts degree in education. This course was developed and is taught collaboratively. The instructors place great emphasis on flexibility and the needs of the students. Hence, this collaborative team decided to offer students specialized topics in an effort to target specific needs (e.g., plagiarism for those who were preparing to teach middle school through high school).

When developing connections across undergraduate instruction, within collaborations connecting to writing and composition, and at the graduate level, consider the following key strategies based on the chapters in this section:

- Expand partnerships with other campus academic support units, such as technology services, graduate student centers, and teaching centers, to work together to increase the impact of instructional initiatives.
- Seek grant funding to enable the development of large-scale programs.
- Offer a wide range of cross-unit assistance to faculty members who are revising their courses to incorporate information literacy elements.
- Consider linking two courses, an information literacy course and a course with an extensive writing component, so that skills learned in the two classes can bolster each other.
- Make the reasoning behind such a linkage very clear to the students—explain how they will benefit from this approach.
- Ground research instruction within a rhetorical context, with real audiences and purposes.
- Investigate opportunities to develop information literacy instruction to graduate students.
- Offer credit-bearing courses that teach critical topics while emphasizing the importance of this material to students.
- Develop and teach such a course collaboratively to best represent the respective knowledge of librarians and faculty.

The discussion of these ideas in the chapters that follow will reinforce the need to engage in collaborative information literacy ventures at the undergraduate and graduate levels. These models for innovation will also encourage librarians and faculty to establish a dialogue about ways to improve existing courses or programs, or perhaps to advance new ones.

1

Information Literacy and Undergraduate Research: Meeting the Challenge at a Large Research University

Elizabeth A. Dupuis, Associate University Librarian for Educational Initiatives and Director of Doe/Moffitt Libraries and Project Director, Mellon Library/Faculty Fellowship for Undergraduate Research
Dr. Christina Maslach, Vice Provost for Undergraduate Education, Professor of Psychology, and Co-Principal Investigator, Mellon Library/Faculty Fellowship for Undergraduate Research
Dr. Cynthia D. Schrager, Special Assistant to the Vice Provost for Undergraduate Education and Steering Committee Member, Mellon Library/Faculty Fellowship for Undergraduate Research
Sarah McDaniel, Instructional Design and Assessment Librarian, Doe/Moffitt Libraries and Assessment Consultant, Mellon Library/Faculty Fellowship for Undergraduate Research
University of California, Berkeley

Since the publication of the Boyer Commission's report, *Reinventing Undergraduate Education: A Blueprint for America's Research Universities* (1998), the higher education community has devoted special attention toward engaging undergraduate students through inquiry-based learning. Intensive capstone experiences and independent studies including substantial research projects have long been features of university curricula. Providing opportunities for all students to experience the thrill of investigation and discovery in a wide array of courses, and at various stages in their academic careers, has been a greater challenge.

As universities began to strategically leverage their research strength to improve the undergraduate teaching mission, academic libraries seized the opportunity to align themselves with the broader campus teaching priorities, to leverage the strength of their research collections, and most important, to underscore their role in cultivating the habits of mind of successful learners. Documents such as the Association of College and Research Libraries' (ACRL) "Information Literacy Competency Standards for Higher Education" (2000) and subsequent discipline-specific iterations provided frameworks for conceptualizing skills and abilities required to locate, evaluate, analyze, synthesize, and communicate findings drawn from a wide range of information sources.

This transformation of undergraduate education demanded that more attention be directed toward developing students' ability to thrive in a research-based learning environment. The institutional support needed to position and develop these skills in meaningful ways within the curriculum required a shared commitment from faculty, librarians, educational technologists, and other pedagogical experts. Models developed by liberal arts colleges provided excellent examples; however, further adaptation and exploration was needed to address characteristics particular to research universities that educate large student bodies and often lack standardized curricula or general education requirements.

At the University of California, Berkeley, a grant from the Andrew W. Mellon Foundation provided the opportunity for the campus community to meet this challenge by redesigning courses across disciplines, re-energizing large enrollment courses, and enabling students to develop their information literacy and critical thinking abilities within and outside the formal classroom. This chapter describes the campus context in which the Mellon Library/Faculty Fellowship for Undergraduate Research was created and three crucial elements of the initiative: a community of faculty dedicated to exploring new approaches for research-based learning, a library reconceived as a center of learning and instructional expertise, and academic support units committed to collaboratively providing consultative support to inform course design and implementation.

The UC Berkeley Environment

In the UC Berkeley student body of more than 23,000 undergraduates one finds an exceptional and diverse group of scholar-learners. Under the California Master Plan for Higher Education, more than 90 percent of undergraduates come from California high schools and community colleges, with the remaining students representing all states and more than 100 countries. The Berkeley student body boasts an exceptional record of academic and extracurricular achievements. Ninety-nine percent of entering freshman graduated in the top 10 percent of their high school class. In keeping with its land grant heritage, Berkeley provides an outstanding educational opportunity to students representing a wide array of economic and cultural backgrounds. Two-thirds of undergraduates have at least one parent who was born outside the United States. One-third of students are the first in their families to go to college, and about one-third are eligible for Pell grants, with family incomes typically less than $35,000. A diversity of student backgrounds, talents, and perspectives is a fundamental aspect of the educational experience.

One of the greatest attractions to campus is the high-caliber faculty. UC Berkeley's longstanding custom has been to hire outstanding faculty at the junior level and to provide them with the support to become preeminent in their chosen fields. This culture of investing in individual faculty has historically served us well, as our reputation as the leading public university attests. In the most recent National Research Council rankings, thirty-five of Berkeley's thirty-six programs placed in the top ten in their field—more than any other institution nationally. Our faculty includes seven Nobel laureates, twenty-eight MacArthur Fellows, and over 200 members of the National Academies of Sciences and of Engineering combined. However, as is common at major research universities, these markers of excellence in research and graduate education have a tendency to overshadow indicators of excellence in teaching and undergraduate education (Boyer, 1998).

The entrepreneurial energy and excellence of our faculty have contributed to a highly decentralized campus culture, which affects many aspects of campus life from governance and decision making to hiring, curriculum, and services. Academic units (colleges, schools, and departments) operate with a high degree of autonomy. An important advantage of this culture is that it recognizes and responds to the unique contexts of the various academic disciplines. Instead of a campus-wide general education curriculum, each of the five undergraduate colleges has its own lower-division curriculum and requirements. The lack of a common curriculum presents challenges for scaling educational initiatives designed to achieve particular learning objectives for all our students.

The strong culture of faculty autonomy is reflected on the course level as well. Faculty have sole ownership of their syllabi and course goals, and pedagogical innovations tend to bloom and die with the individual instructor. If an instructor ceases to teach a particular course in the curriculum, the lifespan and impact of the innovation also typically ends. While this type of approach can produce wonderful results, it can be difficult to link the many "pockets of excellence" across the UC Berkeley campus and to scale innovations to produce a more integrated university vision.

Responding to campus needs and national trends, in 2001 then chancellor Robert Berdahl created a senior administrative position charged with campus-wide oversight for undergraduate education and appointed Professor Christina Maslach to fill the role. The establishment of this position prominently signaled a new campus commitment to make undergraduate education a priority and to place it on a more equal footing with research and graduate education. For the first time, a dedicated advocate for undergraduate education had a seat on the Chancellor's Cabinet. The creation of the new vice provost position converged fortuitously with the campus's ten-year WASC accreditation cycle. The new vice provost was asked to chair the upcoming accreditation effort and to make undergraduate education the focus of the campus self-study. This process, which ultimately engaged a very broad cross-section of campus constituents including faculty, staff, and students, resulted in the development of a set of priorities and recommendations for undergraduate education that serves as a blueprint for the future.

Among the recommendations that surfaced from that effort were: these support a culture that values teaching as a core institutional value and that recognizes teaching and research as mutually enhancing, not antithetical; leverage our strength as a research university on behalf of undergraduates by promoting research-based learning and information literacy competencies in our students; rethink large-enrollment courses that will continue to be an important vehicle for delivering instruction to our undergraduates, especially in the lower division; utilize learning technologies to reduce administrative burdens, improve teaching, and enhance student learning; and promote more effective partnerships between faculty, graduate student instructors (GSIs), librarians, and other academic support staff who contribute to the instructional enterprise.

These emerging visions for undergraduate education and for a reconceived role for the UC Berkeley Library and other academic partners in undergraduate teaching and learning took place within an organizational context of shrinking resources and expanding enrollments. The challenge for the campus was to preserve what is best about the distinctive culture, which has produced and sustained our academic preeminence, while finding ways to respond to its shortcomings and inefficiencies. These administrative changes provided the necessary campus leadership that helped to create an environment conducive to experimenting with a new model for promoting undergraduate instructional innovation, setting the stage for the Mellon initiative.

Mellon Fellowship for Undergraduate Research

The Mellon Library/Faculty Fellowship for Undergraduate Research, funded as a four-year grant by the Andrew W. Mellon Foundation, encourages UC Berkeley faculty to explore creative and effective ways to engage students by integrating research skills into the classroom and the curriculum through the redesign of large-enrollment and high-impact undergraduate courses. The Fellowship begins with an intensive two-week institute held in the early summer and continues with consultations and support throughout the academic year. This initiative focuses on three key strategies: strengthening the community of faculty committed to creating undergraduate research opportunities and able to serve as change agents within the academy; illuminating the library's educational role through the development of research assignments that encourage undergraduates to utilize library collections and build information literacy and research skills; and developing models of collaboration among campus academic partners in support of instructors and instruction.

Strengthening a Community of Faculty

In addition to publicizing a general campus call for applications, for this project we also engage in strategic recruitment by identifying key departments and faculty teaching high-impact courses for personalized recruitment efforts. As part of this strategy, the vice provost for undergraduate education and the Mellon project director meet with chairs of targeted departments to gain a deeper understanding of how undergraduate research and information literacy are—and could potentially be—embedded into their curricula, and to elicit recommendations for specific courses as well as instructors who would be promising candidates for the fellowship. These discussions are particularly important given the absence of a campus-wide general education curriculum, which makes it essential to understand the undergraduate curricular context at the departmental level.

Through the deliberate selection of Faculty Fellows for this project, the vice provost consciously set out to create an inclusive community of faculty change agents who would impact a broader community of peers. All teaching faculty on the Berkeley campus—including tenure-track faculty, adjunct faculty, and lecturers from any discipline—are eligible for this year-long fellowship. The diversity of perspectives afforded by participants from various ranks, disciplines, and length of tenure at the institution is one of the hallmarks of this experience for faculty. In the institute evaluations faculty participants often emphasize their appreciation for the opportunity to develop relationships with peers across departments and express their enthusiasm for sustaining this type of peer learning community beyond the year of their fellowship.

Two instructor development models provided the foundation that informs the design of the Mellon initiative. The "peer-to-peer" model provides the opportunity for faculty to come together across department lines in forums that focus on sharing innovations. Faculty in the research university environment are accustomed to sharing research in progress with respected peers for feedback, and we have found that this approach translates equally well to course development. The inaugural event of the fellowship, an intensive two-week institute in which the faculty participants are exposed to concepts and teaching methods in support of research-based learning, emphasizes an exchange of ideas with peers and academic partners instead of formal lectures. The institute aims to create a supportive environment in which the Faculty Fellows are encouraged to experiment with new pedagogical approaches just as they experiment with new research approaches.

Similarly, the "instructor-entrepreneur" model, in which campus mini-grants are provided for individuals to develop innovations in the classroom, leverages the culture of innovation and risk taking of the research university and provides opportunities for individual faculty creativity to flourish. In addition to their personal $2,000 stipend, faculty are encouraged to apply for Innovation Funds. To obtain these funds, individual faculty members are required to co-develop proposals with another campus faculty member or academic support unit. Proposals must address an issue that will be beneficial to other courses on campus or to their departments and that contributes to the Mellon initiative's overall objectives. Innovation Fund awards of up to $9,000 have been made for a wide range of ideas, from a portable recording station that students can check out to conduct field interviews, to departmental lunches to discuss the Faculty Fellows' experiences with research-based learning.

Illuminating the Library's Instructional Role

The UC Berkeley Library, with approximately ninety librarians and 10 million volumes, registers fourth in the Association of Research Libraries' (ARL) rankings and first among public universities. Like all great research libraries, the UC Berkeley Library tradition is strongly rooted in our extensive collections, the services that support those collections, and the facilities that house those collections. Mirroring the faculty and campus culture, the library culture highly values subject specialization and "selector" or "curator" roles that reward librarians' disciplinary knowledge used to develop the library's deep collections. Many librarians, however, have less experience in the areas of instructional design, student learning, and assessment. Developing these instructional strengths, as complements to subject knowledge, within the library is crucial if the campus is to maximize the potential of research-based learning.

At the heart of the Mellon initiative is a reconceptualization of the UC Berkeley Library's role, extending the traditional focus to include an emphasis on proactively connecting our community of users to our rich print and digital collections through curricular innovation. In this model championed on campus by Patricia Iannuzzi (former associate university librarian at UC Berkeley), librarians and faculty are envisioned as partners in the effort to address challenges such as developing refined research skills among students who increasingly rely on open Internet search engines as the sole research strategy, increasing students' awareness of academic scholarship and library collections overall, and positioning information literacy and research skills in courses as appropriate to the level of student and nature of the discipline.

The Mellon initiative provides a powerful opportunity for rethinking how courses can best utilize library collections, develop research skills, and incorporate library instruction in meaningful ways. The need to develop effective and scaleable approaches for providing library support to students was amplified by the grant's focus on large-enrollment courses (those with enrollments of more than 100 students). In a traditional model, instructors request a standard library class at the start of the semester when the syllabus and assignments are already determined and revisions to those documents are necessarily restricted. In that environment, library instruction may be narrowly viewed as an introduction to a variety of resources relevant to the course content. Positioning the consultation in advance of the semester allows faculty and librarians to approach the design and implementation of the research assignment collaboratively in more creative and more holistic ways. Research assignments may take a variety of forms beyond the typical research paper. Library instruction can be developed to match the nature, format, and goals of the assignment in ways that bring the disciplinary content to life for the students, and instructional support related to library collections and research skills can be embedded in seamless ways into the course materials and the course flow. The faculty-librarian partnership provides the framework for informing the assignment design to ensure that it provides necessary prompts for that audience and is staged and implemented well during the semester.

Each year librarians involved with the Mellon initiative participate in a series of professional development events to better prepare them to support the Faculty Fellows and the students in the courses, and to collaborate effectively with staff from other academic support units. In recent years, each Library Fellow has been partnered with multiple Faculty Fellows, requiring them to broaden their individual expertise to encompass additional disciplinary areas and pedagogical approaches. Over the years the participating librarians have developed and codified good practices that are shared with all library staff and inform our approaches for other courses. Good practices have included topics such as staging library instruction activities around topic formation, using a pre-assignment as homework prior to the instruction session, and leading training sessions for graduate student instructors for large-enrollment courses.

Collaborating among Academic Partners

Campus academic support units—including the UC Berkeley Library, Office of Educational Development, Educational Technology Services, Graduate Student Instructor (GSI) Teaching and Resource Center, and American Cultures Center—share missions that emphasize support for teaching and learning, but they report administratively to different units of the organization. Historically, these academic support units addressed instructional design emphasizing their specialized expertise through a variety of successful models, though largely in isolation from one another. Faculty seeking instructional support had to call upon various units to get help redesigning a single course.

From the beginning, the Mellon initiative drew upon this diverse expertise by forming a steering committee with senior managers from each unit. Collaboration at this level was imperative for the successful initiation and development of the project, as each unit developed a richer appreciation for the multiplicity of skills and perspectives offered by their partners. Collectively, this group informed the design of the institute curricula, recommended Faculty Fellows for selection, guided decisions related to the initiative overall and, perhaps most important, committed their unit's staff and resources to support this shared project with the goal of long-term collaborative relationships. The institute was designed to utilize representatives from all academic partner units as discussion facilitators, and institute topics were intentionally framed to be most meaningful for faculty, often requiring the facilitators to cover content that pushed beyond their unit's traditional boundaries of expertise. For example, sessions about undergraduates as learners, research skills for undergraduates, and crafting and staging assignments, as well as open forums to discuss any issues related to large-enrollment courses, were most effective when informed by the expertise offered by multiple academic partner units.

The redesign of a course relies on a wide range of expertise throughout multiple phases: from the collection of ideas in the institute to the implementation of a specific research assignment during the following academic year. After the first year, the Mellon Steering Committee better understood individual Faculty Fellows' needs as they undertook this process. The framework developed for the Mellon initiative resulted in academic partners pooling their expertise to create a cross-unit, team-based approach to working with faculty. Implementation Teams (I-Teams), composed of one individual from each of the partner units, are assigned to each faculty participant to provide consultative advice and support to the faculty throughout the term of their fellowship. During that period, Faculty Fellows and their I-Teams often meet regularly to revise instructional materials, identify appropriate library collections and student research processes, discuss staging of course-related activities, plan for involving GSIs, and experiment with educational technologies planned for the course.

One of the shared goals of the Mellon grant was to focus on the assessment of student learning by experimenting with various models and collecting data on student research behaviors. Lacking a campus office that provided this type of support, the Mellon Steering Committee developed assessment expertise from current staff by inviting a librarian to take on the role of assessment consultant to work intensively with multiple faculty members each year. Because each Faculty Fellow designs a research assignment suited to unique course goals, needs of a specific group of students, and characteristics of their discipline, assessment methods are tailored for each individual course. To conduct a performance assessment of students' research skills, the assessment consultant works to ensure that key elements are present in the assignment: stated learning outcomes related to the research process, an assignment design that elicits evidence of key learning outcomes, and criteria for evaluating student performance. The experiences gained by working closely with a few courses are useful in identifying strategies for discussing assessment of student learning with faculty, as well as developing assessment models and instruments that can be applied to other courses in the future.

Course Snapshots

During the institute, Faculty Fellows begin working with their I-Team to envision the research assignment appropriate for their course. Early in the process, they articulate the nature of the assignment; identify learning outcomes relating to disciplinary content, information literacy competencies, and research methods; decide on the format of the research product students will complete; and analyze the elements needed to successfully implement that assignment. Those faculty working with the assessment consultant place additional emphasis on selecting assignment models which explicitly evidence outcomes related to the research process, outcomes which are often implicit and invisible in the traditional research paper assignment. In all cases, the final assignment and strategy for carrying it out are the products of conversations and revisions that have benefited from the expertise of multiple collaborators. This chapter provides snapshots of two courses, Chemistry 1A and Sociology 3AC, each of which incorporated a research assignment elegantly despite sizable challenges.

General Chemistry and the Poster Session

Chemistry 1A, General Chemistry, is an introductory course required of non-majors in fields such as integrative biology and earth and planetary science. Because of its significance in the three-course chemistry sequence, Chemistry 1A has a highly structured curriculum and a well-developed course Web site. With approximately 1,200 students enrolled each fall semester, the course is among the highest-impact courses in the lower-division curriculum, serving as an important "gateway" to multiple majors. To manage this large enrollment, the course is assigned two instructors; one instructor organizes the lecture component of the course and the second instructor coordinates the laboratory component and supervises the forty-five GSIs who lead the weekly laboratory sections of approximately twenty-five students each.

Prior to becoming a Mellon Fellow, the laboratory instructor, Dr. Michelle Douskey, had introduced a short assignment where students worked in pairs to apply basic chemistry concepts to real-life problems and communicate their findings in a poster session. Through the assignment, which was intended as a fun, end-of-semester activity, Dr. Douskey hoped to increase student engagement by involving them in research and scientific communication at an introductory level. As a Mellon Fellow, Dr. Douskey refined the research assignment to involve students in a structured process of scientific inquiry. The revised assignment is staged over a longer period of time and guides students more explicitly through the phases of topic selection, hypothesis development, planning a research design, gathering information, and communicating results in a poster session.

Undergraduates in the sciences have some familiarity with the poster format from participation in school science fairs. However, a review of sample student work from the pre-Mellon pilot assignment revealed some areas where students needed a clearer articulation of expectations for a university-level scientific poster. In addition to brief segments in lecture and laboratory sessions introducing the project and emphasizing the role of the poster in professional scientific communication, expectations were communicated using an analytic rubric posted on the course Web site. The new grading rubric emphasized assignment goals related to disciplinary content, information literacy, and presentation skills, and it provided detailed specifications for visual elements of the poster. To supplement these guidelines, links were provided to an online article about effective poster presentations and a scanned student project accompanied by a completed grading rubric to show how evaluation criteria were applied. The final laboratory

"Primary goals of the poster session assignment include: tie Chemistry 1A to the world around you, increase your information literacy, build and improve your presentation skills, and start thinking like a researcher. True research will attempt to answer remaining questions, suggest improvements, or suggest future research directions."

Figure 1.1   Framing the Poster Sessions

section is devoted to a poster session where the GSI and student peers circulate among the posters and evaluate the corresponding presentations in their own sections (see figure 1.1).

Because of the large number of students, the structure of the laboratory sessions, and the range of information sources required, it was impractical for librarians to provide in-person instruction. Instead, the I-Team worked with the instructor to develop two worksheets to guide students through the research process: one for hypothesis development and one for evaluation of sources. These worksheets, which are worth points as laboratory assignments, require students to document their research methods and create opportunities for the GSIs to provide feedback at key points in the research process. The I-Team also worked with the instructor to develop a Web page for the assignment that includes examples, key information resources, and short tutorials.

Dr. Douskey, in consultation with the I-Team, created a detailed schedule that incorporated all assignment-related activities, including a series of sessions to train the GSIs to facilitate the research process. The four GSI training sessions, led by staff from the library and the Graduate Student Instructor Teaching and Resource Center, provided guidance on introducing the poster assignment, locating and evaluating information sources, facilitating hypothesis development, and using the rubric to evaluate the final posters using detailed grading criteria for elements such as "application of chemical principles," "investigative methods," and "organization and communication." In addition, the analytic rubric provided a mechanism for effective and uniform grading in a large course and made it possible to collect performance data on discrete learning outcomes related to the research process.

During her year as a Mellon Fellow, Dr. Douskey worked intensively with the assessment consultant to collect and analyze data on student performance. Both the undergraduates and the GSIs were surveyed to gather information about student research skills and behaviors, as well as to make ongoing improvements to the project. While the I-Team participated in many aspects of the assignment design and implementation, Dr. Douskey retained ownership of all materials and continues to adapt them. The documents and instructional materials designed during the Fellowship allow the assignment to run smoothly as an integrated part of the course, even as GSIs and other course personnel change.

Principles of Sociology and the Research Prospectus

Sociology 3AC, Principles of Sociology, was selected for Mellon because of its placement as a large, lower-division course that fulfills the campus's American Cultures requirement, a comparative analysis of the diverse cultures in the United States and the

"This class has presented statistical evidence that documents group differences in college attendance rates. Explanations for these differences in educational achievement, however, are still debated. This research project invites you to enter this debate. Imagine that you will spend the next year inside one of Oakland's public high schools in search of answers to the following question: why are some groups of people more likely to enter and graduate from college than others?"

Figure 1.2   Framing the Research Prospectus

only campus-wide requirement for undergraduates. The course attracts large numbers of first-year students, many of whom are non-majors. Several instructors teach the course in different semesters, and while there are many commonalties among the courses, the content, size, and methods are determined by each instructor. Dr. Mary Kelsey was the second Sociology 3AC instructor to become a Mellon Fellow. Lacking GSIs and discussion sections, her class of 250 students is taught in a large lecture hall and is supported by four "readers," whose responsibilities are limited to evaluating student work.

Dr. Kelsey had not included a research assignment in previous iterations of the course, in part because of concerns about not having enough support to provide students with feedback. As a Mellon Fellow, she became committed to promoting her students' future success by developing their research skills. She wanted to design a research assignment that would place individual students' experiences in the context of larger social forces. She also believed that a research project would support departmental goals by engaging students in "public sociology," an approach to the discipline that serves to promote and inform the public debate and provides one of the primary frameworks to the teaching of sociology at UC Berkeley (see figure 1.2).

The project goals included items such as "understand how larger social forces may constrain or expand the life changes of individuals," "understand the complex role of schools in perpetuating or countering social inequality," "learn library search skills by exploring article databases," and "learn how to write a literature review as a component of research papers." After considering a variety of projects, Dr. Kelsey decided to have each student develop a research prospectus to address a particular area of inequality in an Oakland public school. Students were assigned one of four public high schools and provided with a wealth of data about the school and the community. Students organized themselves into small groups based on the theme (race, class, or gender) they were interested in researching. The peer groups provided the students with support throughout the research process, which included discussing the data, writing an initial research question, and conducting a literature review. The prospectus—consisting of introduction, literature review, research hypothesis, and research plan—was an individual assignment, for which the students turned in both a rough draft and a revised final paper.

Because this large course had no GSI-led discussion sections and a limited amount of reader labor to draw on, the I-Team focused their efforts on developing a streamlined research project that student groups could move through with a large degree of independence. Two intermediate worksheets, called Group Progress Check Sheets, provided an assignment design strategy that guided the students through the research process, evidenced the learning outcomes, and provided a mechanism for effective feedback to students at key points during the research process.

The first check sheet required students to utilize data and course readings to discuss a problem and articulate a research question. Rather than requiring these first-year students to carry out all aspects of locating, analyzing, and interpreting data, the instructor provided the data and had the students focus on analyzing that data to define a problem. This decision allowed the I-Team to focus the limited instructional support toward the literature review, the second portion of the research process, which was considered to be more appropriate for a lower-division course. Dr. Kelsey met with many groups during office hours to provide feedback as students formulated their research questions, a critical and challenging phase of the research process.

The second check sheet required each student to locate, summarize, and cite two scholarly articles relevant to their research question. To prepare students, the librarian conducted an instruction session in the lecture hall, which engaged students in practice and principles of locating and evaluating articles. Students shared the article summaries with their group members to create a pool of articles related to the research question. During a mid-semester group reading, Dr. Kelsey and the I-Team met to evaluate the students' performance on Group Progress Check Sheet 2. This evaluation provided an opportunity to identify common challenges and adjust instruction to address them with the class as a whole. Systematically gathering information on the progress of the class through formative assessments is particularly beneficial in large classes where instructors have less opportunity to consult with individual students about their research progress.

The I-Team worked with Dr. Kelsey to develop a detailed grading rubric, which was used to provide students with feedback on the draft prospectus and to grade the final versions. At the end of the semester, Dr. Kelsey and the I-Team met to evaluate sample final prospectuses using the evaluation criteria in the grading rubric, and to confer with the four readers about the research assignment. Analysis of students' progress through the check sheets to the final draft of the prospectus led to the overall agreement that the scaffolded assignment design had resulted in a higher degree of student success than would normally be expected in an introductory course. It was also noted, however, that it was challenging to offer the level of support and feedback required in a large-enrollment course without GSIs.

Evaluation and Impact

In the past three years, thirty-five faculty representing the sciences, social sciences, and humanities have participated in the Mellon initiative. Collectively they have redesigned thirty-three lower-division and upper-division courses to include research components influencing nearly 8,000 students. Through their experiences as Mellon Faculty Fellows, many faculty have been inspired to incorporate research-based learning and information literacy development into other courses they teach. In addition, through formal events and informal conversations, these faculty members continue to spark interest in research-based learning among colleagues on campus, providing a form of grassroots publicity and increased credibility for the initiative.

The initial gathering of faculty for the institute is a crucial time for introducing the philosophy and approaches related to research-based learning, suggesting models that can be tailored, and providing a venue for faculty to exchange ideas with peers and academic support partners. Of the experience, one participant said: "During the Institute, I spent an intensive period of time with colleagues deeply reflecting on the practice and art of teaching. The Fellowship experience invigorated my teaching a great deal. It was clearer to the students what I was trying to do, because it was clearer to me. I am a much better educator and, if I am a better educator, then the students are learning more and that's what we're here for." Because the faculty's reflections about their own experiences and their observations about student learning are so powerful, we chose to capture their comments through videotaped interviews. In addition to serving as a creative method to collect qualitative data from faculty, the video clips are an effective way of bringing these stories to life in a vibrant way for a broader audience.

For the UC Berkeley Library, the Mellon initiative has energized a new focus on the library's instructional role. Recently an associate university librarian position was revised to include responsibility for educational initiatives library-wide. Mirroring the success of the new campus position of vice provost for undergraduate education, this senior leadership position is designed to initiate stronger connections between various units and staff within the library in support of teaching and learning, as well as to sustain the library's involvement with other related initiatives across campus. Library instructor development programs are currently being designed to support a greater number of library staff as they explore this extension of their roles, and to ensure the ongoing evolution of the methods developed through the Mellon initiative. In 2003 the UC Berkeley Library developed the Library Prize for Undergraduate Research, which draws additional attention to undergraduate research projects that show evidence of significant inquiry using library resources and collections and reflection about research and information-gathering process itself. Survey and performance data from Mellon courses inform our understanding of students' attitudes toward research assignments, as well as their research behaviors and skills. The exploratory work related to assessment of student learning may translate into the identification of models and strategies that could be incorporated in a wider array of courses.

The collaborative models of academic support are one of the most difficult and yet crucial elements to sustain as growing campus consensus develops about the need to establish more centralized organizational structures to improve effectiveness. An important outcome of the initiative has been closer working relationships among the various units that support faculty in their teaching. One mechanism for the long-term institutionalization of the collaboration is the establishment of the Council of Academic Partners, a consortium of academic support units that includes the Mellon partners and extends to include other units on campus. The Council of Academic Partners has contributed to a number of other initiatives related to teaching and learning such as the biannual eBerkeley Symposium and the annual New Faculty Orientation. The 2005 eBerkeley Symposium—Teaching and Critical Thinking in the "Point-and-Click" Age—spotlighted several successful models from the Mellon initiative and provided an important opportunity to disseminate best practices emerging from the project to the broader campus community.

Conclusion

The Mellon Library/Faculty Fellowship for Undergraduate Research has been a watershed initiative for UC Berkeley. Over the past few years, campus energy has been effectively channeled toward key priorities for undergraduate education. Campus discussions with deans and department chairs have increased focus about the dual teaching and research missions, just as faculty who have experimented with research-based learning have become advocates for more widespread implementation. The UC Berkeley Library has garnered heightened visibility with faculty, campus administrators, and students while experiencing an increased use of library collections for undergraduate research projects. Academic support units have developed stronger relationships and deeper collaborations in support of course instructional design and faculty development.

While the benefits have been significant, the challenges that remain are equally substantial. Models for collaborative course development and partnerships need to be further refined to match the needs of a broader range of faculty than those who have been early and avid adopters. To create seamless student-centered instructional environments, successful models must continue to push the traditional boundaries of course ownership in ways that easily draw in appropriate support from other campus experts as it is needed and institutionalize course innovations across instructional personnel changes. For the greatest impact on campus, these models must continue to allow for faculty's individual creativity but provide ways for wider adoption of teaching approaches that prove effective. Increasing departmental commitment to these issues is crucial if the curriculum within many colleges is to be impacted across courses. Similarly, we need to sustain our focus on developing institutional financial resources, identifying and developing needed expertise, and creating organizational structures to ensure the development and support of teaching and learning initiatives that cross the traditional departmental and organizational silos.

Given the Berkeley campus culture, one must accept that substantive changes are likely to be slow and incremental. Although the successes of this initiative are tempered by a substantial list of remaining challenges, they give our campus reason to be inspired by this collaborative initiative thus far and provide us with the momentum to continue moving forward.

References

Association of College and Research Libraries (ACRL). 2000. "Information Literacy Competency Standards for Higher Education." American Library Association. Retrieved April 3, 2006, from http://www.ala.org/ala/acrl/acrlstandards/informationliteracycompetency.htm.

Association of College and Research Libraries (ACRL). Instruction Section. Teaching Methods Committee. 2004. "Information Literacy in the Disciplines." Retrieved April 3, 2006, from www.ala.org/ala/acrlbucket/is/projectsacrl/infolitdisciplines/.

The Boyer Commission on Educating Undergraduates in the Research University. 1998. "Reinventing Undergraduate Education: A Blueprint for America's Research Universities." Retrieved April 3, 2006, from www.naples.cc.sunysb.edu/ Pres/boyer.nsf.

University of California, Berkeley. 2002. "Educational Effectiveness Review." Retrieved April 3, 2006, from http://education.berkeley.edu/accreditation/ee_toc.html.

University of California, Berkeley. Mellon Library/Faculty Fellowship for Undergraduate Research. 2003a. "Institute Program." Retrieved April 3, 2006, from www.lib.berkeley.edu/Mellon Institute/institute.html.

———. 2003b. "Video Gallery." Retrieved April 3, 2006, from http://www.lib.berkeley.edu/ MellonInstitute/video_gallery.htm.

University of California, Berkeley Library. 2003. "The Library Prize for Undergraduate Research." Retrieved April 3, 2006, from www.lib.berkeley.edu/researchprize/.

2

Building an Informed Citizenry: Information Literacy, First-Year Writing, and the Civic Goals of Education

*Dominic DelliCarpini, Associate Professor of English/Writing Program
    Administrator, Department of English and Humanities*
Joel Burkholder, Information Literacy Coordinator, Schmidt Library
Susan Campbell, Director, Schmidt Library
York College of Pennsylvania

Among the many goals served by general education within a democratic culture, preparing citizens to base their civic deliberations upon available and reliable information is among the most crucial. As the Association of College and Research Libraries (ACRL) has noted, "The uncertain quality and expanding quantity of information pose large challenges for society" and "the sheer abundance of information will not itself create a more informed citizenry without a complementary cluster of abilities to use information effectively" (2000). For these reasons, the goals of information literacy education are not merely academic; they also envision an informed and reflective populace with the ability to locate, evaluate, and synthesize information, as well as the ability to form and communicate informed positions. And as James Madison wrote in a letter to W. T. Barry, "A popular government, without popular information or the means of acquiring it, is but a prologue to farce, or a tragedy, or perhaps both" (Madison, 1910; vol. 1: 276). In our information age, we might add another line—"without the means to interpret and evaluate that information"—to Madison's warning.[1]

First-year composition (FYC), likewise, has its roots in a rhetorical tradition that has, from Greek and Roman rhetoricians such as Isocrates and Cicero to recent composition theorists, treated the creation of good citizens as its primary role.[2] As James Berlin writes, "For democracy to function . . . citizens must actively engage in public debate, applying reading and writing practices in the service of articulating their positions and their critiques of positions of others. To have citizens who are unable to write and read for the public forum thus defeats the central purpose of democracy" (Berlin, 1992: 417).

Information literacy and FYC share not only civic goals; they also share curricular methods. As the Middle States Commission on Higher Education (MSCHE) has suggested, "Students gain critical insights about information literacy through their own production of information which is likely to be the result of some form of active learning opportunities. . . . especially as they try to formulate a response" (2002: 5). This chapter describes the ways in which the shared goals of information literacy and rhetoric/composition—and more specifically, goals that are central to encouraging more informed citizenship skills—emerged in linked courses designed to provide students with a more cohesive understanding of academic research and writing processes. The teaching and early assessments of this course not only revealed important points of contact between the disciplines of information literacy and composition studies but also suggested that a productive union between the disciplines can help to overcome a key problem identified by ACRL: that the availability of information does not automatically translate into a more informed populace. As early as 1989, the American Library Association (ALA) had articulated the fact that the knowledge of "facts" was no longer an adequate measure of students' ability to be active and productive citizens; rather, the ALA asserted that

> to any thoughtful person, it must be clear that teaching facts is a poor substitute for teaching people how to learn, i.e., giving them the skills to be able to locate, evaluate, and effectively use information for any given need. What is called for is not a new information studies curriculum but, rather, a restructuring of the learning process. (ALA, 1989)

In our collaborative efforts, it is this restructured form of learning that is given precedence.

We first overview the theoretical and historical backgrounds of the well-established information literacy program at York College and its context within the college's general education program. We then illustrate the shared disciplinary goals that informed our decision to link the information literacy course with one of our first-year writing courses. We go on to describe the practices used in these linked courses and how the synergy that developed between these courses has helped us to model for our students civically responsible treatments of information. To demonstrate the successes and further potential of this collaboration, we include excerpts from students' oral presentation materials, research portfolios, and observations on the course both immediately following its completion and later in their academic careers. The chapter concludes with a discussion of the ways that this initiative (currently part of our honors program) has begun to affect the goals of general education and the teaching of varied literacies at the college more generally.

A Genealogy of Information Literacy and First-Year Writing at York College of Pennsylvania

The library and composition faculties at York College of Pennsylvania (YCP) have worked together for decades, but the creation of a new core curriculum, including a two-credit course in information literacy (IFL 101), enhanced opportunities for collaboration and widened the scope of the library faculty's role in the college.[3] The IFL course arose from the exigencies of an information age, in which students' abilities to employ electronic information retrieval and communication lagged behind the potential for its use. Early versions of the course required the delivery of basic skills that are now taken for granted—students' abilities to access electronic information, to use e-mail, to perform basic searches, and so on. When the course was first piloted a decade ago, no such assumptions could be made; in a typical class of twenty-four, perhaps three or four would come to college with even rudimentary skills like using e-mail. That changed rapidly, forcing annual re-evaluations of the course goals, methods, and assessments to keep pace with students who were increasingly skilled in the technological aspects of information literacy. This rapid growth in computer skills, however, did not come with an equally rapid growth in higher-order abilities—locating *credible* information, evaluating that information, reasoning from that information, presenting that information coherently, and synthesizing the information with other sources and their own arguments. York College was already on the bleeding edge of these new challenges when the ACRL approved its Information Literacy Competency Standards for Higher Education on January 18, 2000. The standards asserted that successful college students should be able to do the following:

- Determine the extent of information needed
- Access the needed information effectively and efficiently
- Evaluate information and its sources critically
- Incorporate selected information into one's knowledge base
- Use information effectively to accomplish a specific purpose
- Understand the economic, legal, and social issues surrounding the use of information, and access and use information ethically and legally (ACRL, 2000)

From the start, then, ACRL envisioned the educational goals of information literacy as going beyond basic retrieval skills. The information literacy initiative at York College was likewise part of a visionary plan for liberal education that looked to higher-order activities. The new YCP mission statement, crafted by a task force and approved by the Academic Senate on May 3, 1994, articulated the following educational philosophy and student learning outcome statements for the York College general education program,

> The faculty and staff of York College seek to create an environment which encourages the intellectual, social, and physical development of students. This environment is designed to promote an appreciation of life-long learning, community service, and ethical decision making. Moreover, we are committed to helping our students gain an awareness of the interrelationships among various fields of knowledge to enhance their understanding of themselves, of others, and of our world. (York College Mission Statement)

Among the most notable features of this educational philosophy is its express commitment to two goals that go beyond that which might be narrowly defined as "academic." First, it extends the college's goals to matters beyond its classrooms—community service and ethical decision making. Second, it illustrates the college's commitment to interdisciplinarity, not only in academic incarnations ("interrelationships among various fields of knowledge") but in wider civic ideals as well ("to enhance their [students] understanding of themselves, of others, and of our world"). All undergraduates are required to complete a sequence of general education courses toward the following learning outcomes:

I.   Development of Essential Educational Abilities:

- The ability to communicate (reading, writing, listening, and speaking)
- The ability to utilize quantitative reasoning

- The ability to think critically and creatively
- The ability to conduct research and utilize information technology as a foundation for learning

II.   Development of an Expanded Foundation of Learning:

- A knowledge and appreciation of the arts and the humanities
- A knowledge of the nature of science and its methodology
- A knowledge of human behavior and the social environment
- A knowledge of our nation's historical and cultural heritage
- A knowledge of international cultures and an awareness of the global Community (York College Student Learning Outcomes)

The task force then conducted an extensive evaluation of core curricula, which included a literature review, an examination of other institutions' curricula, and faculty hearings. They brought forth a proposal for a new sixteen-credit core curriculum and asked faculty in appropriate departments to design the following courses, which were ultimately approved by the Academic Senate in 1996: Information Literacy (2 credits), English Composition (3 credits), Writing about Literature (3 credits), Critical Thinking and Problem Solving in Mathematics (3 credits), Human Communication (3 credits), and Physical Education (2 credits). However, as many colleges have learned, the existence of general education courses does not automatically translate into an interdisciplinary, liberal education. Without encouragement to make connections, students often treat general education requirements as a type of cafeteria menu whose various dishes must be sampled, rather than fathoming the "interrelationships among various fields of knowledge."[4]

As the information literacy course at York College was extending its curriculum beyond a "basic skills" approach—perhaps the simplest version of what "information literacy" means—so was the composition program expanding its charge as part of the new general education core, moving from "current traditional" pedagogy (which focuses upon surface features of student writing such as grammar, format, and error counting) to a rhetorical approach. A "rhetorical" pedagogy extends the goals of instruction beyond formulaic versions of academic writing toward greater attention to the varied and specific writing occasions used by educated, expert discourse communities.[5] This change in focus mirrored curricular movements in IFL 101 toward higher-order activities (source evaluation, integration and synthesis of sources, ethical considerations in information retrieval and use), activities that also meshed closely with the Council of Writing Program Administrators (WPA) "Outcomes Statement for First-Year Composition," adopted in April 2000—just three months after the ACRL's adoption of standards for information literacy. The Outcomes Statement reinforced developments in the discipline of composition studies, moving beyond composition's sole focus upon the production of papers whose formal characteristics conformed to standardized written English toward higher-order concerns in the two other areas:[6]

1.   "Rhetorical Knowledge," which develop students' abilities to

- Focus on a purpose
- Respond to the needs of different audiences

- Respond appropriately to different kinds of rhetorical situations
- Use conventions of format and structure appropriate to the rhetorical situation
- Adopt appropriate voice, tone, and level of formality
- Understand how genres shape reading and writing
- Write in several genres

2. "Critical Thinking, Reading, and Writing," which developed students' ability to

- Use writing and reading for inquiry, learning, thinking, and communicating
- Understand a writing assignment as a series of tasks, including finding, evaluating, analyzing, and synthesizing appropriate primary and secondary sources
- Integrate their own ideas with those of others
- Understand the relationships among language, knowledge, and power (WPA Outcomes Statement for First-Year Composition, 2001)

Thus, while reflecting current practices in their respective disciplines, each program was moving toward a common ground that recognized more complex cognitive processes required for the production of sound arguments.[7]

Many studies demonstrate that attending to higher-order cognitive abilities benefits students in both disciplines, and that each discipline suffers when the other is neglected. From the perspective of composition pedagogy, control of available information is crucial to the production of well-written arguments because with the growing amount of information available through various means, it is increasingly unlikely that a student will possess enough prior knowledge on any topic to produce a paper of significant detail and length (Davis and Winek, 1989; Tracey, 1997). Simply stated, being information literate improves an individual's ability to communicate. Barbara McKenna and John McKenna (2000), drawing upon the work of John McLaren and Suzanne Hidi, have demonstrated that "student writing is much stronger qualitatively and quantitatively when the student has sufficient knowledge of the topic" (54–55). They go on to assert that the "totality of student's knowledge about a subject . . . is the single most important factor in a student's success as an expository writer" (55). Thus, library instruction is needed to address the skills required to develop sound writing. At the same time, information literacy instructors recognize the need for elements of the writing process, from early attempts to form arguments to the "delivery" or "presentation" stage of the information literacy continuum. Students experience the full process of accessing information only when that search for information is contextualized within a project with real audiences and purposes—in other words, in a rhetorical situation. Further, when research is divorced from its rhetorical contexts, we do little to overcome weaknesses in the civic deliberations of our democracy more generally. That is, when we treat the goals of research as merely "academic"—as the demonstration of skills or the completion of tasks—we do not help students see the natural connections between their "academic" work and its implications for their role as citizens.

From *Writing about Literature* to *Writing from Literatures*: Our Linked Courses

WRT 200, Writing about Literature, is the second course in our required two-course composition sequence. The title of the course reflects a curricular compromise, a compromise designed to retain a "Literature" course in the core curriculum of the college while still focusing upon students' academic writing abilities; but from the start, the well-worn disconnect between the teaching of writing and the teaching of literature was problematic.[8] To address the academic goals of the core curriculum (which serves students of all majors) instructors were asked to use the readings in the course as a springboard for the production of student texts rather than as *belles lettres* to be analyzed by standards of traditional literary analysis. The capstone of WRT 200 is the production of a researched essay, in which students demonstrate their achievement of a key outcome for the two-course sequence—the ability to write a multi-source academic essay that integrates research findings into their own argument. After several shorter essays, in which students focus upon skills of critical reading and writing techniques, students choose a topic for further research (which emerges from the conflation of course readings and students' own disciplinary and personal interests), develop a detailed proposal for their research accompanied by a working annotated bibliography, and then develop an argument-based paper that integrates the research into their own critical perspectives. In practice, then, the course is less focused upon writing *about literature* and more upon writing *from literatures*—that is, developing arguments that demonstrate solid control of the "literature" (i.e., disciplinary texts) that surrounds any topic. As such, the success of WRT 200 students is based at least partially upon their information literacy.

Goals and Effects of the Linked Courses

Although the interdependence of writing and information literacy was certainly no revelation to us, it was increasingly clear that we had not made those connections explicit enough to our students. To bridge this disconnect, library faculty members (Professor Kimberly Donnelly, and later Professor Greg Szczyrbak[9]) and the writing program director (Dominic Delli Carpini), piloted a program that highlighted the interrelated work of the courses. Though each course remained distinct—students received credit and a grade for each—the same population of students attended each of the courses, the faculty members regularly attended each other's class, and the syllabus explicitly reflected the interdependence of the work done in each course. The librarian's role went beyond being the purveyor of skills that will be useful in other courses *someday* (as we assure our students); instead, it offered immediate and substantive techniques used while researching a topic that mattered to them on many levels: as a student, as an individual, and (we hope) as a citizen. To stress this immediacy, the two curricula were developed as parallel structures. (Even the course Web site was designed in two columns, illustrating how the two fit together.) Assignments were purposefully intertwined, with each course raising questions that could be fully answered only through the activities of the other course. For example, when students in WRT 200 were asked to develop an overview of the available research on a topic, they needed information literacy skills to find and assess the most important arguments available; at the same time, when students in IFL were asked to develop keywords for searches, conversations and writing exercises in WRT 200 were used as heuristics to uncover a wider range of key terms and approaches.

Because of its link with IFL 101, this version of WRT 200 shifted even further toward developing wider critical literacies, leaving the traditional study of literature behind rather explicitly in its syllabus: "Though 'Literature' (with a capital 'L') often refers to imaginative writing like stories, poems, and plays, 'literature' (more broadly defined) refers to the writing associated with any field. That is, psychology, biology, business, history, etc., each have a 'literature' associated with it." This version of literature focused explicitly upon students' need to consider the available information on any topic, re-defining literature as "a long record of other writers' work which can extend our own thoughts on a topic." Treating "literature" as the "writing associated with any field" encourages students, as the ACRL standards suggest, first to determine the need for in-formation, and then to move toward accessing, evaluating, and incorporating the infor-mation into its specific contexts and into an "intellectual community" whose members test the credibility of one another's work. This method also models a well-functioning "intellectual community," using class discussions, research interest groups (groups of students researching similar topics), and shared readings to, as stated on the syllabus, "help each other to think critically about the various topics we'll discuss, and to critique one another's writing. That's what makes an intellectual community: careful reading, thoughtful writing, and a willingness to push one another (gently and gracefully) to-wards the best work we can produce."

Finally, the course grounded students' research in their own academic motives. Rather than treating "civic engagement" as disconnected from the private goals of college students—the vast majority of whom attend college to move toward a profession—the course connected those motives with the cultural contexts surrounding their own pro-fessional goals. Drawing upon concepts discussed in John Dewey's pragmatism, which treat one's "occupation" as "a life's work" rather than merely a way of making a living,[10] students were invited to "use writing as a way to explore your goals as a person, as a stu-dent preparing for a profession, and as a citizen" and to "bring together your goals as an individual and your responsibilities as a citizen or the various communities to which you belong—civic, professional, and private." In this way, students were asked to see their proposed "occupations" as more than individual jobs or private goals, and instead to in-vestigate the occupations' place within the context of a wider community. What does it mean to be a biologist? A lawyer? A politician? Or a teacher? What roles do they fulfill within the larger society, and what impact do those professions have upon the wider community?[11] This rhetoric-based pedagogy changes the ways that students engage with information they find, widening what it means to be information literate. Specifically, the course asks students to consider how discursive styles reveal the underlying assump-tions, methods, and aims of a given disciplinary or professional community.

A Rhetorical Approach to Information Literacy

From a rhetorical perspective, information is always situated within its uses—and within the *ethos* (character) of the individual who uses it. Situating information retrieval, assessment, and use in this way can help librarians to demonstrate its uses to students, asking them to consider how credibility is nurtured within a written piece by projecting the *ethos* of, say, a scientist using sound empirical method or a literary critic who is grounded in careful attention to critical theory, language analysis, and close reading. This attention to *ethos* can then be transferred to expectations for student writing as they enter into a specific rhetorical situation (purpose and audience), encouraging them to consider the occasion and preferred discursive style of its audience. In this way, students are able to learn more about how researched writing in intellectual and professional communities requires their attention to the preferred methods of those communities, as well as to gain a wider understanding of how discourse communities interact with one another to comprise a polis.

The rhetorical concept of the commonplace helped students to further explore that need for coming to terms with other members of the community. Rhetorically, "commonplaces" refer not only to the core set of values, beliefs, and ideas a community holds but also to the discourses it uses to express them—discourses that shape and contain a community's beliefs. As Hendricks and Quinn (2000) have asserted, through "common access to others' views," members continuously define the important terms of their community through discussion and debate (448). To fully engage with the information they locate, students need to understand how the creation of specialized vocabularies can shape a community and identify its members. As they begin to learn those vocabularies, they can begin to imitate the language and infuse it into their own voice (LaBaugh, 1995: 29).

Traditional models, however, often neglect this attention to discursive differences. They portray research as a series of linear steps that students follow in an orderly fashion. Students receive an assignment. They choose a topic, formulate a question, and find information.[12] First, reference materials are consulted for background information. Second, catalogs are searched for relevant books. Third, periodical indexes are consulted for appropriate articles. And finally, the Web is explored for credible Web sites. When all information is gathered and evaluated, the search process is closed as the writing begins; hence, this model suggests erroneously that the writing stage is separate from the research stage. In effect, it teaches students that "research" is a simple process of gathering (devoid of serious reflection), and that writing is appropriate only to the latter stages, which focus largely on matters of form, incorporation of requisite numbers of sources, and proper citation, rather than on ongoing attention to matters of content, such as locating potential gaps in their knowledge base.

There are several problems with this model, problems that can be alleviated by explicitly linking composition and information literacy. First, traditional approaches often give students the impression that a journey through each of the major information formats yields a definitive answer to the research question. It does not assume that information discovered will present contradictory perspectives, perspectives that force students to pursue new leads—in other words, the research question is treated as permanent and unchanging. This "one size fits all" approach instructs students on idealized mechanics for searching a particular tool, but it does not help them to recognize that all research questions (and attempts to answer them) are different. Without a context, students often predetermine a thesis and attempt to make all information fit it, pursuing a path of least resistance and using sources that are readily available to meet requirements, rather than choosing sources that are the best for the project (Tracey, 1997: 2). It also assumes students already understand the importance of this connection between the question and the tool (Gibson, 1995: 60). It was these problems we sought to alleviate by focusing upon the often-neglected intermediate stages of mature research.

Discovering Shared Goals: Synergy and Development of the Collaborative Model

The process of planning and delivering the linked courses revealed a rich new space between our disciplines, a space that offers promise for both academic and civic purposes. In composition, the focus had been upon continually asking rhetorically based questions: Who is the primary audience and what information do they need? What information do I need to make my case? What genres will be best suited to presenting information to my audience? From the librarian's perspective, research had focused on critical elements of information retrieval (such as the use of keywords and synonyms) and evaluation, practical skills designed to help students target information that is at once credible and relevant to the research. To bring these approaches together, we first considered the possibility that IFL could act as a laboratory component, where students could carry out the research assigned in WRT 200. But it did not take long to recognize the flaws in this simplistic approach; that type of superficial linkage did little to overcome the serious shortcomings of each course's approach to research. Left as separate processes, the version of research taught in each course ignored many of the complex cognitive strategies that inform actual research: that success in research is defined by the rhetorical goals established in the question, that the question itself frequently changes as we perform research, that success in research is not determined by some predetermined number of resources collected, and that research is anything but linear. It became increasingly clear that our individual courses did not provide students with realistic perspectives on research—perspectives that are often at odds with more regimented methods of scholastic research learned in secondary education. Simply linking two courses that kept to their disciplinary business-as-usual would not get the job done.

As our course planning proceeded, curricular discussions focused largely upon alleviating the problems outlined above, and from those discussions, our central goal emerged—helping students understand how *scholastic* research can become truly *scholarly* and *civically responsible* research. Helping students to this more complex understanding of a "research question" quickly became the linchpin of our collaborative course, as well as its central contribution to the preparation of more reflective citizens.

What has emerged instead are, in effect, two new courses, each of which is more in keeping with the recursive, often messy stages of researched writing that we want students to encounter. After all, we concluded, if students take the time to investigate a topic's background knowledge, they will discover (as we do) that not every question is worth asking—something only an in-depth investigation of the literature can reveal. As Kirscht asserts, the "function of research is to provide better questions . . . not final answers" (1996: 14). A large body of research suggests that mature information literacy requires experience with the recursive process of searching and re-searching the available literature (Mellon, 1984). Rather than present research as a linear and seamless process of steps, our course design forces students to move through their research in varied sequences, often involving them in more than one stage at the same time, and reminding students that research does not merely *precede* writing but circulates back and forth with it. To highlight the spiraling, rather than linear, nature of the process, students are required

- to formulate a research question that was related to their proposed major area of study or professional aspirations, but that also was of interest to the wider public;
- to write first an initial, and then an increasingly more developed, research proposal with an accompanying annotated bibliography,[13]
- to develop a progress report that details how their question has changed over time and how their research has responded to those changes;
- to present their research findings and initial conclusions to the class orally, using PowerPoint or other visual aids, and to respond to feedback on their report;
- to produce a researched essay that is responsive to the feedback they received during conferences with both faculty members and the oral presentation.

These assignments—along with classroom exercises accompanying them—encourage students to continually revise their questions, to pursue new and promising leads, and to search new keywords as they are discovered—something that happens only when the research processes of information literacy are linked intimately with a series of written and oral performances. In this way, students learn that the act of writing, rather than being just an endgame, *continuously* reveals the need for more information, different information, and better information. At the same time, these written and oral performances become testing grounds, improving the student's "ability to use the literature . . . and the student's talent for writing clearly" (Kohl and Wilson, 1986: 210). This design enacts rhetorical processes of research and writing that are evident in both the WPA Outcomes Statement and the ACRL's Standards for Information Literacy. Specifically, it requires students to continuously ask "what information is needed" as they develop their research proposals, to access and evaluate the most pertinent information as they prepare the annotated bibliography, to synthesize that information within their own "knowledge base" in written and oral progress reports, and to put that information to use "to accomplish a specific purpose."

To reinforce connections between this "messy" research and its uses for civic participation, students were asked to write about public issues related to their proposed majors, disciplines, and future professions—questions that would involve them in learning about the discourses of their field as well as their relation to the wider polis.[14] So an engineering major used disciplinary knowledge to examine the conspiracy theories about whether it was a plane or a missile that struck the Pentagon; one prospective teacher examined public discussions about year-round schooling and another the debate about the growing number of home-schooled children; and a political science major investigated issues related to academic freedom, examining in depth the Ward Churchill case; and so forth.[15]

But such examinations, if kept between student and teacher, still lack the public performances necessary to help students become active participants in civic discourses. To simulate what the oratorical tradition calls the "delivery" stage, and drawing upon knowledge of contemporary information technology provided by the library faculty, we asked students to "go public" in two ways: in a Web-based research site and in an oral report using visual technologies.

Web-Based Research Portfolios: Information Management, Multi-modal Composing, and the Public Sphere

To highlight the public nature of research, we ask students to develop electronic research portfolios, an innovation added to the course in 2004 that reflects both disciplines' increasing interests in moving beyond paper-based media. The library faculty member provides students with a basic introduction to WYSIWYG (What You See Is What You Get) tools for Web site building (though an increasing number of students are now coming to the course with advanced HTML skills). Each student then develops a Web site that becomes, in effect, a flexible and public record of his or her research activities. The sites are used for a number of purposes. On the most basic level, they are a temporal and spatial record of each student's work in the course, a location to collect formal and informal writing assignments and to share them with the teacher and fellow students. But students are also encouraged to use the site as a location to reflect upon research—to store and annotate information, try out arguments, and develop writing skills.

The electronic format allows students to establish a personal, interactive relationship with information sources, perhaps because those sites share an (albeit small) corner of the cyberspace with many of their information sources. Their online work, rather than existing in an isolated classroom space, is *public*; as seen in figures 2.1 and 2.2, it quite explicitly reaches out to its audience on its welcome pages and through the selection of images, art, writings, and links that define the students' *ethos*.

Since these sites include both scholarly efforts and other, more personal forms of expression, the boundary between the personal and the academic is not as sharp as it might have been otherwise. Internal links ask students to arrange the site into a reasonable and coherent depiction of its author and his or her work; but the site is also *connected* to the wider public through external links to the Internet and the library subscription services, making that which is "out there" part of that author's *ethos* and knowledge base as well (see figure 2.3). In this way, students gain rudimentary experience with public dialogue, and they do so in an increasingly important form: electronic media.

To further enhance the public nature of this work, students are encouraged to consider this site an ongoing project, an electronic portfolio of resources and writings that they should maintain throughout their college years and beyond, and to share with others. Indeed, some students continued to develop their sites in subsequent years, extending these habits beyond the general education curriculum to later courses and to wider public interactions, as did the student whose work is seen in figure 2.4.[16]

Encouraging Dialogue through Oral Presentations

Another method for simulating public dialogue around students' research questions is the use of oral progress reports that ask students to summarize their research findings for the class before they write their final papers. Pausing for reflection and feedback at this

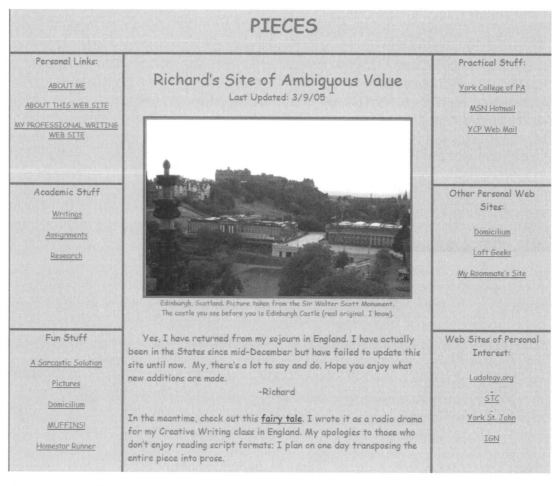

Figure 2.1   Richard Rabil's Homepage (This page illustrates how students used their Web pages to connect their personal and academic interests.)

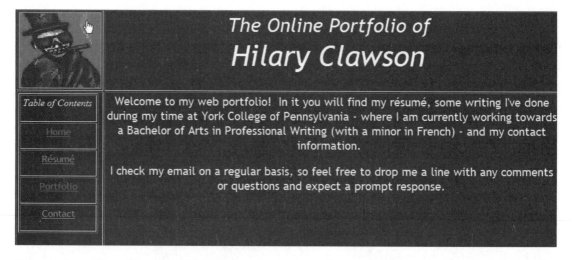

Figure 2.2   Hilary Clawson's Homepage (This page captures her personality and illustrates the use of the web portfolio to invite response and interaction on both personal and academic contents.)

Keywords: piercing, jewelry, body piercing, body modification, self expression, sociology, psychology, anthropology

Journal

Searched: www.yahoo.com

Term: "history of piercing"

Results: http://www.holejunkie.com/history.htm

http://www.body-jewellery-shop.co.uk/info/pierce_info_historyofpiercing.htm

http://www.sexscrolls.net/bodmod.html

http://www.chargerweb.org/lawson/tattoo/piercing_history.htm

http://www.fluxpiercing.co.uk/history.html

http://freespace.virgin.net/crystal.commissions/Penetrate%20Body%20Piercing/Penetrate%20Body%20Piercing/history.htm

http://www.sandydandy.com/writings/piercings/history.html

http://www.guns2roses.com/piercing_history.htm

Comments: This search turned up a ton of webpages! It was a little too vague, however, because tons of pages turned up that were not appropriate. This biggest problem here is that the webpages are not what I would refer to as "credible" pages; they are links from small piercing shops. I need to narrow my search down.

Figure 2.3   Jenny Freudenberg's Site's Research Journal (This page illustrates the ways in which external hyperlinks are blended with her research questions and keywords, and how her personal interests are tied to academic research.)

Figure 2.4   Later Development of Hilary Clawson's Web Site (This page shows how the original site blossomed into an online record of her academic coursework (in progress) in the years that followed.)

intermediate stage encourages students to treat research as a recursive process, a process that requires them to "re-search" for further information based upon audience responses. This reiterates the fact that research is neither a linear process nor one that is carried out in isolation from other voices. Students, under the pressure of presenting findings to their colleagues and teachers, are compelled to locate the most pertinent information—and ways to articulate synthesized and reflective versions of that information. Both the formal presentations and the question-and-answer periods that follow encourage higher-order critical thinking, challenging students to make sense of the information they find, to try out defenses of positions they are staking out, and—in some cases—to retrench from those positions. This helps them to see, as Isbell (1995) has noted, that "scholarly writing is a dialogue between the writer, his or her sources, and colleagues."[17]

The need to articulate their findings in an interactive setting also forces students to begin the process of organizing and synthesizing their information. Two elements of the oral presentations were particularly useful in this sense, one temporal and one visual. First, by its very nature, oral presentation is structured as a sequence of moments that need to be linked one to another by rational transitions—or risk losing the audience. In this way, the temporally based oral report forced students to think through the logical connections between various pieces of information and parts of their argument, so as to lead the listener through a logical progression of ideas. As such, a natural organization of ideas (which can also inform the later, written version) emerges as students "talk through" those ideas with a real audience—something we reinforce in our feedback.

Second, students are required to incorporate visuals—usually PowerPoint—into their oral reports. This helps students to literally *see* the shape of their argument as they play it out on the slides and consider the transitions from one point to another. Whatever the shortcomings of PowerPoint as a tool for polished oral presentation, the visual nature of the slides (and the need to arrange them logically) enhances students' ability to find a shape for their argument. Figure 2.5 illustrates the ways in which one student shaped the information she had obtained into a coherent organizational structure. This process also nurtures their abilities to use visual presentation of information effectively, another key facet of current composition techniques.[18]

Finally, from a civic perspective, these presentations helped students to work within an (albeit idealized) polis. This rhetorical moment, linking composition back to its oral roots, prepares students for the civic duty of speaking on issues from informed positions and for responding to their fellow citizens in ways that are at once reasonable and civil.

Assessing the Effects of the Linked Courses on Information and Civic Literacies

The goals of civic education, like those of research and rhetoric, are based in recursive processes that ask students to reserve judgment, to listen closely to expert arguments, and to find ways to synthesize and test information by communicating it in their own words. For students to become self-sufficient, responsible, and information literate citizens within any community, they must first find and understand what discourses it uses to express the issues and arguments it believes are important. They must also develop the ability to ask questions about the issues and arguments of the community. And finally, they

MINIMAL GROUP PARADIGM:
The Connector Between Religion and Conflict

Sara Barshinger
Honors Information Literacy
Writing About Literature
20 April 2005

What is the Minimal Group Paradigm?

❖ A sociological condition
  ➤ Group identity
  ➤ Self-image/ self esteem
  ➤ Case Study & Examples
❖ Conflict
  ➤ Intergroup conflict
  ➤ The "Us" versus "Them" ideology

Connection to Religion
❖ Division
  ➤ Religions, being different, form groups
  ➤ Minimal Group Paradigm emphasizes differences
  ➤ Religion is a part of our identity

❖ Leads to Conflict
  ➤ Theologically, religions are pacifistic (mostly)
  ➤ Historically, religions are involved in war

War's Justification
❖ Why needed?
  ➤ Dehumanize enemy
  ➤ Build moral in troops

❖ Through Religion
  ➤ Holy War against evil
❖ Through Minimal Group Paradigm
  ➤ Survival
  ➤ "We" are superior to "them"

Why does this Matter?
❖ Current Application
  ➤ Religious "Holy Wars"
  ➤ Current Iraq Conflict
  ➤ Media Attitude toward War
    ▪ Often called war against Islam (Muslims)
    ▪ Not the religion to be blamed
    ▪ We have grouped enemy

Summary
❖ Religion=One of War's Justifications
❖ Minimal Group Paradigm=reason for conflict
  ➤ Division/grouping
  ➤ Dehumanized enemy/ raise self-esteem
  ➤ Survival

❖ Questions?
  ➤ Why categorization lowers self-esteem?
  ➤ Any more?

Selected Bibliography
- Encyclopedia of Violence, Peace & Conflict. Volume 3. Academic Press, 1999.

- Hinde, Robert. "Is War a Consequence of Human Aggression?". Aggression: Biological, Developmental, and Social Perspectives. Ed. Seymour Feshbach and Jolanta Zagrodzka. New York: Plenum Press, 1997.

- Lemyre, L. and P.M. Smith. "Intergroup Relations". Journal of Personality and Social Psychology. 1985. The Blackwell Reader in Social Psychology. Ed. Miles Hewstone, Antony S.R. Manstead, and Wolfgang Stroebe. Malden, Maine: Blackwell Publishers Ltd., 1997.

- Nessan, Craig L. "Sex, Aggression, And Pain; Sociobiological Implications For Theological Anthropology". Zygon: Journal of Religion and Science. Vol. 33, no.3. Joint Publication Board of Zygon: ISSN 0591-2385, September 1998. P443-454.

- Paul, Anne Murphy. "Psychology's Own Peace Corps". Psychology Today. July/August 1998. Reprinted, "Many Factors Can Lead to War". War: Opposing Viewpoints. Pages 56-61. See Roleff.

- Roleff, Tamara L. Ed. War: Opposing Viewpoints. Publ. David L. Bender. San Diego, California: Greenhaven Press, Inc, 1999.

- Wilson, Edward O. On Human Nature. 1978. Cambridge, Massachusetts: Harvard University Press, 2001.

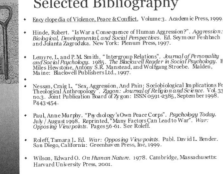

Figure 2.5   Sara Barshinger's PowerPoint Slides (This figure illustrates how students used their oral presentation and accompanying visual displays to organize their ideas into a resonable and audience-sensitive arrangement.)

must develop processes that recognize and engage with the various perspectives that are held in any given community. In these ways, the goals of academic research and those of civic action are not so separate from one another as they might first seem. Indeed, the planning and execution of this course, as demonstrated earlier, finds key points of contact between the shared intellectual activities of becoming a "good student"—that is, a student engaged in a process of inquiry based in asking pertinent questions, seeking answers and perspectives in pertinent and credible information, and processing that information through recursive writing processes. In those ways, the story is a positive one, one that demonstrates the ways that general education initiatives linking the shared and rhetorically based goals of information literacy and composition have great potential to serve the goals of civic literacy as well. But assessing the effectiveness of any writing or information literacy course, let alone a set of courses with such complex civic goals, is not an easy task. For initial assessment, we have relied largely upon student observations on the course and a survey of students who had completed the course one, two, and three years earlier.

Students reported that the intensive research they performed helped them to widen their understanding of how research can inform civic deliberations. One student with aspirations of attending law school, and who researched international law in the course, reported that "one of my criteria is a program that will allow me to further explore international law, because of the interest I gained doing my research in WRT 200." Another student reported that "I think about available information now in terms of politics—both globally and locally," while a third, a fine arts major who explored the local art community, noted that "it opened my mind to specific community issues and allowed me to make several lasting and important contacts," that "writing my paper opened my eyes to not just the art community, but also to the state of the community, particularly in York's urban areas," and that "no matter which side of an issue you choose, you must be willing to compromise with your opposition in order to solve problems." Other students reported that they had developed more critical perspectives on information, one noting that it "forced me to question information, sources, and the ways of gathering information," another that "I try to find out information from all sides of the issue before I assert my position," and a third that "I definitely have become more critical of sources and the person holding the arguments."

However, the course also revealed some deeper problems in students' predispositions toward information, toward the processes of gathering it, and toward its evaluation and use. These problems remind us of crises in civic literacy and engagement that affect the functioning of our democracy more generally. Many students tended to consider research a process of "defending" an already fixed thesis, at least at the outset of the course (and sometimes even at its end). One student noted that her research "helped to affirm her beliefs" more than question them, and another stated that finding "a lot of contrary information to my topic would only strengthen my beliefs even further." That is, students demonstrated habits of research that tended toward justifying predispositions and already fixed positions, rather than following the facts and arguments surrounding a topic where they led. In a civic environment already splintered by polemical media outlets (talk radio, news networks, Internet sites, and blogs) that have explicit and hegemonic ideological and political positions, such a research process can be especially dangerous. That version of "research," namely, finding information to support a "thesis" that really amounts to a pre-existing ideological position, defeats the spirit of liberal thought upon which informa-tion literacy and rhetorical inquiry is based. Even when students are asked to find and ad-dress "counterarguments," a common requirement of writing and information literacy projects, students often treat the activity in ways that amount to the "straw man" fallacy—a fallacy that is rampant in political discussions in the media as well.

Despite the problems of the polarized civic environs within which we work, we did find reasons to believe that our efforts were having some success. One student noted, for example, that "through this course, I learned that research and writing are compan-ion processes. Research informs thinking and writing, but when you write, you make your own argument and support it with research, instead of merely summarizing oth-ers' arguments." Many student comments also suggested that they had achieved one of our key goals (reflective thought and reserving judgments), reporting that it was only in the *late* stages of the process that they discovered what it was they were really writing about—a sign that they had truly been open to the learning involved in the research process. That is, they had come to understand that promising leads often terminate in a series of dead-ends, and that how well an individual adapts to these problems is the hallmark of a successful researcher. Of course, such moments can be frustrating to stu-dents who wish to find the shortest distance between two points; weathering those frustrations is a very real—and often difficult—part of success in using these methods.

Another measure of success has been seen through the ways that some students have continued to develop their research Web sites in the years following the course. Such sites serve as a model for ongoing, informed civic deliberations that they can carry forth into a public sphere, one that increasingly includes electronic environments. As one stu-dent reported, "I found the greatest application of the website was as a forum in which we could share our work with our classmates, but more importantly those in our lives that we chose to invite to read our work. I often send my website link to my parents and former classmates, to keep them abreast of my current studies/projects." Those who found the site useful also commented upon its technological advantages, pointing to its capabilities for hyperlinks and other communicative tools that might be added in the fu-ture. One student noted that "I was able to link websites I found helpful directly into the pages where I published my own papers," while others envisioned ways to extend their interactive nature: "I think it would be interesting if we were able to add some sort of commenting function or a blog with the websites so professors or other students could offer suggestions after reading my work."

In fact, students reported in surveys that it was the higher level and consistency of feedback of their peers that set the course apart, both through the electronic research site and even more so from the oral reports. Students noted that "being in the audience for my classmates' reports allowed me to see the many different ways of approaching a presentation," that "being able to speak to other motivated students about your topic pushes you to be exceptionally prepared and knowledgeable about your own topic," and that "it allows peers to give an assessment of the presentations" rather than "being only critiqued or questioned by those viewed as superiors or educators." Other students re-ported that the presentations were valuable to help them find useful ways to arrange the information they had found, making comments such as "I was able to establish an order for my thoughts that would help me in composing my final paper" and "It forced me to be able to articulate the arguments presented in my paper and it was a good organizational tool because I presented an outline of my paper."

Students also noted that the oral presentations helped them to develop "public speaking confidence" and the "use of PowerPoint as a tool in effective and informative speeches to either peers or superiors." Such comments, while certainly not a definitive or summative assessment, have nonetheless offered formative information that can help us to better define how we might know success when we see it.

Conclusion: Rhetoric, Information Literacy, and Civic Education

Ideally, the habits of research and communication learned in this linked course develop students' ability to investigate, evaluate, and publicly experiment with varied perspectives before drawing conclusions; this, in turn, can help to encourage them to become responsible, self-sufficient, and continuous learners—and hence, better citizens. By slowing down and articulating the full, recursive process of becoming an information literate individual—from forming questions to producing arguments based upon the fruits of their inquiry—their work becomes a pattern for future learning, as well as for future civic deliberation and action. After all, these practices not only are useful in the academy, which Dewey saw as a laboratory for civic action, but are crucial for our work in disciplines, occupations, and political action.

It is for this reason that the processes described here—which have had a great deal of success, but which also revealed a good deal of resistance toward any information that contradicts predispositions—need continuing attention in a democratic culture. We cannot expect students in the early years of their college experience to emerge from our courses with the fully developed civic literacies that come with serious academic research. To be effective, such initiatives need to be broadened, using the natural (but sometimes overlooked) connections between information literacy and rhetoric as an architectonic for a college curriculum that consistently reinforces civic imperatives, imperatives that measure successful research by its use toward forming well-reasoned positions.

Our work in this course has already inspired not only proposed changes to our first-year writing curriculum but also wider discussions about our general education curriculum among coordinators of other core course—especially Human Communication (a course in interpersonal communication) and Critical Thinking and Problem Solving (our course in mathematics and quantitative reasoning). We hope to reinforce the disciplinary connections that our curricula already share, many of which are grounded in the conventions of the rhetorical tradition—the teaching of logical fallacies, methods for group interaction and communication, and the processes of critical thinking, just to name the most obvious. Despite the fact that such components already exist in each curriculum, we have perhaps been remiss in failing to help students to see how the various forms of quantitative and qualitative research, and the various oral and written performances that are based on that research, should inform not only academic research but responsible civic decisions as well. In this way, the marriage of composition and information literacy represents a starting point from which higher education might once again take seriously its role in the formation of active and informed citizens.

Notes

1. Michael X. Delli Carpini and Scott Keeter argue against the view espoused by some political scientists that "citizens are able to make reasonably good low-information decisions, and indeed are reasonable in doing so." They instead develop the case for "the importance of a broadly and equitably informed citizenry." Melissa Comber (2005) takes this contention further, using the IEA Civic Education Study to illustrate that not only information but "the skill of interpreting political information is a cognitive skill that is important for political participation." Comber also illustrates the importance of civic communication skills, both oral and written.

2. See, for example, the work of Ellen Cushman, David Bleich, Lisa Ede, Gerard Houser, Thomas P. Miller, Susan Wells, John Schilb, James Sledd, and John Trimbur, just to name a few of the best-known recent theorists who have demonstrated links between composition and the civic goals of the rhetorical tradition.

3. At York College, there are currently seven librarians with full-time faculty status, as well as a varying number of adjunct faculty members who also teach the Information Literacy course; the course is required for all of our nearly 5,000 students as part of their core curriculum.

4. Another limiting factor for information literacy initiatives and for general education curricula more generally is a developmental one: the relative inexperience of students in the early stages of their college career. As the Middle States Commission (2002) has argued, information literacy initiatives that are limited to inexperienced students in their first two years of general education cannot "achieve fully the higher order information literacy skills, such as thinking more critically about content, pursuing even deeper lines of inquiry with more sophisticated methods" (2).

5. Defining an "educated" or "expert" voice in this way simulates the classical *trivium*, a system of education that suggests that liberal education begins from grammar (having the facts of a case) on to logic (the ability to reason and draw conclusions from those facts) to rhetoric (the ability to form good arguments based upon that reasoning).

6. The goals of current traditional rhetoric, of course, have not been wholly abandoned. The WPA Outcomes Statement includes a section on the "Knowledge of Conventions," which retains the control of "such surface features as syntax, grammar, punctuation, and spelling" as important learning goals.

7. The similarities are striking; as library instruction was moving beyond the model of "bibliographic instruction" by worksheets and library lectures, so was the writing program abandoning simplified models of composition based upon "skill and drill," the "five paragraph essay" template, and error counting.

8. The uneasy relationship between literature and composition in English departments is well documented in the literature. See, for example, Sharon Crowley's (1998) "Literature and Composition: Not Separate but Certainly Unequal," the essays in Winifred Horner's (1983) edited collection, *Composition and Literature: Bridging the Gap*, the debate between Erika Lindemann and Gary Tate (1993) on the topic, "Two Views on the Use of Literature in Composition," and the most recent collection on the topic, *Composition and/or Literature: The Ends of Education*, edited by Linda S. Bergmann and Edith M. Baker (2006).

9. We would like to acknowledge the important work in developing this course through its early years by Professors Donnelly and Szczyrbak.

10. See, for example, Dewey's discussion of occupations in *The School and Society*, 132–37, and *Democracy and Education*, 231–32.

11. This approach, based in Dewey's theories on occupations, is developed further in the course textbook, *Composing a Life's Work: Writing, Citizenship, and Your Occupation* Longman (2004).

12. See, for example, Kathleen McCormick's (1994) aptly titled "On a topic of your own choosing and with a clear position of your own, use at least seven unbiased, accurate, and authoritative sources to write a balanced and objective paper that gives a complete picture of the subject you are investigating." McCormick's hyperbolic title caricatures the oversimplified and nearly unachievable nature of many assignments in courses and textbooks, and the "contradictory advice" that such assignments often give students.

13. Our work with annotated bibliographies supports Isbell's (1995) similar findings on the value of careful, and shared, annotations of research sources.

14. As Deborah Huerta and Victoria E. McMillan (2005) have noted, students struggle with disciplinary discourses and so often are intellectually unable to access the content necessary for rich writing. Our course is designed to help students become more familiar with reading those discourses.

15. Students also wrote about other topics that related their fields of study to community issues: for example, a literary studies major wrote about textbook censorship; a fine arts major wrote about the role of the arts within a community; a psychology major wrote about media representations of obsessive-compulsive disorders; and a communications major investigated media bias.

16. As such, our use of electronic portfolios goes beyond the use of portfolios as polished products that allow for a moment of holistic assessment noted by Snavely and Wright (2003). Our use of portfolios is more in keeping with process movements. This, however, was not always the case. One student reported, "I did not feel like I could really make it *my* website, because it has to contain information for the course and it was being graded. Therefore, it lacked personality, and so I did not care about it." This comment is crucial to our understanding of the research sites' goals, as those that are richest with individual personality, those that combined the information that students located with their own personal fields of interest, were clearly the most effective in motivating students toward ongoing research.

17. As with Isbell (1995), our course is based in a social-constructionist model, articulated by Kenneth Bruffee, within which knowledge is created collaboratively through interaction among individuals.

18. Visual rhetoric has become an increasingly important area of composition studies through the work of Cynthia Selfe, David Blakesly, Lester Faigley, Dennis Lynch, Ann Wysocki, and many others.

References

American Library Association (ALA). 1989. "ALA Presidential Committee on Information Literacy: Final Report." Retrieved June 14, 2006, from http://www.ala.org/ala/acrl/acrlpubs/whitepapers/presidential.htm.

Association of College and Research Libraries (ACRL). 2000. "Information Literacy Competency Standards for Higher Education." American Library Association Retrieved November 15, 2005, from http://www.ala.org/ala/acrl/acrlstandards/informationliteracy competency.htm.

Bergmann, Linda S., and Edith M. Baker, eds. 2006. *Composition and/or Literature: The Ends of Education*. Urbana-Champaign, IL: NCTE.

Berlin, James A. 1992. "Freirean Pedagogy in the U.S.: A Response." *Journal of Advanced Composition* 12: 414–421.

Braun, M. J., and Sarah Prineas. 2002. "First-Year Composition as an Introduction to Academic Discourse." In *Strategies for Teaching in First-Year Composition*. Edited by Duane Roen. Urbana: NCTE.

Bruffee, Kenneth. 1993. *Collaborative Learning: Higher Education, Interdependence, and the Authority of Knowledge*. Baltimore: Johns Hopkins UP.

Comber, Melissa. 2005. "The Effects of Civic Education on Civic Skills." Center for Information and Research on Civic Learning and Engagement. Retrieved September 10, 2005, from www.**civic**youth.org/PopUps/FactSheets/FS_05_effects_of_**civic_education**_on_**civic**_skills .pdf.

Crowley, Sharon. 1998. *Composition in the University: Historical and Polemical Essays*. U of Pittsburgh P.

Cushman, Ellen. 1996. "The Rhetorician as an Agent of Social Change." CCC 47, no. 1 (February): 7–28.

Davis, Susan J., and Janice Winek. 1989. "Improving Expository Writing by Increasing Background Knowledge." *Journal of Reading* 33, no. 3 (December): 178–181.

Delli, Carpini, Michael, and Scott Keeter. 1997. *What Americans Know about Politics and Why It Matters*. New Haven: Yale UP.

Dewey, John. 1916. *Democracy and Education*. New York: McMillan.

———. *The School and Society*. 1943. Chicago: U of Chicago.

Elmborg, James K. 2003. "Information Literacy and Writing across the Curriculum: Sharing the Vision." *Reference Services Review* 31, no. 1: 68–80.

Gibson, Craig. 1995. "Research Skills across the Curriculum: Connections with Writing-across-the-Curriculum." In *Writing-across-the-Curriculum and the Academic Library*. Edited by J. Sheridan. Westport, CT: Greenwood Press: 55–70.

Hendricks, Monica, and Lynn Quinn. 2000. "Teaching Referencing as an Introduction to Epistemological Empowerment." *Teaching in Higher Education* 5, no. 4: 447–457.

Horner, Winifred Bryan, ed. 1983. *Composition and Literature: Bridging the Gap*. Chicago: U of Chicago P.

Huerta, Deborah, and Victoria E. McMillan. 2005. "Collaborative Instruction by Writing and Library Faculty: A Two-Tiered Approach to the Teaching of Scientific Writing." *Issues in Science and Technology Librarianship* 28. Retrieved September 1, 2005, from http://www.library .ucsb.edu/istl/00-fall/article1.html.

Isbell, Dennis. 1995. "Teaching Writing and Research as Inseparable: A Faculty-Librarian Teaching Team." *Reference Services Review* 23, no. 4: 51–62.

Kirscht, Judy. 1996. "Cross Talk: Opening Disciplinary Boundaries for Faculty and Students Alike." Presentation at the 47th Annual Meeting of the Conference on College Composition and Communication, Milwaukee, WI, March 1996.

Kohl, David. F., and Lizabeth A. Wilson. 1986. "Effectiveness of Course-Integrated Bibliographic Instruction in Improving Coursework." *RQ* 26 (Winter): 206–211.

LaBaugh, Ross. 1995. "Talking the Discourse: Composition Theory." In *Writing-Across-the-Curriculum and the Academic Library*. Edited by J. Sheridan. Westport, CT: Greenwood: 23–51.

Lindemann, Erika, and Gary Tate. 1993. "Two Views on the Use of Literature in Composition." *College English* 55 (March): 311–321.

Madison, James. 1910. *The Founders' Constitution*. Vol. 1, chap. 18, doc. 35. Chicago: U of Chicago: 276. Retrieved January 10, 2006, from http://press-pubs.uchicago.edu/founders/documents/ v1ch18s35.html.

McCormick, Kathleen. 1994. "On a topic of your own choosing and with a clear position of your own, use at least seven unbiased, accurate, and authoritative sources to write a balanced and objective paper that gives a complete picture of the subject you are investigating." In *Writing Theory and Critical Theory*. Edited by John Clifford and John Schilb. New York: MLA.

McKenna, Barbara J., and John J. McKenna. 2000. "Selecting Topics for Research Writing Projects." *English Journal* 89, no. 6 (July): 53–58.

Mellon, Constance A. 1984. "Process Not Product in Course-Integrated Instruction: A Generic Model of Library Research." *College and Research Libraries* 45, no. 6: 471–478.

Middle States Commission on Higher Education. 2002. "Developing Research and Communication Skills: Guidelines for Information Literacy in the Curriculum." Retrieved October 9, 2005, from http://www.msache.org/msache/content/pdf_files/devskill.pdf.

Snavely, Loanne L., and Carol A. Wright. 2003. "Research Portfolio Use in Undergraduate Honors Education: Assessment Tool and Model for Future Work." *Journal of Academic Librarianship* 29, no. 5: 298–303.

Tracey, Karen. 1997. "Teaching Freshman to Understand Research as a Process of Inquiry." Presentation at the 48th Annual Meeting of the Conference on College Composition and Communication, Phoenix, AZ, March 1997.

Valentine, Barbara. 2001. "The Legitimate Effort in Research Papers: Student Commitment versus Faculty Expectations." *Journal of Academic Librarianship* 27, no. 2 (March): 107–115.

Wilder, Stanley. 2005. "Information Literacy Makes All the Wrong Assumptions." *Chronicle Review*. B13: January 7.

"WPA Outcomes Statement for First-Year Composition." 2001. *College English* 63, no. 1 (January): 321–325.

York College of Pennsylvania Mission Statement, York College Long-Range Planning Committee, 1991–1992.

York College of Pennsylvania Student Learning Outcomes, Approved by Academic Senate, Spring 1994.

3
Responding to the Needs of Our Graduate Students: A Pilot Information Literacy Course in Graduate Education

Alice Crosetto, Acquisitions Librarian, University Libraries, University of Toledo, Formerly Head of Instructional Media & Technical Services, Ursuline College
Polly Wilkenfeld, Head of Reference Services & Instruction
Dianne Runnestrand, PhD MAP: Master Apprenticeship Program, Program Director
Ursuline College

Academic librarians spend much of their time addressing undergraduate needs, providing orientations to the library and library resources, facilitating sessions for core research courses, and teaching bibliographic sessions in the disciplines. Undergraduates constitute the majority of students on most college campuses, which may contribute to the perception of faculty and librarians that the information literacy needs of this student population are greater than those of the more experienced, older graduate students. Instructors may even assume that graduate students already possess the skills required for more advanced research. From the experiences at Ursuline College, however, graduate students are equally in need of library resources and instruction. In many instances the needs of the graduate students are even more extensive than the needs of undergraduates because of the master's thesis requirement in many graduate programs. At this level the academic research expectations may require extensive interlibrary loans and referrals to other local institutions.

Both the graduate faculty and the librarians on campus have been witnessing an alarming and disturbing trend—namely, that many of the graduate students are not prepared for the research requirements of graduate work. Many of these students have never used an online catalog, and most do not have experience using a database or a periodical index. They also lack familiarity with library classification and arrangement.

Developing and enhancing the graduate student's basic academic skills present several identifiable challenges: limited instructional time, the part-time nature of many graduate programs, and the extensive material that must be covered within a short time. At Ursuline College, the librarian and the classroom instructor, by creating a true collaborative endeavor, found that the needs of the graduate student can be effectively addressed.

Nothing New under the Sun: The Literature Review

In a study on the "academic problems" of graduate students in education, students reported that library problems constituted 87 percent of all their study problems. Among the five most prevalent problems reported, those related to the library were

1. difficulty in learning to use the library,
2. difficulty in getting material desired, and
3. time lost looking for books.

Sound familiar? These findings were from a 1933 study by Dorothy Stratton at Teacher's College of Columbia University (Stratton, 1933). In a separate publication five years later, Webb was quoted as saying, "Watching potentially good graduate students wander around the library, floundering in their attempts to find material, and so pathetically grateful for help has caused many to search continually for a solution." (Alire, 1984: 39, quoting Webb, 1938).

Between the 1930s and the present there has been a plethora of articles and books about information literacy, bibliographic instruction, and information fluency. Very little of that work, however, applies to graduate students and even less to graduate education students.

A doctoral thesis by recent Association of College and Research Libraries (ACRL) president Camila A. Alire found that more than one-half of the surveyed doctoral students in education felt a need for bibliographic instruction. The majority also agreed that a course in library research methodology should be required in programs where dissertations are mandatory (Alire, 1984).

In an essay entitled "Information Retrieval and Evaluation Skills for Education Students," the authors describe a library-centered program that conveys research skills to undergraduate and graduate students in education (Gratch et al., 1992). Although faculty members were not specifically involved with this instruction, the authors articulated information literacy goals similar to those later adapted by ACRL (Gratch et al., 1992). Authors from the University of Arkansas confirm our own assessment that graduate students should be skilled in basic library research (Murry, McKee, and Hammons, 1997). Based on their experience with graduate students in their College of Education's Higher Education Leadership program, they concluded that library research skills were either inadequate or nonexistent among the majority of their new students (Murry, McKee, and Hammons, 1997).

At the same time that we started to investigate the need for action in 2000, Michelle Toth (2005) describes a research and writing class for the Master's of Liberal Arts program at SUNY, Plattsburgh. In 2002, a needs assessment survey by Washington-Hoagland and Clougherty found that graduate and professional students recognize their need for more assistance using the library. Based on this survey, students were familiar with checking out materials and using photo-copiers. 46 percent of students lacked an awareness of any further library sources and resources, particularly online. (Washington-Hoagland and Clougherty, 2002). A recent study at the Australian National University suggests that this is an international phenomenon. In a survey of 107 graduate students, 9 students had never used a database (Perrett, 2004). In addition, thirty-nine of the students overestimated their searching skills when comparing perceived ability with actual ability (Perrett, 2004).

John W. Holmes of the University of Washington focuses on the special needs of the re-entry student. We identified with his findings (Holmes, 2000) because it seemed to effectively describe most of the students in our Master Apprenticeship Program (MAP).

For example, Holmes describes the lack of technological skills by students when engaging in scholarly research, even if they have professional technology experience from their work environment. He suggested that many re-entry students are quite anxious about using these new technologies (Holmes, 2000). Anthony J. Onwuegbuzie and Qun G. Jiao (2000 and 2004) confirmed our suspicions that library anxiety creates a barrier for all graduate students when conducting research. For example, in one study the authors demonstrated a high correlation between library anxiety and the creation of poor research proposals (Onwuegbuzie and Jiao, 2000 and 2004).

Behr (2004) created online modules for education students after administering a pretest of their skills. At Ecole Polytechnique de Montreal librarians took on part of a research methodology course for graduate students. They create a portfolio assignment that they also grade for all PhD students (Dumont et al., 2005).

Helene Williams (2000) summarizes much of our twentieth-century knowledge of graduate students' information literacy skills. She cites a survey showing that 81 percent of faculty members assume that students have necessary research skills. She proves that they do not. Williams wisely asserts that one cannot assume that graduate students have had any library instruction at the undergraduate level. She reinforces the claim that technical knowledge for employment is often not the same as research skills.

Harriet Lightman and Ruth Reingold illustrate how graduate students often fall into an "instruction gap" between workshops for undergraduates and those for faculty (2005, p. 26). In response, they created a mandatory one-day training session for doctoral students at Northwestern University. The session highlighted digital resources from EndNote to subject-specific materials. Feedback after the first year was mostly positive. It continued to improve over the next two years as the librarians responded to student surveys and other anecdotal evidence. (Lightman and Reingold, 2005).

As the literature shows, there was no substantive research on graduate information literacy until the beginning of 2000. When we realized that we needed to address graduate skills at Ursuline College, there was little on which to pattern a course. Therefore, to create the Ursuline Academic Skills course no single program reported in the literature could be replicated. Specific techniques that were adapted to our program included the integration of online strategies, a modified portfolio assignment, a separate and required class, and a focus on writing and research skills.

The Department of Graduate Education at Ursuline College

Founded in 1871, Ursuline College in Pepper Pike, Ohio, is one of the oldest Catholic women's liberal arts colleges in the United States. Ursuline College offers thirty-five undergraduate and seven graduate programs to more than 1,400 students. Commitment to the mission of the College as a Catholic institution of higher learning is essential (Ursuline College Web site, 2006).

The Education Department at Ursuline College offers graduate and undergraduate licensure programs in the areas of early childhood, middle childhood, adolescent/young adult, multi-age visual arts, and special education. A graduate program in educational administration is also offered. The Graduate School teacher preparation program offers a master of arts degree in education. The teacher preparation program is an apprenticeship-based program designed for baccalaureate-prepared students who were non-education majors. The MAP is offered jointly with east and west side schools in the Cleveland metropolitan area. This one-year, site-based program is designed to lead to both a master's degree and eligibility for state teaching licensure. Intended for the recent college graduate or for those making a career change to education, this full-time, intensive program encompasses forty-one to forty-four graduate semester hours (56 for special education) in professional education core curriculum and a full-time assignment to a K-12 classroom.

Finding Solutions Together

Over the past years, as Ursuline College expanded its graduate programs, both the graduate faculty and the librarians witnessed a disturbing trend: many of the graduate students were not prepared to do advanced research. These students lacked fundamental and appropriate academic skills for graduate study. The identified deficiencies included locating literature appropriate to the area of investigation, reading the literature with a critical eye, and exhibiting the writing skills necessary for participation in ongoing academic conversations. The graduate faculty members saw a need to develop and enhance these basic skills.

From the librarians' perspective, assistance was provided to the graduate students on a sporadic, one-on-one basis. Basic questions related to directions within the library and the location of specific resources were common—"Where are the Education magazines?" and "How can I find books on third grade reading?" It became clear that the librarians were addressing the students' needs one at a time, a very inefficient, time-consuming, and repetitive process. In addition, these fundamental questions were addressed only if the graduate student entered the library and was willing to ask for assistance from the library staff.

Concurrently, as the librarians were noticing and discussing a need for change, the director of MAP was identifying concerns of her own. Because of time and staff constraints, the librarians were struggling to provide sporadic and individual assistance to MAP students. The director continued to receive substandard research papers. These mutual concerns led to an initial meeting in order to explore options for solutions. During this and subsequent meetings, this new collaborative team developed objectives for the pilot information literacy course.

The Course

During the initial two years of MAP, the librarians continued to provide the standard introductory sessions to the library: a library tour; a brief introduction to the library's Web page; brief searching lessons highlighting specific education topics; and a brief introduction to OhioLINK, the Ohio Library and Information Network that provides shared borrowing privileges and accessibility to multi-disciplinary databases.

After the team met, we came to the conclusion that a discipline-specific course with structured sessions and assignments was needed. We agreed that it would be successful only if it were offered as a credit course spanning the twelve-month MAP year. During MAP's second year, the team developed a working syllabus based on collaborative teaching.

The course itself was developed by the librarians and the program director. Some sessions were co-taught by the librarians and the program director, and some sessions were taught exclusively by the librarians. The majority of the sessions were taught solely by the director. The director accompanied the students to the library sessions so she could immediately answer any questions they might have regarding assignments. During her sessions, the director prepared the students for the library sessions by providing assignments or by engaging in follow-up activities that resulted from the library sessions. Still other sessions addressed graduate research expectations.

The students were grouped into cohorts based on the grade levels they intended to teach: preschool to grade 3, grades 4–9, or grades 7–12. Although the graduate research skills taught were similar, the librarians quickly recognized that this grouping allowed for appropriate grade-level resources, especially for children's literature, lesson plans, Web sites, and other classroom resources. Customized grade-level handouts for each cohort were prepared for students to maintain in folders provided by the library.

In addition to the individualized sessions for each cohort, a Web site was created highlighting online resources including activity sheets, handouts, and resource links for the students. The librarians worked with the director to identify the required graduate research skills and to design instruction based on discipline-specific objectives. One of the first tasks was to identify, from the list of generated topics, which ones would be covered during the librarians' sessions and which to cover in the director's sessions.

Figure 3.1 describes the purpose, objectives, skills, dispositions, and topics covered during the initial year. Sessions are divided for the twelve-month MAP academic year. It also includes topics covered in individual sessions. An asterisk following the individual session number denotes those sessions taught by the librarians.

While most of these topics were required for all the MAP students, several topics were aimed at a specific grade-level cohort. For example, the topic of plagiarism is more likely to be encountered in the middle grades through high school and was therefore more important for the future teacher of these specific grade levels; whereas the classroom teacher of preschool through elementary grades is more likely to need the additional resources for classroom activities available on Web sites provided by major textbook publishers. During the extensive planning meetings to develop course objectives, scope, sequence, and assessment procedures, it was agreed that flexibility and respect for individual roles was vital, but most important, the instructors were required to keep the course student-focused.

Course Sessions

The librarians addressed the skills necessary to access research materials in education and to identify appropriate classroom resources. The classroom portion of the first session began with a discussion of the Digital Divide and how it affects classroom learning. Statistics about student access to Internet resources in our inner-city environment were included. In addition, the first session involved demonstrations of how to use the library

ACADEMIC SKILLS FOR GRADUATE STUDY

Purpose: The purpose of this course is to introduce the graduate student to library resources, research approaches, and academic writing. This course will lay the foundation for life-long competency in information literacy and provide the basic skills for evaluating and utilizing information and academic writing.

Objectives: At the end of this course the student will be able to:
➤ Utilize the various electronic resources to locate information
➤ Write at a level to submit articles to academic journals and/or to enter a PhD. Program
➤ Evaluate information resources and distinguish between scholarly and non-scholarly works.

Skills: At the end of this course student will have the following skills:
➤ Students will be familiar and be able to execute searches on ERIC, periodical indices, and other electronic resources.
➤ Be able to write at a level to submit articles to academic journals and/or to enter a PhD. Program.
➤ Be able to develop a resource packet for the preparation of lessons and units for the k – 12 class room.
➤ Be able to evaluate textbooks for appropriateness of material for specific grades and purposes.

Dispositions: At the end of this course students will exhibit the following dispositions and values:
➤ Students will have a respect for the role information literacy can play in their lives as teachers.
➤ Students will value this information and be enthusiastic about sharing and encouraging this literacy with their students.
➤ Students will feel confident and proud of their ability to communicate ideas at a level commensurate with a Masters prepared student.

Course content and schedule: The course schedule includes sessions on the following topics:

Summer

Session 1	Welcome to Graduate School: The journey ahead.
Session 2*	What is information literacy? Library tour and introduction to Oracle.
Session 3*	Using databases. Electronic journals.
Session 4	An examination of articles and their structure: Who are you writing for and what do they need?
Session 5	APA standards: How to do it and why.
Session 6	Organizing your first paper: The controlling idea.
Session 7*	Educational sites: Finding them and using them.
Session 8	Reviewing your first paper and making corrections.

Fall

Session 9*	Developing an Educational Resource Packet I: lesson plans, maps, pictures, hands-on activities.
Session 10*	Developing an Educational Resource Packet II: lesson plans, maps, pictures, hands-on activities (ECH only).
Session 10*	Plagiarism (AYA and MCH students only)

Spring

Session 11*	Unit Planning
Session 12*	Textbook evaluation

*Provided by Library Staff

Figure 3.1   Academic Skills for Graduate Study

catalog, how to order books from OhioLINK, and how to use databases to access periodical articles. Major reference books such as *Encyclopedia of Education, Education and Sociology: An Encyclopedia*, and the reference handbooks in the ABC-CLIO Contemporary Education Issues series were shown. This knowledge was applied immediately by students when they were given an assignment that required them to locate information on an education topic of their choice. After they completed the in-class assignment, it was evaluated by the MAP director.

After the first session, it became clear to the instructors that while most of the information presented was very basic, it was new to the students. Many had never used a library catalog. None had used periodical indexes. When the librarians asked the class to identify the term "Digital Divide," only one student raised her hand. It became apparent that more in-depth resources were required. The librarians developed a basic Web page containing links to online resources on Boolean searching, the Digital Divide, information on differentiating popular, professional, and peer-reviewed journals, and information on the searching techniques for the various education indexes: *ERIC, Education Abstracts,* and *Professional Development Collection.*

Later sessions were scheduled after the students were already involved in their specific classrooms assignments. These included textbook evaluation, locating lesson plans for a specific unit, online and print resources for selecting children and young adult literature, and media resources. This information was reinforced in handouts for the students to keep in their library folders and as links on the MAP Web page.

Because many of the online proprietary databases are offered statewide at no cost to public and private K-12 school libraries, resources available to students in their K-12 schools were also covered. The librarians often discussed the concept of lifelong professional learning skills. As former school librarians, we know the important and valuable role that the school librarian plays within the K-12 building. The school librarian supports and enhances the curriculum with research and resources.

A special session was offered to those students planning to teach in middle schools or high schools. This session explored plagiarism and cheating. It examined the reasons that students cheat, how to design assignments that prevent plagiarism, and how to detect plagiarism and cheating. This session received the highest evaluation of all sessions taught to this cohort.

Positive Results

After three years of fine-tuning the course, the director, librarians, and students indicate that the course has been successful in meeting the needs of the graduate students. During MAP's first year of existence and prior to the implementation of this course, twelve of the twenty-eight students did not pass the state's PRAXIS exam the first time the test was taken. During the first year of implementation, the course instructors witnessed a 100 percent passing rate, with only two students having to take the test twice. During the second year of implementation, the test scores of the students rose dramatically. Comparing the students' scores pre-course to the students' scores after the third year, the mean score rose from 171 to 186. Using the student t test, this increase was significant ($a \geq .05$).

Our success was further demonstrated by the enthusiasm generated by the graduate faculty and college administration to create curricula for other disciplines. We are currently discussing the design of similar courses for other graduate programs. Education faculty verified that their students' papers showed a dramatic increase in the number of references used and cited. In addition, the faculty noted that the students' ability to use technology to support their teaching and research increased dramatically.

Always Room for Improvement

Now in its third year, the course has evolved from an expanded bibliographic instructional session to a comprehensive research course. This enhanced research course includes new

Session 1	Library tour and introduction to Oracle. What is Information Literacy?
Session 2	Using databases. Locating information.
Session 3	An examination of articles and their structure: for whom are you writing and what do you wish to communicate?
Session 4	APA standards: how to do it and why is it important?
Session 5	APA standards: how to do it and why is it important?
Session 6	The controlling the idea of a paper: organizing your first paper: creating sections and writing your introductions.
Session 7	The controlling the idea of a paper: organizing your first paper: creating sections and writing your introductions.
Session 8	Reviewing your first paper and making corrections.
Session 9	Reviewing your first paper and making corrections.
Session 10	Working with PowerPoint.
Session 11	Building an electronic grade book.
Session 12	Writing performance papers.
Session 13	Building an electronic grade book.
Session 14	Building a Web page.
Session 15	Building a Web page.
Session 16	Creating labels and their uses in the classroom.
Session 17	Information Literacy and applications for your classroom.
Session 18	Building a table of contents and putting your portfolio together.

Figure 3.2   Academic Skills—2005 Sessions, 90 Minute Sessions

assignments, assessment strategies, scheduling, and content. To guide this evolution, four assessment strategies were used: annual student evaluations, the librarians' and director's critique after individual sessions, the education professors' assessment of writing and research skills, and student performance on required state tests. During the first year of implementation, the librarians and the MAP director met after individual sessions to discuss what worked and what did not. As productive and beneficial as this immediate assessment was, it became clear that time was against continuing this assessment strategy. In lieu of assessing every session, discussions of concerns occurred periodically.

The four assessment strategies were used to make changes to improve the course. Several aspects of the course were successful and needed to be maintained; not surprising, however, was the recognition that extensive changes in course structure and content were needed. We made four major changes. The first change was lengthening each session to one and one-half hours from the current one hour. This first change allowed us to make the second change—the sessions became more interactive. The third change involved integrating classroom exercises with other course requirements. And the last change was to limit database searching instruction to one database. It also became clear that the course needed to expand from one credit to two credits to accommodate the new information and technology standards adopted by the college. Figure 3.2 illustrates the changes and current topics of the course.

The MAP director and librarians concluded that each session needed to be longer. Although one-hour sessions were sufficient to impart information, they were not sufficient to accommodate hands-on activities. Figure 3.3 gives an excellent example of how

Ralph M. Besse Library
Self Guided Tour

Where can you borrow a laptop?

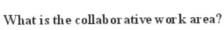

What is the collaborative work area?

What is the name of a journal (magazine) we are currently receiving?
(Hint: Find where we keep the most recent issues.)

Where would you go for help finding research information?

Where do we keep sample textbooks and teachers' guides?

Where do we keep children's literature?

Where are the Library restrooms located?

Extra Credit:
Find two places in the Library where you can eat and read.

Figure 3.3   Virtual Library Tour Activity

1. Find three articles on a topic related to your first paper in Human Growth and Development (one should be a literature search). Two of the articles may be online and one should be from a journal in the Library. The articles should all be in APA format and include a reference list. One of your articles must be a review of the literature about the topic. This is not a book review, but rather a review of the literature about the topic.

2. Read the articles. Identify the sentence(s) in the articles that describe(s) what the articles are about and what is going to be covered. (This is found in the body of the articles, not the abstract.) Underline the sentence(s).

3. Identify the headings in the articles and highlight them. Do the headings in the articles relate to the organization laid out in the introduction that you underlined?

4. Pick the one article that you thought was the easiest to understand and explain what made it easy for you to read and understand.

Figure 3.4   Graduate Skills Assignment 1

a lecture, previously a canned presentation, was changed to an interactive, fun exercise. The librarians created a Virtual Library Tour activity that was undertaken during the students' first visit.

This hands-on, interactive activity addressed the needs of those students who were new to the library. It also allowed the students to familiarize themselves with the services and support offered. For the adult student, this was a non-threatening, self-paced learning activity. It allowed students to practice new skills while still in the classroom where librarians and faculty were available to guide and encourage student activities.

Other strategies were used to improve the course. For example, we reduced the total number of sessions every semester by lengthening the time of each class. This change also allowed for more efficient scheduling. Similarly, another strategy to improve the course was to integrate library assignments with the MAP course requirements. For instance, the first library assignment, a database-searching exercise, required the students to conduct a literature search on a current education topic. The assignment found in Figure 3.4 provides an example of how a database-searching exercise can be improved by asking the students to perform a literature search already required in one of the academic courses. In the course's initial year, the students could search on any topic in the field of education for the assignment. By requiring the students to conduct the literature search on a topic with which they were familiar and have researched, the students were able to focus on building their database-searching skills.

Another example of integration was the integration of the requirement to design a lesson plan with the library session on Web resources for lesson plans and classroom activities. Structuring the library sessions around real-course requirements made the library sessions more authentic and relevant to the students.

During the initial two years of MAP, the librarians demonstrated multiple databases. The director, in evaluating student work and reviewing student assessments, recommended that only one education database be used to teach database-searching skills. Searching multiple databases often frustrated the students and produced superficial

Ursuline College
Computer and Information Literacy Requirement

Understanding the Operation and Use of Technology

1. have a working knowledge of **hardware and network** concepts
2. be proficient in the use of an **operating system**
3. determine whether technology is needed and **which technology tools** are appropriate in order to solve problems in a work environment
4. develop **positive attitudes** toward technology uses that support lifelong learning.
5. understand the **cultural, organizational and societal issues** related to technology

Using Technology to Retrieve, Interpret, and Present Information

6. determine the **nature and extent** of the information needed
7. **access** needed information from technology and non-technology sources **effectively and efficiently**
8. **evaluate information** and its sources critically and incorporate selected information into his or her knowledge base and value system
9. **use information effectively** to accomplish a specific purpose
10. use and create **structured electronic documents**
11. use electronic tools to analyze **qualitative and quantitative data**, discern trends and patterns and perform basic statistical operations
12. understand appropriate use of **graphs and charts** to aggregate and display information
13. use **databases** to manage information
14. use **presentation software as well as graphical and multimedia technologies** to organize text, data, charts, and graphics to design a persuasive presentation suitable for a certain audience
15. access and use information **ethically and legally**
16. understand many of the **economic, legal, and social issues** surrounding the use of information

Engaging in Electronic Collaboration

17. send and receive **e-mail**
18. participate in **electronic discussions**
19. understand **netiquette and impact** of electronic communication

Figure 3.5   Campus-wide Information Literacy Standards

results. Focusing on one database allowed the librarians to demonstrate the skills necessary to produce successful searches. A great deal of discussion surrounded the selection of the one database. Eventually, *Professional Development Collection* was chosen because it was a comprehensive database and would be available to these future educators in their K-12 schools. *Professional Development Collection*, provided by EBSCOhost, is designed for professional educators and provides indexing for a highly specialized collection of more than 550 high-quality education journals, including more than 350 peer-reviewed titles. It also contains more than 200 educational reports and a large number of full-text articles.

The librarians created and maintained a Web page dedicated to the MAP course. The online resources included e-documents of activity sheets and handouts that had been distributed during the individual sessions. Students were able to utilize the active links that were listed on the handouts. Links to Web sites demonstrated in sessions and utilized during the instructional units were provided in order to allow MAP students to use library activities in their own teaching sessions.

Changing the course from one credit to two credits was necessary to address both the information technology standards and the information literacy standards. In 2002, Ursuline College adopted campus-wide the information literacy standards listed in figure 3.5.

These standards are very similar to those adopted by the Association of College and Research Libraries and later endorsed by the American Association for Higher Education and the Council of Independent Colleges. The additional credit requirement accommodated the information literacy standards adopted by the college. The course was designed to allow students to "test out" of the second credit if they could demonstrate competency in Web page design, Excel, PowerPoint, and the more sophisticated aspects of Word.

As would be expected, our early successes, though satisfying, served to encourage us to explore further methods to improve our students' information literacy skills. This past year Ursuline College was awarded a $15,000 grant from the Ohio Department of Education to develop strategies to improve the literacy skills of our students. One problem that students identified was the consistency of feedback from the various professors who evaluated the students' written work. To address this problem the staff developed a routing sheet for each student. This sheet, which "travels" with the student from course to course and documents improvements in the students' writing throughout the course of the program, is shown in figure 3.6.

Once this strategy is tested, the faculty plan to develop Web access to the written and graded work. This approach, if successful, will allow students and faculty to have access to the students' work from previous classes. It is hoped that these strategies will improve consistency in feedback to students and provide a usable assessment tool to demonstrate to the students that improving literacy skills is a team effort among students, librarians, and faculty; literacy skills can be improved over time with diligent and consistent effort by student and faculty alike.

MAP 2005-6
Name _____   Advisor _____

Topic	Date/Name Grading Professor/Grade of Paper												
I. Content													
A. Introduction is too short													
B. Ideas need further development													
C. Theory into practice not developed													
D. Content inaccurate													
E. Content not comprehensive													
F. Introduction is not a "hook"													
II. Organization													
A. Structure is not delineated													
B. Structure is not suitable for the topic													
C. Topic sentence is too narrow for the content													
D. Paragraph/sentence is too long													
E. Unbalanced structure													
III. Analysis													
A. Analysis not linked to paper													
B. Analysis is not grounded in the literature													
C. Analysis is just an opinion													
D. Needs multiple points of view													
E. Too Brief (Min. 2 pages)													
IV. APA													
A. Agreement													
B. Changed tense													
C. Changed person													
D. Incomplete sentence													
E. Sentence unclear													
F. Misplaced modifier													
G. Misuse of semicolon													
H. Misuse of colon													
I. Parallelism													
J. Stay in present tense													
K. Headings/spacing inaccurate													
L. Cite only once in paragraph													
M. Citation not in reference													
N. Need quotations													
O. Plagiarism													
P. Reference/citation: Incorrect format													
Q. Need more references													
R. Capitalization													
S. Word Usage													

Figure 3.6   Student Routing Sheet

Librarians—Willing and Able

The librarians involved in this project were particularly qualified to address the needs of the graduate students in the field of education. Both had worked with the Education Department faculty on a variety of projects and had taught bibliographic instruction sessions for numerous education courses, including the graduate course Educational Research. Both librarians held positions as school librarians: one in a private K-12 facility for seventeen years and the other in public elementary and high school libraries for thirteen years. These experiences allowed the librarians to address the needs of the current graduate students in education. Working with the MAP director, the librarians identified the required graduate research skills and collaborated in designing instruction based on discipline-specific objectives.

Experiences at Ursuline College confirmed the findings of the previous, limited research on graduate students' information literacy abilities: students could not demonstrate the most basic skills necessary to perform research (e.g., searching online sources, using indexes, and evaluating resources). Offering a twelve-month course that progressed in depth as students improved their professional abilities worked to develop these skills.

Over the last three years, other experiences have confirmed the need for librarians to focus their attention on the graduate student. At a roundtable discussion at the 2005 Conference of the Association of College and Research Libraries, librarians from across the country joined us in lamenting the scarcity of material written about teaching information literacy to graduate students. Sharing the materials created for our program generated enormous enthusiasm among our librarian colleagues. Meeting the needs of graduate students encompassed all levels of higher education: state-sponsored universities, private colleges, community colleges, and specialized colleges. One librarian shared that law school librarians are experiencing the same dilemma: under-developed academic skills for graduate research.

A similar session offered at the 2005 Annual Academic Library Association of Ohio (ALAO) Conference generated equal enthusiasm. Our presentation detailed the Academic Skills course and provided the blueprints for other academic librarians. The ALAO presentation and subsequent discussion indicated that the librarians felt that the course was innovative and, in some ways, unique. The discussion at ALAO revealed that many librarians felt a need to serve the graduate in a more meaningful and significant venue; the audience's questions reflected the frustration on the part of librarians and confirmed that librarians want to be part of the solution.

During one of the sessions taught by the librarians during the first year of this course, a simple but poignant question provided a humorous interlude for all of us. But more important, it represented the very essence of this collaborative endeavor and illustrated the need more vividly than even we could have expressed ourselves. After we discussed the various indexes that would be helpful for the graduate education student, one student who was returning to school after raising her children slowly raised her hand and said, "I've heard of Windex, but I've never heard of index!" As we looked at each other and started to chuckle, we realized that in this one question, we were facing our challenge—the challenge that had propelled us to undertake this collaborative endeavor in the very beginning. This one question seemed to validate the whole course and all our efforts. There was indeed a need for information literacy in our graduate education program. We had to start with the basics of information literacy for the graduate student, and this included defining the most rudimentary terms.

Conclusion

Our graduate education students needed help. Students could not demonstrate the most basic skills necessary to perform research (e.g., searching online sources, using indexes, and evaluating resources). Experiences at our institution confirmed the previous limited research on graduate students' information literacy abilities. Offering a year-long course that progressed in depth as students' professional abilities improved helped students to develop their skills.

Nothing in the literature provided direction for a graduate skills course. By using authentic learning experiences designed by the program director and librarians, a course was created that became vital to the graduate program. Synergy between the director and librarians created a program that was superior to one that either group could have created alone. Not only did the students benefit but the instructors developed new perspectives on their respective fields. It is our feeling that this collaborative effort provided the best possible outcome for all involved.

Personality factors were crucial in assuring the success of our endeavor. The three staff members worked well together. All were open to new ideas and enjoyed the time spent together. All worked hard, with no one person feeling disgruntled at being overburdened. All were focused on the needs of our students.

The success of the program was demonstrated in the improved scores on the PRAXIS exams and the improved ability of the students to use the library and to translate their new knowledge to improved writing skills. Open-ended survey questions generated subjective data indicating the usefulness of skills learned.

The development and revision of this course was extremely time-consuming. None of the instructors received release time to work on the course, but the results seemed worth the effort. The program runs smoothly, with only small adjustments made. There are wonderful resources for graduate research in the library, but without instruction they remain unused. The authors hope that this program will be expanded to other graduate departments in the authors' school as well as in the schools of others reading this chapter.

References

Alire, Camila A. 1984. "A Nationwide Survey of Education Doctoral Students' Attitudes Regarding the Importance of the Library and the Need for Bibliographic Instruction." PhD thesis, University of Northern Colorado.

Behr, Michele D. 2004. "On Ramp to Research: Creation of a Multimedia Library Instruction Presentation for Off-campus Students." *Journal of Library Administration* 41, no. 1/2: 19–30.

Dumont, Richard et al. 2005. "Innovative Approaches by Ecole Polytechnique de Montreal Library in Support of Research Activities." *IATUL Proceedings* 2005: 1–10.

Gratch, Bonnie, et al. 1992. *Information Retrieval and Evaluation Skills for Education Students.* ERIC Document 351038.

Holmes, John W. 2000. "Just in Case, Just in Time, Just for You: User Education for the Re-entry Student." In *Teaching the New Library to Today's Users: Reaching International, Minority, Senior Citizens, Gay/Lesbian, First Generation, At-Risk, Graduate and Returning Students, and Distance Learners.* Edited by Trudi E. Jacobson and Helene C. Williams. New York: Neal-Schuman.

Lightman, Harriet, and Ruth N. Reingold. 2005. "A Collaborative Model for Teaching e-Resources: Northwestern University's Graduate Training Day." *portal: Libraries and the Academy* 5, no. 1: 23–32.

Murry, John W., Jr., Elizabeth Chadbourn McKee, and James O. Hammons. 1997. "Faculty and Librarian Collaboration: The Road to Information Literacy for Graduate Students." *Journal on Excellence in College Teaching* 8, no. 2: 107–121.

Onwuegbuzie, Anthony J., and Qun G. Jiao. 2000. "I'll Go to the Library Later: The Relationship between Academic Procrastination and Library Anxiety." *College and Research Libraries* 61, no. 1 (January): 45–54.

———. 2004. "Information Search Performance and Research Achievement: An Empirical Test of the Anxiety-Expectation Mediation Model of Library Anxiety." *Journal of the American Society for Information Science and Technology* 55, no. 6 (January 1): 41–54.

Perrett, Valerie. 2004. "Graduate Information Literacy Skills: The 2003 ANU Skills Audit." *Australian Library Journal* 53, no. 2: 161–171.

Stratton, Dorothy C. 1933. *Problems of Students in a Graduate School of Education.* New York: Teachers College, Columbia University.

Toth, Michelle. 2005. "Research and Writing and Theses—Oh My! The Journey of a Collaboratively Taught Graduate Research and Writing Course." In *Relationships between Teaching Faculty and Teaching Librarians.* Edited by Susan B. Kraat. New York: Haworth Information Press.

Ursuline College. 2006. "Web site." Pepper Pike, Ohio: Ursuline College. Retrieved January 10, 2006, from www.ursuline.edu.

Washington-Hoagland, Carlette, and Leo Clougherty. 2002. "Identifying the Resource and Service Needs of Graduate and Professional Students." *portal: Libraries and the Academy* 2, no. 2: 125–143.

Williams, Helene C. 2000. "User Education for Today's Graduate Students: Never a Given, and Not Always Received." In *Teaching the New Library to Today's Users: Reaching International, Minority, Senior Citizens, Gay/Lesbian, First Generation, At-Risk, Graduate and Returning Students, and Distance Learners.* Edited by Trudi E. Jacobson and Helene C. Williams. New York: Neal-Schuman.

Part II
The Disciplines and Information Literacy Collaboration: Building Partnerships with the Humanities, Social Sciences, and Sciences

Most instruction librarians work with faculty members in various departments in order to teach information literacy skills to students within the context of a particular discipline. These students might be taught in lower-level courses or in courses required for the major—possibly even in capstone courses. Discipline-specific instruction is a critical arena that allows librarians to build on student interest in a particular subject area with a deeper understanding of information-related issues.

While some faculty members might invite a librarian to come to class once during the semester to teach needed topics, rarely do they go in depth. The chapters in this section provide a wealth of ideas for more intensive and extensive collaborative ventures, ones that will have a much greater impact on student learning. The faculty members who are receptive to single sessions may be willing to consider a more in-depth approach.

It is often difficult, or at least time-consuming, to build close relationships that allow for the types of endeavors presented in this section. Faculty members face a host of issues connected to their course and to their goals for student learning, and they may or may not have a developed conception of what they would like addressed by information literacy instruction. Librarians' concerns may overlap those of a faculty member to a large extent, but they may not completely coincide. These chapters have the advantage of presenting both points of view and considering what accommodations may need to be made to make a partnership successful. Obviously, such issues must be addressed anew in each collaborative venture. The background information presented in these chapters will be extremely helpful in thinking about the issues faced in collaborations. Librarians who are newer to teaching and to working with faculty members may find this to be particularly true.

While these chapters cover the humanities, social sciences, and sciences, we encourage readers who might work exclusively within one of these disciplines to read widely in this section. The ideas proposed will often work just as well in another subject as in the one being discussed. For example, in Chapter 9, Elsa E. Winch and Shonah A. Hunter of Lock Haven University describe a poster project that they substituted for a more traditional research assignment. While theirs is a biology course, the poster project idea might easily be used in a wide variety of courses in different disciplines. James B. Tuttle and Steve McKinzie explain in Chapter 7 a collaboration at Dickinson College that was designed to conquer students' fear of the research project. Obviously, students in all disciplines have similar worries, and instruction that specifically targets the relationship between research and writing is widely applicable.

In Chapter 5, Margaret Fain, Sara Sanders, and Linda Martin of Coastal Carolina University describe how an inquiry-based assignment, that of researching the history and use of a word, was initially developed to teach information literacy skills in a linguistics course, but has been successfully adapted to be used with first-year composition students and English-as-a-Second-Language (ESL) teachers.

Karin E. Westman, Sara K. Kearns, and Marcia G. Stockham of Kansas State University (Chapter 4) developed the idea of a collaborative triangle, with the points comprised of "engaged faculty seeking pedagogical support for teaching information literacy, engaged librarians familiar with the assigned project and its learning outcomes, and engaged students ready for assistance." Their collaboration is in an English literature course, but what course would not benefit from such a model? In Chapter 10, Lori J. Toedter and Dorothy F. Glew collaborated on an interdisciplinary course at Moravian College that challenged students "to investigate the consequences to individuals and society when the scientific method is poorly, mistakenly, or incompletely applied." With the increasing importance of interdisciplinarity in today's academy, this model might be adapted for other such courses.

Several chapters in this section look beyond individual collaborations and single courses to address information literacy instruction within a major or program of study. Grace Peña Delgado and Susan C. Luévano describe an effort to incorporate information literacy in a curriculum reform in the Chicano and Latino Studies Department at California State University, Long Beach. "At the center of the *Semillas* model . . . [is] a focused training of faculty in information literacy skills, assignment development, learning outcomes and assessments." This idea would be applicable in a wide range of departments. Christy R. Stevens and Patricia J. Campbell describe the integration of information literacy into the political science curriculum at the University of West Georgia (Chapter 8), whereas Laurie A. Kutner and Cecelia Danks worked within the Environmental Studies core curriculum at the University of Vermont to effect changes (Chapter 11).

Some key strategies to incorporate in effective discipline-based collaborations, based on the chapters in this section, include these:

- Discuss the goals of and constraints upon each partner in the collaboration.
- Integrate the need for information literacy skills throughout the course, not just as a means of completing one assignment.
- Provide students with multiple opportunities to use and practice the skills they are learning.
- Develop innovative methods for students to present the results of their research.
- Adapt ideas from one discipline to another, using relevant pieces and building on them.
- Target interdisciplinary courses and curricula to teach students information-seeking skills and strategies.
- Work with departments and programs to broaden the scope and impact of student learning of information literacy skills in a progressive manner.

- Expand a particular collaboration by involving other faculty members in the venture.
- Build assessment of student learning into the collaboration from the very beginning.

While all these ideas are not entirely new, seeing how they played out in innovative, successful partnerships will spark ideas in all teaching librarians. These successful models for collaboration should also inspire faculty members to envision similar approaches in a variety of courses and disciplines.

.4

Regenerating the Collaborative Triangle: Point-of-Need Assistance for English Literature Students

Karin E. Westman, Associate Professor of English
Sara K. Kearns, Assistant Professor and Library Instruction Coordinator
Marcia G. Stockham, Associate Professor and Education Librarian
Kansas State University

While librarians and English faculty have frequently collaborated to assist undergraduates enrolled in required introductory writing courses, there are few documented examples of collaborations for undergraduates enrolled in required literature courses toward the English major or minor. At Kansas State University, subject librarians and English faculty have shared similar concerns about students' ability to meet the Association of College and Research Libraries' Information Literacy Competency Standards (American Library Association, 2005). Librarians and faculty noted two standards that they particularly wished to foster in their students: students' ability to determine the type of information they need (Standard 1), and students' ability to evaluate and then incorporate information into a final project (Standard 3). The goal was to create the optimal collaborative environment to foster these information literacy skills. To this end, faculty and librarians decided to collaborate at that moment when student engagement is likely to be at its highest: right before the project is due. By energizing all three points of the collaborative triangle—engaged faculty seeking pedagogical support for teaching information literacy, engaged librarians familiar with the assigned project and its learning outcomes, and engaged students ready for assistance—faculty and librarians created a successful model for faculty-librarian-student collaboration to foster information literacy skills connected to the discipline.

Related Literature

The collaboration between teaching faculty and librarians has cut across disciplines from the arts to the sciences. However, and perhaps surprisingly, there are few published cases of faculty-librarian collaboration in the field of English literature, as distinguished from the expository writing or composition courses that the majority of college freshmen complete.

Some partnerships bring the librarian to the students and faculty, while others bring the students and faculty to the library. A collaborative effort at Daniel Webster College in New Hampshire "embedded" the librarian in a college writing and research course. The librarian provided instruction sessions, participated in online discussion, and reviewed and partially graded student papers (Hearn, 2005). By contrast, Paterson and White at the University of New Hampshire at Manchester worked with an introductory-level English literature class for majors where students and professor met in the library for at least one class session. As with many collaborative efforts, the teaching faculty and librarian felt that, by meeting in the library, students would grow more comfortable with the building and any library anxiety would ease. The objective was to teach students how to conduct research using a specific database through a "lecture/demonstration format to teach the more mechanical aspects" and "actively question[ing] students and allow[ing] them to 'figure out' the database" (Paterson and White, 2004: 168).

Two other collaborations are intriguing, if not for the actual partnership, then certainly for the learning processes and outcomes of the classes. The first bears some resemblance to the student project described in this chapter in that students wrote for an Internet audience. Prompted by a situation in which "students made extensive, but inappropriate, use of Web-based information resources in their academic research," a professor of English and a librarian at the University of Missouri, Kansas City, wanted to instill in students the critical thinking skills necessary for evaluating information found on the Internet (Walter, 2000: 36). Students were required to search out and review Web sites that would be relevant to their coursework for this class on Chaucer. Throughout the semester, and over several class sessions, the librarian and teaching faculty both provided instruction and evaluated the reviews. The final versions of the reviews were posted on the course Web site (available at www.umkc.edu/lib/engelond), where they served as guidance for subsequent students and the general public.

A final collaboration fully immersed English literature students into not just the library but also the research processes of expert researchers, as students explored the 1930s. Through several projects, students at the University of Louisville, Kentucky, were first introduced to and then set free in the library. The initial project required students to respond to artifacts (photographs and music) in the library collection. Subsequent papers required students to research "an area of the 1930s . . . in six different library venues" (Yohannes and Johnson, 2004: 121). This team effort involved several librarians from many areas of the library, although it is not clear to what extent or in what manner the collaboration occurred. The authors do provide this note:

> A better model is when librarians and teaching faculty collaborate in the design and implementation of an assignment. The teaching faculty is responsible for the library research instruction, the librarians respond to the assignment design by indicating if they think it would work and what materials students might actually be able to find, and both the teaching and library faculty can act as consultants with the students as they engage in actual research. (Yohannes and Johnson, 2004: 123)

The authors report that this collaboration yielded a greater transference of research methods because students did not simply learn the mechanics of research, but the concepts. Set free in the library, students had to make decisions about what research questions to ask and what research paths to follow as they also learned how to locate and integrate their selected resources.

Overall, the literature describing collaborations between librarians and faculty in English literature approached the collaboration from a variety of perspectives and levels of engagement. However, all cite the need to incorporate information literacy skills into literature courses. Ultimately, as Hearn states, "no one model of collaboration can apply to every campus, and academic librarians are regularly trying to develop programs to fit their own scenarios" (Hearn, 2005: 219).

Information Literacy Instruction at Kansas State University

Kansas State University is a comprehensive research and land-grant university of 23,000 students and nine colleges. As the largest of the colleges, the College of Arts and Sciences enrolls over 7,000 students and contains more than twenty departments, including the Department of English. This department serves students from across the university, but several courses are dedicated to English majors and minors, as well as education majors specializing in English. One of these courses is English 310, Introduction to Literary Studies, the department's foundational course for the English major and minor. Designed as a writing-intensive class, the course caps at fifteen students and therefore allows opportunity for the discussion and evaluation of students' critical writing skills. As taught for this collaborative project, the course had the following four learning outcomes:

1. Students will become familiar with major genres in and conventions of literature.
2. Students will become familiar with the literary terms commonly used in later courses.
3. Students will develop and apply critical skills for reading, thinking, and writing about literature.
4. Students will acquire new skills and develop existing skills related to research in English literature and to communication through various technologies.

Learning outcomes 3 and 4 illustrate the degree to which skills for literary analysis and for information literacy overlap: for both outcomes, students must be able to determine the kind of information they need from literary or other texts, retrieve the information, and then evaluate and incorporate that information into a new document for a particular purpose or audience. This point of intersection prompted collaboration between librarians and English faculty, as the case study below describes.

Points of Intersection at Kansas State University: Our Case Study

The case study below describes the interactions and points of collaboration between faculty, librarians, and students during spring 2004 for one section of English 310. The semester-long class met in a computer lab classroom; the class was held twice a week for seventy-five-minute sessions. The collaboration occurred in the second half of the semester and over a three-week period. The final product was a series of short, online essays for Pat Barker's *Regeneration* (1991) that provided cultural, historical, and literary context for her best-selling novel.

The Assignment

As part of their work for English 310, Introduction to Literary Studies, students completed a final writing assignment (five pages in length) that asked them to synthesize skills in information literacy and literary analysis. Students read and discussed Pat Barker's *Regeneration* (1991), and then each student researched a person, place, or cultural reference that Barker introduces into her historical novel about World War I. These references ranged from the well known—"Freudian" (Barker, 1991: 29) and "No Man's Land" (Barker, 1991: 214)—to the more obscure, such as "Hymn No. 373" (Barker, 1991: 149), a hymn sung at a church service during the war, and "a man's private life" (Barker, 1991: 55), an allusion to homosexuality in Britain during World War I. After gathering information for the selected topic and reviewing the novel in light of this research, each student wrote a short critical context essay as an entry for a group Web site on Barker's novel, *Pat Barker's Regeneration: Critical Contexts*, available at www.ksu .edu/english/westmank/regeneration. Faculty, who had designed the Web site in advance, formatted and uploaded successful student essays at the end of the semester.

In the first section of the essay, students were asked to summarize the results of their research on their topic using at least three and no more than six published sources, available online or from print periodicals or books. For this first section, students needed to locate information on their topic; determine which information they should include, given the length restrictions of the assignment and the topic's appearance in the novel; and decide on the best way to organize their selected research for their readers. In the second section of the essay, students were asked to develop a "close reading" of the passage in which the person, place, or cultural reference appears, answering the question, "What is the significance of the reference within this particular scene?" Finally, students had to demonstrate how the topic contributes to the development of the novel's themes. The second and third sections of the essay primarily evaluated students' skills in literary interpretation, though their information literacy skills—retrieval, selection, and integration of information—are certainly still in use. (To view the assignment sheet distributed to the students, see www.ksu.edu/english/westmank/regeneration/ assignment.html.)

Student Preparation for the Assignment

In preparation for students' completing this assignment, the English faculty member led discussion about Barker's novel for two class sessions so that students could become familiar with the novel's structure, characters, and themes. Students selected their topic during this time in order to begin thinking about their critical context essay. During the second week of the unit, the English faculty member provided several in-class activities targeted specifically to the fourth learning outcome for the course—"To acquire new skills and to develop existing skills related to research in English literature and to communication through various technologies"—to ensure that students were familiar with basic online searches for a specific topic and claim before beginning their own research.

When they finished discussion of the novel at the end of the first week, students completed a preliminary Research Survey. The Research Survey asked the following questions:

- When you are assigned a project that requires research, what's the first step you take to gather information, as you begin your research?
- In the past, have you received instruction or guidance for using online resources for research from a high school teacher, college instructor, librarian, or other source?
- Have you used a database like Expanded Academic or Lexis-Nexis for research in the past six months?
- Have you used a search engine like Google or Yahoo for research in the past six months?
- The primary URL of a Web page will contain an ending such as .com, .net, .edu, .gov, and .org. Do you know what each of these endings indicates about the Web page?
- How confident are you about your ability to use library resources for research?
- How confident are you about your ability to locate the correct bibliographic information for a book, database article, or Web page when you include it in your "Works Cited" and in the text of your paper?

Of the fifteen students in the class, all but two had used free-access Web pages in the previous six months; during that same time period, just over half had used resources in the library, and only five had used a database. Not surprisingly, students were most likely to go online to free-access sites for information before asking a librarian for assistance. Students were therefore familiar with the *process* of searching free-access Web pages, even if they may not be experienced evaluators of the information they retrieved. Finally, many had not realized the type of resources available through the library's collection or databases.

Given that the class met in a computer lab, the classroom's word-processing software, ELMO Visual Presenter, and Internet connection provided resources for modeling research skills as well as for student practice of those skills during class time. At the start of the second week, these resources were put to use for a class session about online information literacy skills. With the Research Survey information in hand, the English faculty member first provided a brief introduction to online information literacy skills, including a review of the five criteria for evaluating the credibility and suitability of resources, both subscription and free-access: authority, objectivity (clear disclosure of advocacy), coverage, accuracy, and currency. Second, the faculty member modeled a search on the free-access portion of the Web for one of the students' topics, and students briefly discussed the challenges and benefits of several sites retrieved by two or three keyword searches. In the third and final portion of the class session, students moved to their own computers in the lab classroom and began reviewing online, free-access Web pages for their own topics; as they completed a worksheet using the five standard criteria for evaluation, the faculty member was available to answer questions and advise, thereby modeling further the research process.

Faculty-Librarian Collaboration

Concurrent with the first week of the unit and the students' selecting their topic, the English faculty member paired each student with one of three librarians, so that each librarian had five students. The librarians were the English librarian, the education librarian, and the business librarian, who had a BA in English. Previous to this pairing, the English faculty member conferred with the librarians to (1) introduce the assignment and its learning outcomes (2) confirm the timeframe for the three-week unit, and (3) confirm the availability of the librarians to attend one class session and to schedule meetings with the students. Most important, at this meeting faculty and librarians also confirmed the role the librarians would play in the collaborative triangle: librarians would be the students' research guide and resource for the first part of the essay. To complement the librarians' role, faculty would assist students in developing the second and third parts of the essay; help them draft, revise, and format the essay as a whole; and grade the final draft. Thus, when meeting with the students for the first time, the librarians were familiar with the assigned project, its learning outcomes, and their contribution to the collaboration.

Librarian-Student Collaboration

Librarians attended class to introduce themselves to the students at the start of the second week of the unit. During this week—also the initial research phase—librarians met with students one on one for scheduled thirty-minute appointments to review the students' preliminary research and to assist them in locating further print and online resources related to their selected topic. Prior to the meetings, the librarians conducted preliminary research to locate material they thought could be relevant to the students' research. None of the librarians had read the novel, although they did know it was set in Great Britain during World War I. During the meetings with students, librarians learned that many of the students approached their topics from directions the librarians had never considered. Essentially, the librarians could not neglect the reference interview. In some instances, the topics became only a small part of a larger social framework the students wanted to research. One consultation became a philosophical discussion regarding the meaning behind an event in the book; the discussion was intellectually stimulating for librarian and student and resulted in a new approach to the paper. Other students had already located resources that the librarian had not yet encountered, but, once known, led them to discover related sources together. Throughout the consultation, the students maintained control of the research process: they used the librarians' staff computers, they had the final say as to whether a resource was appropriate to their research, and they decided when they had enough information. Some meetings lasted far less than the scheduled thirty minutes; others went longer and extended into e-mails and follow-up phone calls or appointments.

Faculty-Student Collaboration

As the librarians completed their consultations with the students, the English faculty member re-entered the collaborative relationship to assist students with drafting and revising their essay. During class and in conference, the English faculty member discussed strategies for organizing information, developing the close reading for the second part of the essay, and developing the argument for the third part of the essay—those two sections where students would demonstrate their skills in literary analysis and persuasive writing as well as information literacy. A writing workshop before the essay's due date asked students to review each other's drafts with attention to the selection and organization of information and the development of their ideas, as well as the citation and documentation of their sources.

Faculty evaluated the final drafts according to a rubric that distinguished between the different parts of the essay and the skills required. Students could receive "Excellent," "Good," "Adequate," or "Insufficient/Needs revision" in the following categories:

- Focus and Purpose: Does the essay have a clear thesis that addresses the assignment?
- Development of Part I: Is there sufficient research provided and explained for Part I?
- Development of Part II: Is there sufficient and appropriate explication of the topic and passage provided for Part II?
- Development of Part III: Are there enough examples, detail, explanation for Part III?
- Organization: Is the arrangement of information and ideas logical and easy to follow? Do paragraphs have topic and concluding sentences and transitions?
- Tone and Style: Does the writing show control, variety, and complexity of prose?
- Editing and Proofreading: Is the essay relatively free of distracting surface errors in grammar, punctuation, MLA citation style, and formatting?

Essays that received "Excellent" or "Good" in all categories were approved for inclusion on the dedicated Web site *Pat Barker's Regeneration: Critical Contexts*. The English faculty member, who designed and maintains the site, formatted and then posted the essays online.

Point-of-Need Collaborative Instruction for Information Literacy

The contributions and innovations of this collaboration were fourfold:

First, the collaboration engaged students at their point of need in a low-risk learning environment rather than in a general or one-shot library class. This learning environment allowed librarians to serve as informed and interested partners, not graders, of the students' efforts. However approachable the English faculty member was, students knew that she had literally written the book about Barker's *Regeneration* as the author of *Regeneration: A Reader's Guide*. (Westman, 2001). The librarians had not even read Barker's novel, so the student became the de facto expert about their topic and contexts. This situation placed the librarian and student on a more equal, collaborative footing during the consultation: one acting as the subject expert and the other as the research process expert. For example, in the case of "Hymn No. 373," librarians began exploring the possibilities but were unable to determine which hymn of the several so-numbered was the hymn in question. The student, however, being the subject expert, was able to establish the proper hymn and focus the direction of the research. In other cases, preparations, even misguided, on the part of both librarians and students allowed them to use the scheduled time efficiently. The students were able to place what they learned with the librarians in the context of an immediate and specific research need. By meeting with librarians who maintained a consultative approach, the students learned through an experiential process how they might conduct research using a recursive process of reading, research, and writing. Allowing the students to take the lead in the process also contributed to the feeling of partnership.

Further, students had time dedicated to their individual research needs. Because librarians were familiar with the assignment and expected learning outcomes, librarians could tailor their questions and assistance to the students' needs—an opportunity often missing with students who inquire at a general reference desk or walk-in students who "need some help with a paper." A common statement heard from students asking for help is, "I'm sorry for disturbing you." Indeed, surveys and focus groups report college students either (1) are afraid to expose their ignorance, (2) do not want to disturb the librarian, or (3) do not know the librarian is there to help them (Egan, 1992; Fister, 2002; Jenkins, 2001; Leckie, 1996; Valentine, 1993). As a result, students tend to rely on what is familiar (Google or Yahoo!), what is readily accessible (physically or intellectually), and what they learn from their friends or classmates (Burton and Chadwick, 2000; Holliday and Li, 2004; OCLC, 2002; Valentine, 1993 and 2001). Because the meetings for this collaboration were scheduled, students displayed less concern about interrupting the librarians and asked many follow-up questions. Students thus had the opportunity to learn as much as they needed.

These scheduled, collaborative partnerships also modeled what one-shot or general library instruction sessions often cannot address because of time and pedagogical purpose: the vagaries of the research process. When librarians teach one-shot sessions, for consistency they sometimes prepare a script that demonstrates the use of various research resources in a procedural step-by-step manner. These demonstrations illustrate a framework or a process that seasoned researchers know is never so linear. Students who begin research after a one-shot session can be frustrated that they do not progress through the research process as smoothly as the librarian did. In this case study collaboration, by contrast, librarians modeled non-linear research as students developed their own skills, thereby minimizing student frustration. In partnership, students and librarians moved through the research process together. Alternative keywords were identified, searches were re-run in different databases, and the online catalog was consulted to determine if the library owned a book referenced in a Web site. The librarians consulted with each other, other librarians, and the teaching faculty when they needed further ideas. In many cases, the students and librarians discovered together invaluable resources in unexpected places. For example, the librarian expected that the *Hydra*, the journal of the Craiglockhart War Hospital, would be found only in a remote archive or, at best, on microfilm. However, a search on the free-access Web located digitized copies of the *Hydra* within seconds. This discovery reminds librarians, students, and faculty of the valuable and appropriate resources available through the free-access Web.

Second, the one-on-one sessions provided important "field-work" opportunities for librarians, so they could learn how students approach and pursue research tasks and explore non-traditional literary resources. Each librarian knew prior to a consultative meeting what a student's topic would be, although not the angle from which the student was approaching a topic. Because the students began the research prior to the meetings, those identified resources became the starting point for these discussions: how students located the information, if the resource contained the needed information, if they felt it was a credible source, where they felt it was lacking, or what information or perspectives they still needed. Then, as the librarians and students explored additional resources during the consultation, the librarian could directly observe the decision-making process of the student. While working in a database such as JSTOR, the librarian observed the process by which the student deemed one article irrelevant but selected another as significant to his research. Thus the librarians gained insight into the student research process that could be valuable in future teaching interactions.

Third, assistance from the librarians in locating resources allowed English faculty to spend more time in class and in conference discussing the evaluation of resources and the integration of resources into the critical context essay. Confident about the range and type of information they had located with their librarian's assistance, students were able to concentrate on selecting and organizing the information for the first part of the essay, and they could then turn their attention to the remaining portions of the essay. Thanks to the librarian-student collaboration in the second week of the unit, the research process did not shortchange the English faculty's or the students' attention to the second and third sections of the essay, where students would demonstrate their skills in literary analysis and persuasive writing. Instead, during the third and final week of the unit, faculty and students could dedicate time in class and in conference on the development, organization, and formatting of the essay as a whole.

Fourth, the collaboration resulted in a real-world resource for others to consult. Since the assigned essay was written not just for the instructor but for a real-world online audience, students were more concerned about succeeding in the project, and success depended on their skills in information literacy and literary analysis. Although *Regeneration* is a best-selling novel in the United Kingdom and often used for university entrance exams, there is very little about Barker's novel on the Web. Writing for a real-world audience of interested readers therefore provided exigency for the students' writing task while also contributing to the international conversation about this award-winning novel. Having just used a variety of resources, in print and online, to gather information for their topics, students had grown increasingly aware of how authors constructed their texts. In turn, they were becoming aware of how their own text was constructed: the types of resources they located, the quality of the resources they selected, and the criteria for including or excluding resources. The possibility that someone might do a free-access Web search, discover the Web page with their essay, and then consult their essay's content and sources made them more careful about the selection and integration of their research and the development of their ideas.

Assessment of the Instruction

Students, faculty, and librarians assessed the collaborative project. During the collaboration, English faculty checked in with the librarians and the students to confirm that meetings had taken place and to receive informal feedback from the librarians on the students' progress. Most assessment occurred at the project's completion: students completed a survey of their experience, librarians and faculty offered informal evaluation to the faculty, and faculty evaluated the completed essays using a rubric that tracked separately the development of students' skills in information literacy and literary analysis.

In a survey following the completion of their essays, the majority of students agreed or strongly agreed that the librarians' assistance

- was valuable;
- improved their ability to locate appropriate print and online resources;
- made library technology more accessible;
- allowed them to locate resources they would not have otherwise discovered; and
- encouraged them to consult their librarian or another librarian for future projects, especially early in the research process.

Faculty assessment of the students' essays corroborated several of the students' responses. The English faculty member was impressed by the range of resources students were able to locate with librarian assistance, particularly in comparison to the resources students had located for a similar assignment the previous year. Further, the librarians' assistance in locating and retrieving information allowed students and faculty to dedicate more time to the evaluation and integration of that information, a crucial information literacy skill. As a result, nearly all students achieved an "Excellent" or "Good" for the research portion of their essays. Librarians valued the preparation that students brought with them to the collaborative relationship, given the time spent in class discussing the novel and the goals for the assignment. Librarians also valued the intellectual challenges posed by the students and their research needs. They enjoyed working with students to identify and locate a greater range of resources than anticipated, both traditional and serendipitous, as well as having in-depth conversations with the students about their research and analytical goals. Finally, while librarians did preparatory research in advance of meeting with the students, in their assessment they noted that the collaborative learning environment of the project indicates that such preparation is not necessary for a successful collaboration.

Conclusion

Every semester, in colleges and universities, thousands of students are assigned research papers or otherwise required to locate information. While the case study model described in this chapter may not be possible for each of those students, the benefits were clear. First, the faculty-librarian-student collaboration allowed students to produce better essays for the Web site. Students were able to locate a greater range of resources for their research, thereby improving their skills at locating and selecting information for their purpose and audience. Being guided through the research process—both how to find and how to evaluate resources—offered students a model they could apply to future research in English and other disciplines. Second, the collaboration encouraged students to consult librarians for future projects, especially early in the research process. Students came to recognize the assistance that librarians could provide. Finally, for English faculty and librarians, the collaboration reinforced their shared mission in fostering information literacy for lifelong learning. The three-week assignment required minimal preparation time between faculty and librarians, but the benefits extend beyond the initial project, as they continue to collaborate on efforts to instill an understanding of information literacy in other faculty, librarians, and students across the university. Faculty and librarians at other institutions could easily implement a collaborative triangle similar to the one described above, starting with just one research assignment in English or another discipline. Such collaborations can be successful with a minimal amount of planning and the willingness to provide open communication to make it work.

References

American Library Association. 2005. "Information Literacy Competency Standards for Higher Education." Retrieved March 10, 2006, from www.ala.org/acrl/ilcomstan.html.

Barker, Pat. 1991. *Regeneration*. New York: Vintage.

Burton, Vicki T., and Scott A. Chadwick. 2000. "Investigating the Practices of Student Researchers: Patterns of Use and Criteria for Use of Internet and Library Sources." *Computers and Composition* 17, no. 3: 309–328.

Egan, Philip J. 1992. "Bridging the Gap between the Student and the Library." *College Teaching* 40: 67–70.

Fister, Barbara. 2002. "Fear of Reference." *Chronicle of Higher Education: The Chronicle Review*, June 14: 20.

Hearn, Michael R. 2005. "Embedding a Librarian in the Classroom: An Intensive Information Literacy Model." *Reference Services Review* 33, no. 2: 219–227.

Holliday, Wendy, and Qin Li. 2004. "Understanding the Millennials: Updating Our Knowledge about Students." *Reference Services Review* 32, no. 4: 356.

Jenkins, Sandra. 2001. "Undergraduate Perceptions of the Reference Collection and the Reference Librarian in an Academic Library." *Reference Librarian*, no. 73: 229–241.

Leckie, Gloria J. 1996. "Desperately Seeking Citations: Uncovering Faculty Assumptions about the Undergraduate Research Process." *Journal of Academic Librarianship* 22: 201–208.

OCLC White Paper on the Information Habits of College Students: How Academic Librarians Can Influence Students' Web-Based Information Choices. 2002. Dublin, OH: OCLC Online Computer Library Center.

Paterson, Susanne F., and Carolyn B. White. 2004. "A Collaborative Approach to Information Literacy." *Academic Exchange* 8, no. 4: 165–171.

Valentine, Barbara. 1993. "Undergraduate Research Behavior: Using Focus Groups to Generate Theory." *Journal of Academic Librarianship* 19: 300–304.

———. 2001. "The Legitimate Effort in Research Papers: Student Commitment versus Faculty Expectations." *Journal of Academic Librarianship* 27, no. 2: 107–115.

Walter, Scott. 2000. "Engelond: A Model for Faculty-Librarian Collaboration in the Information Age." *Information Technology and Libraries* 19, no. 1: 34–41.

Westman, Karin E. 2001. *Regeneration: A Reader's Guide*. New York: Continuum.

Yohannes, Tamara, and Anna M. Johnson. 2004. "A Writing Course Faculty-Librarian Collaboration." *Academic Exchange* 8, no. 4: 120–124.

5

Inquiry-Based Word Study: Threads of Collaboration

Margaret Fain, Librarian, Head of Public Services, Kimbel Library
Sara Sanders, Professor and Chair of the Department of English,
  Communication, and Journalism
Linda Martin, Teaching Associate, English
Coastal Carolina University

About nine years ago a group of faculty interested in improving student learning at Coastal Carolina University began meeting to read and discuss books and articles related to teaching. Sanders was part of that group and was intrigued by William Ayers's story in his memoir *To Teach: The Journey of a Teacher*, where he told of teaching everything from one inquiry-based project his students selected (1993). He wanted them to study water ecology, but the students were fascinated by the bridge they saw on their field trip to a local river. Ayers and his middle school students began an inquiry about bridges that included lessons in physics and mathematics as they built bridges of various sorts in their classroom and lessons in photography, art, and metaphor as they considered bridges from all those perspectives. Based on this experience, Ayers said, "You can learn everything from anything" (Ayers, 1993: 86).

Sara Sanders, a linguist, began to think about how to apply this concept in her own teaching of introductory linguistics. While Sanders was excited about introducing students to the study of language, they routinely had difficulty applying the theoretical concepts in the course to real-world data. After reading Ayers, Sanders wondered whether it would be possible to learn everything about linguistic principles from the study of a single word. She asked her friend, colleague, and librarian collaborator Margaret Fain about her idea of introducing a word study project into English 451, Introduction to the Study of Language and Modern Grammar. Fain was enthusiastic, and the pair developed the word study project for this upper-level course. Because of its success as an inquiry-based project, the word study has now been adapted for use with first-year composition students and English-as-a-Second-Language (ESL) teachers. For the past nine years, this constantly evolving project has served as a model for faculty-librarian cooperation at Coastal Carolina University. With the introduction of the Association of College and Research Libraries (ACRL) Information Literacy Competency Standards to Kimbel Library's instruction program, the project has also served to model successful integration of key standards into the curriculum. The inquiry-based word study project is a case study that illustrates one way to develop and sustain a mutually successful long-term information literacy collaboration.

Background

Constructivist learning is based on the idea that new knowledge is built on the foundation of a student's prior knowledge; it is the activity of "making [new knowledge] their own" that creates the learning space (Good and Brophy, 2003: 408). Meaningful learning comes when students internalize the processes through "authentic" tasks (Cooperstein and Kovecar-Weidinger, 2004). With the word study project, the tasks are directly related to both the assignment and the underlying linguistic concepts. One advantage of this project is that many of the resources are largely pre-selected; thus students concentrate primarily on making sense of the resources in hand. For upper-level students, this focuses their attention on examining and comparing the information found in the various texts. Students must begin to understand the scope and content of the recommended dictionaries and the rationales behind inclusion or exclusion of words and meanings. They must be able to evaluate the information they find and then incorporate it into their reflections and class presentations. These activities directly parallel the performance indicators of Standard 3 of the Information Literacy Competency Standards: "The information literate student evaluates information and its sources critically and incorporates information into his or her knowledge base and value system" (ACRL, 2000).

The National Council of Teachers of English and the National Council for Accreditation of Teacher Education Program Standards: Program for Initial Preparation for Teachers of Secondary English Language Arts Grades 7–12, 2003 revision, emphasizes the importance of knowledge about language through seven target skills in section 3.1 related to information provided in linguistic classes. Linguistic principles are best understood and retained through experiential learning. For the linguist, all the language used in the world is a source of information. Helping students to understand how to use such things as Internet search engines as databases for the study of authentic language use was one of our project goals. Identifying and analyzing "authentic text" is a new concept to students. Most of the students in the Introduction to the Study of Language and Modern Grammar class are English majors in their junior or senior year. They have learned a lot about researching literary topics (we hope) and often have a sense that they know all they need to know about research. The word study project provides a different perspective on what it means to do research and requires use of sources the students may not even know exist. When Sanders began this work, she was focused on improving student learning of linguistic concepts; Fain was focused on improving student research and critical thinking skills. Both have been gratified to see the tremendous gains students make as a result of this project in increasing their understanding of what it means to do research and in using, assessing, and writing critically about a wide variety of sources.

Information Literacy Program at Coastal Carolina University

Coastal Carolina University is a rapidly growing state-supported institution that offers undergraduate and selected master's degrees to approximately 7,000 students. The English Department has grown from 125 majors when this project began to 186. A course in linguistics is required of all majors, and Introduction to the Study of Language and Modern Grammar is one of two linguistic courses offered by the department that meets this requirement. On average, twenty to thirty-five students enroll in this course.

The information literacy program at Kimbel Library is well established and conducts over 220 sessions a year reaching nearly two-thirds of Coastal students. Sessions are course integrated, and collaboration with faculty is encouraged in developing library sessions. The librarians are proactive in approaching professors to develop research assignments that address both the needs of the particular class and the overall objectives of the information literacy program. They are not hesitant about talking with instructors when assignments create problems for students. The information literacy librarians continually reach out to new faculty and faculty teaching new courses. This ensures that professors are aware of both the available resources and the contributions the instruction program makes to their students' success. As Gilson and Michel (2002) point out, successful library assignments are dependent on faculty participation. Librarians cannot sit back and wait to be approached; they must take the initiative and promote instruction on a personal, departmental, and institutional level (Gilson and Michel, 2002; Iannuzzi, 1998).

While many faculty support the principles of information literacy, they just do not call it that. It is important for librarians to make connections with discipline specific research. Translating "our" language to "their" language often makes a stronger point. By demonstrating parallels, librarians can offer faculty constructive advice on designing and developing "authentic tasks" that accomplish the objectives of the class. The word project involved offering up Internet search engines and directories of brand names as potential authentic texts. Often, just asking faculty to define the objectives of the assignment is enough to start a dialogue. When talking with professors about proposed topics, the main question is, "What do you want the students to be able to do when they have finished the project?" When that has been answered, the follow up question for faculty is, "What is not being accomplished with your current assignment?" Most of the time, the problems with an existing research assignment are directly related to the students' level of information literacy and the disconnect between that stage and the construction of the assignment. Well-designed assignments that operate on a variety of levels, like the word study, are more effective in teaching both the content and the process in ways that "stick" with the student.

When the word study first started in 1996, the library, like many other small academic libraries (student enrollment at Coastal was then 3,656), offered only locally owned print materials or cost-prohibitive access to mediated search databases. Internet searching was in its infancy, and few linguistic resources were available online. The use of corpus-based research was beginning to be a factor in linguistics research and teaching (Thomas and Short, 1996; Tribble and Jones, 1990; Wichmann et al., 1997). Over the past ten years, while the outcomes of the project have not changed, the resources have evolved and become more complex. One of the eye openers for students continues to be the sheer variety and complexity of potential resources for what seems at first to be a very simple assignment. With this in mind, the assignment is revised annually, by the librarian and the professor jointly, to incorporate newly available resources such as online dictionaries and linguistic databases.

Linguistics Perspective

The initial goal of the word study was to give beginning linguistics students an opportunity to conduct basic linguistic research and to apply theoretical concepts introduced in the course by carrying out a series of nine research assignments focused on their chosen word. Interestingly, while the word study was developed prior to the establishment of the ACRL Information Literacy Competency Standards, the complementary goals of the librarian and the professor led to a project that entails students' demonstrating an understanding of all five standards. The professor wanted students to be able to select a word that offered opportunities for both research and reflection. The librarian wanted students to select a word that offered opportunities to develop a critical approach to research. In assignment 1, "Choose Your Word," students select a word that has personal appeal. With the word in hand, they must select three unabridged dictionaries owned by the library and locate the word in all three. In their project notebook, they then write a reflective essay on their personal connection to the word and what they have learned so far. Thus the basic act of locating appropriate resources is tied to critically thinking about why the definitions vary from dictionary to dictionary and what implications this has for their research. For upper-level and graduate students this is often the first time that they have paused to consider why and how resources, like dictionaries, are constructed. The succeeding assignments build on this foundation of locating and critically analyzing both the information found and the sources used. Based on several years of grading data, we can generalize that students who successfully integrate research and theory usually earn a grade of A in both the project and in the course. These students demonstrate their ability to determine the nature and extent of information needed, access that information effectively and efficiently, evaluate the information and incorporate it into their linguistic knowledge base, and use information to accomplish a specific purpose (ACRL, 2000).

Linda Martin says of her student experience in Introduction to the Study of Language and Modern Grammar:

My biggest problem with the word study project was assignment 1, selecting the one word out of the thousands encountered daily that would actually work (and help me earn a good grade). The words I was first considering just didn't seem to have the spark that would keep me interested for four months. Dr. Moye, my medieval studies professor, suggested three words that might be fun and might lend themselves well to exploration: *kin*, *kettle*, and *jack*. After rejecting *kin* and *kettle*, *Jack*, to my utter delight, became my new best friend. Jack and I went back to the eighth century and met his ancestor Jacques. The continuing search for Jack's relatives led to other discoveries not only about the word but also about the times themselves. As Jack evolved, he has become, among many things, a sailor, a part of a piano, a game played, and has become invaluable in the modern world of technology. Imagine a computer without a computer jack or a car without a tire jack. And do not forget Halloween and Jack O'Lantern.

The Word Study Project

The goals of the word study project are tied closely to the proficiency goals of the core curriculum for Coastal Carolina University, which state that courses in each major will introduce students to research methods and resources relevant to their discipline. But instead of one small project, the students in the course are engaged in a semester-long word study project with each project assignment directly linked to applying material from the chapter concurrently being studied. The word study project consists of nine separate assignments, each tied to a distinct section of the text (complete assignments for the word study project can be found in appendices 5.1 and 5.2). The project is accomplished in stages throughout the semester. The sequential assignments build on the knowledge and skills gained in previous assignments. Students do not just learn to locate tools. Through their reflective writings about each assignment, they engage in a dialogue with the professor and themselves about how and why the tools have been developed. They must consider why editors choose to include or exclude meanings, definitions, or even the word itself. They begin to ask questions such as why do English-foreign language dictionaries differ in translation? What are the reasons definitions are or are not included in different dictionaries? Where are errors and how often do they appear? Why do words appear in some resources and not in others?

Through the project students use a variety of sources, including the following: both the print and online versions of the *Oxford English Dictionary*, general and subject dictionaries, foreign language dictionaries, slang and other specialized dictionaries, online catalogs, indexes, databases, Internet search engines, quotation and proverb books, and any other resource they can locate that sheds light on the use and history of their word. Students start with a list of recommended sources, but they are encouraged to expand beyond that list. Part of the success of the assignment is that students learn the value of serendipitous discovery, that browsing the shelves or the Internet may lead them to new and intriguing resources as they follow the threads of their word.

Integration with Information Literacy Standards

To complete the sections successfully, students must constantly ask themselves questions about the sources located. Does the source meet the needs of the assignment? Is it appropriate? What does it cover? What does it not cover? How does it compare with similar sources? Students must develop many of the core performance indicators as outlined in the ACRL Information Literacy Competency Standards in order to demonstrate how linguistic principles are applied to the sources selected. Assignment 1, "Choose Your Word," covers aspects of Standards 1 and 2, as students determine the nature and extent of information needed and begin accessing that information for their selected word. In word study assignment 4, students are asked to conduct word association interviews with at least three people as a method to "retrieve primary information," as stated in Standard 3.d (ACRL, 2000). In assignment 6, "Your Word in Translation," students are asked to look up their word in German/English–English/German, French/English–English/French, Spanish/English–English/Spanish dictionaries and two other foreign languages of their choice. They photocopy (or copy) the words given in the target language that translate their English word. Students then look up the target language words and see what English definition is given for each. This reverse translation exercise exposes students to translation issues in the cultural context of language as it is reflected semantically.

This exercise also reveals relationships between languages in the same "family" that students are typically not aware of. Afterward they write about what this research tells them about translation, about language, and about the relationship of languages to each other. In addition, students interview someone who is a native speaker of one of the languages they have investigated for this exercise about the meaning and use of their word in that language. If there are multiple translations offered for the word, then the students must ask their informant how these words are related to each other. Finally, students write a summary of the interview and their response to it. This particular assignment comes after students have examined and used a variety of English language dictionaries and have written reflectively on those experiences. The students have also previously conducted word association interviews with others in their class and with friends. Thus, while this assignment introduces new resources and a new method of examining language, the basic skills have already been introduced and the students can draw on those as they examine the complexities and semantics of language translation. The various elements of this assignment directly relate to Standard 3.2 and 3.3, where students comparatively examine various sources and then synthesize the "main ideas to construct new concepts" (ACRL, 2000).

In word study assignment 7, students examine the way their word is currently used in the world. Students must be able to construct searches in at least four different contexts. Options include searching the online catalog, appropriating periodical indexes, and using three Internet search engines. Students may also choose to locate their word as a brand or trade name. They can search for quotations or the use of their word as slang or taboo language. They can be creative and locate "wordplay" uses in song lyrics, bumper stickers, games, puns, and song, movie, or book titles. In order to complete this assignment, students must be able to construct searches in a variety of formats and use different classification schemes, as stated in Standard 2 (ACRL, 2000). In the linguistics course, students are encouraged to explore indexes and databases in a variety of disciplines to see where their word appears and in what context.

Designing the Word Study Project

The genesis of the word study project was a seemingly simple request. Inspired by her reading of Ayers, Sanders wondered if the hook of studying a single word all semester would enable her students to make connections between the linguistic principles presented in the textbook, *An Introduction to Language* by Fromkin and Rodman, and real-life applications. In previous semesters, Sanders had been frustrated by the inability of many of her students to understand linguistic theory. Sanders wanted students to be able to apply theory to real-world language data. Isolated projects and exercises were not producing the desired results. She had been considering different approaches when she encountered the Ayers quote. Sanders approached Fain with the idea of having students select one word, all semester collect data related to the history, structure, and use of the word, and write reflectively about the data incorporating principles of linguistic analysis. A semester-long course-integrated project offered the possibility of heightened student engagement and authentic learning. Sanders's initial concern was whether the project was feasible, given limited library resources at that time. The librarian recognized that the idea was feasible not only for linguistics but also for information literacy skill development. At this time, the instruction program at Coastal was moving toward a course-integrated model that encouraged collaboration with faculty to design and develop research projects that addressed both the needs of the course and critical thinking skills.

This project, if successful, would be an excellent marketing tool and would encourage similar collaborations to take place before projects were assigned to students. Before the word study project, most collaboration was taking place after the fact. Librarians were contacting faculty when students had problems with assignments and assisting with redesigning the assignment, usually after an entire class had been unnecessarily frustrated. With the word study project, the librarian was given the opportunity not only to try out the project before it was assigned but also to revise it to incorporate resources unfamiliar to the professor.

After talking with Fain about her ideas and receiving initial feedback, Sanders completed a preliminary draft of the project assignments. Using this draft and the word *smocking*, a decorative embroidery technique, Fain read the class text and conducted research in the potential resources identified by Sanders. Over the course of two weeks, she not only verified that these resources would indeed work but also provided additional suggestions for resources. In section 7 of the assignment "Your Word in Use," she suggested, students could use the "new" Internet search engines and to try trademark name searches. A few years later, the first generation of citation databases prompted the inclusion of searching in one or more databases to determine the use of the word in a variety of disciplines. Fain and Sanders have continued to review the exercise in terms of the class objectives and the resources available to students. The collaboration continues as the project is refined annually to meet the evolving objectives of the class.

The syllabus for the linguistics class states, "Your word will be the thread you follow to learn all you can about language and the study of language." The guiding objective behind this project was the need for a semester-long application project to help students apply and understand theory. In the past, students had read the text but did not seem able to transfer that linguistic knowledge to real-world language applications. The goal was to enable students to understand and apply the linguistic theory presented in the text through the study of one word. Words that work well in this project have a "story": something about their history, changes in use over time, their complex web of meanings, and the impact of other languages on them offer a multitude of areas for exploration. Words in the past that have proved fruitful include *celestial, jack, hand, knock, board, carousel, celebration, academy, saucer,* and *toilet.* Students use both tools and processes for linguistic research. They are exposed to a variety of resources, ranging from print (dictionaries), electronic (Helsinki database, Plumbline virtual thesaurus, *OED,* and Internet search engines), interviews (a sociolinguistic application); and they also are confronted with translation issues. Working in a small university library, students initially did not have access to the variety and range of resources available at larger institutions.

> **Of the initial work Margaret Fain says:**
>
> When Sara [Sanders] first approached me about the assignment, it was midsummer and she was heading off to Vermont for a five-week teaching stint. She stopped by the library and said, "I have a great idea, do you think this is feasible?" We talked for a bit and when I looked over the first draft I immediately recognized the possibilities of using the assignment to achieve not only her objectives, but also to help senior English majors develop their research skills in a meaningful manner. With a copy of the text in one hand, and my word in another, I started the search process. In doing this, I kept track of my progress, copied everything I found, tried out different resources, and presented Sara with a completed notebook on her return. What was exciting for me was the opportunity to try out an idea for an assignment before it was given to students and to contribute significantly to its development. Sara was extremely receptive to my suggestions for improving the variety and number of resources that students could use, particularly in assignment 7. She and I had already done some collaboration on smaller projects, but this was the first truly course-integrated project I had worked on.

Designing the assignments around local resources gives students more opportunities to be successful.

Continuing Development

For the first seven years of the word study project, library instruction took place in the classroom or reference area of the library. Students were given a handout listing sample sources for each assignment and were shown sample resources (the handout for the project's library orientation session can be found in appendix 5.3).

As library instruction resources expanded to computers, and then a classroom with laptops, the session was adjusted to accommodate new technologies, new resources, and new instructional space. Currently, students are provided with an online listing of Kimbel Library resources through ChantSource, a mySQL database that allows lists of resources to be generated by topic or class, and are given the opportunity for hands-on searching in the online *Oxford English Dictionary*. Most students arrive at the session with several possible words in mind. One of the goals of the instruction session is to assist students in determining which of these potential words offers the most opportunities for exploration. Words that are older and have undergone significant meaning changes usually work well with this project.

One of the most important factors with both seniors and first-year students is the students' interest in and commitment to their word. This is the first step in making the connections that take this project beyond a series of exercises. Many of the students are not aware of all they are learning during the project. As they write the reflective pieces and make the presentations, their understanding of the underlying linguistic and information literacy theories are articulated.

Sara Sanders on using the project with other classes:

I taught some of these graduate seminars in linguistics at St. Michael's College in Vermont, where the librarians helping me with the project were delighted to have a copy of Margaret's library orientation handout to adapt to the sources available in the library at St. Michael's College. Inspired by the application of the project in ESL classes, I later taught an English 101 freshman composition class focused on the theme of language study using *Language Awareness: Readings for College Writers* by Escholz, Rosa, and Clark (2002) as the text and an adaptation of the Word Study project for the class research.

Adapting the Project

The success of the word study project with undergraduate students has led to its adaptation for graduate-level ESL teachers and for use in undergraduate first-year composition classes. At least one former Coastal student adapted the assignment for use by high school students during her Master of Arts in Teaching (MAT) practicum. Sanders has used the project with graduate linguistics seminars for ESL teachers and has discussed with them ways to use parts of the assignment with their ESL students. Many of these graduate students are non-native speakers of English themselves and have found the exploration of semantic fields for words across languages to be interesting and enlightening. They have also enjoyed the sociolinguistic interviews with native speakers about their words, and both the native and non-native speakers of English who teach ESL often incorporate the word association interviews into the vocabulary work they do with ESL students.

First-Year Students and the Word Study Project

In English composition and literature library instruction sessions, first-year students are introduced to the concepts of selecting and using potential sources, retrieving information through a variety of methods, evaluating selected resources, and communicating about the project to others. All students are exposed to issues of fee-versus-free information in gathering their sources and are required to provide copies or printouts of all materials used for citations to deter unintended plagiarism. Most English classes expect students to use the library and its resources to provide support for a series of small papers or projects that culminate in the final assignment for the semester. After becoming an instructor at Coastal Carolina University, Linda Martin began to adapt for first-year students the word study project she had loved as a senior. Using the most recent edition of the project, she made very few changes and embarked on her first project as instructor, not student. She briefly discussed her goals of encouraging students to spend hours gazing in wonder at all the material available to them with the librarians. The librarians, ever courteous, smiled and pulled the requested dictionaries to put on reserve. The seasoned librarians, unlike the new instructor of English, knew there are college students and then there are first-year college students.

Linda Martin as a new instructor:

My first mistake in incorporating the word study project was forgetting that an eighteen-year-old marine science major or a nineteen-year-old professional golf major would not have the same interest in linguistics as an English major. They did not know there were dictionaries that would provide more information than what would be needed on Friday's vocabulary test. They were terrified by the *OED* [*Oxford English Dictionary*] and its vast amount of information. Interviewing anyone seemed to be pure agony to students who were just coming out of their shells during class discussions. The idea of looking up their word in foreign language dictionaries was equally daunting.

My error in judging the interest and skills level of freshmen students was compounded by the fact that I had no trouble as a student asking the librarians for help but felt uncomfortable requesting help as an instructor.

The next semester that Martin used the word study project, she met with the librarians, who asked her what had and had not worked. It took a long time to explain what had not worked but very little time to explain what had worked. The librarians helped her reorganize the project in such a way as to use the library resources, in combination with selected Internet resources, more effectively. The result kept the dictionary component and incorporated famous quotes and Internet searches for brand name connections or lyrics using the words of choice. Each student was asked to prepare a presentation that would introduce his or her word to the rest of the class. Over the succeeding years, the project has been trimmed and adjusted again and again. Gone was the lofty goal that students would love a project simply because the instructor did. The current goal is instead one of cooperation between the professor and the library staff, cooperative research between students and the library staff, and a partnership between the professor, the library staff, and the students to help students develop and refine their research skills.

The underlying information literacy standards enabled this project to be adapted successfully for a variety of students. Prior to college, most students have had contact with librarians only through annual mandatory meetings in high school. They do not yet understand how crucial establishing a relationship with the librarians is for their collegiate success. First-year students often believe that conducting research using Ask Jeeves is the best way to obtain the data necessary for assignments. This project shows freshmen the first steps that will help them recognize the material necessary for successful research in more complicated assignments, how to use this material, and how to correctly give credit to primary researchers. Most important, the project engages students, whether they are first-year or seniors. The more involved students are in the learning process, the more likely it is that they will retain the knowledge or skill (Bicknell-Holmes and Hoffman, 2000).

The freshman word study project, like Sanders's linguistic-based project, requires students to do more than simply photocopy entries out of dictionaries. Students are

Linda Martin's perspective:

Overall, the first-year project has been a labor of love. Each time I delete a segment I go into depression because I know exactly what students are missing when it comes to gaining individual awareness and knowledge. Each time I add a segment it is like a rebirth. In the coming semesters I will again be working with the library staff to revise the project. The dictionary segment will be far more hands-on during a library orientation session, and students will do part of their research with the combined help and guidance of professor and reference librarian. I will also be re-incorporating the quotation segment, which will include a tie-in to each individual student's major and will continue with the presentation component.

expected to consider the implications of why and how the meanings of words have changed and how these changes are reflected in everyday speech. Students then make connections between the spoken word and the written word after researching how words are used, for example, by corporate America. These independent threads of linguistic data are then woven into written assignments that ask students to explain why they selected their individual words and what their research led them to consider about the power of language. The final component of the freshman project has always been to share what they have learned with their fellow students. The librarians have proved invaluable to students in their willingness to help students sift through the various types of materials (posters, visual aids, music, etc.) housed in the library that have consistently made the presentation segment a success. Students engaged in the study have created powerful presentations. One student traced the journey of *court* from *courtroom* to *courtesan* using PowerPoint. Another student created an illustrated children's book using the each letter of the word on an individual page to tell the story of the word. One music major composed and performed an original piece based on his experiences with his word. As a professor, Martin was awed by the power of language and the power of connections students can make.

Martin's experience in transferring the project to first-year students is not uncommon. First-year students are just beginning to learn to identify resources. By reducing the number of assignments and focusing the project on the goals of cooperation, basic research, and proper citations, Martin was able to create a positive experience for her students. As important, it increased her comfort level in working with librarians as peers. Ensuring student success in meeting assignment requirements is a critical factor in creating motivated students who "get" what research is and who begin to build the skills that the upper-level students already possess. The difference in research abilities between the two classes demonstrates that students do improve with time and also shows how information literate students develop. The basic underlying information literacy skills facilitated the transfer of this project to both first-year and graduate student courses.

Our Reflections on the Collaborative Process and Its Outcomes

Margaret Fain reflects:

On a personal level, collaborating with faculty colleagues has been one of the most enriching aspects of working at Coastal Carolina University. Through my experiences, I have become a better teacher, a better collaborator, and a better librarian. In true collaboration, everyone has an equal say. We might not always like what we hear, but as a learning tool it is invaluable. As Raspa and Ward (2000) point out, true collaboration is a "pervasive long term relationship" where the participants share goals and tasks and "participate in extensive planning and participation." This is exactly my experience. Participating in the give and take of creating assignments and creating book chapters (like this one) has been a rewarding experience. Being invited into students' learning and not being a tacked-on addition to a course creates a space where true learning takes place for all the participants.

Sara Sanders on collaboration:

In a values clarification workshop, I discovered that my core value is connection, so it is not surprising to me that collaboration is my default mode for planning projects, for creating assignments, for designing courses, and for writing. In all real collaboration the collected wisdom transcends the sum of each individual's contributions. I count on Margaret [Fain] to help me think through research ideas for my classes and to collaborate with me in giving presentations and writing articles about our findings. When I introduce her to my students at the beginning of library orientation sessions I tell them that Margaret knows everything (which is almost true); and, on the rare occasion she isn't sure about something, she knows where to find the answer. The students smile, but I am very serious!

Before the word study project, Margaret and I had developed a metaphor-based project for a freshman honors seminar. We used cognitive metaphors as described by Lakoff and Johnson in *Metaphors We Live By* (1980) as a method of creating a meaningful research assignment that would engage honors students in a fresh appreciation of what it can mean to use library resources to investigate a topic, in this case a cognitive metaphor, without a written paper as the final product. We have presented at linguistic conferences and published an article and a book chapter based on our work together and with other faculty on this metaphor project

Collaborating with Linda [Martin] on the word study project when she was a student in English 451, and later when she became my colleague in the English Department and adapted the project for use with her students in English 102, and now as we write this piece together has been the culmination of a web of wondrous connections! I'm teaching an English 102 class this semester and have asked Linda if I may use her adaptation of the word study project with my students. She enthusiastically agreed.

Linda Martin:

As an English major who was a senior, and nearing the advanced years of being considered a senior in real life, I had already discovered what a valuable resource librarians were. The librarians here at Coastal Carolina University are incredibly approachable, have unbounded enthusiasm for new topics to help students research and are invariably kind and dedicated to making students aware of the many types of material available. My first experience with the project would not have been nearly as successful without the librarians explaining to me that it was OK to include *The Dictionary of Slang* or *Musical Morphology: A Discourse and a Dictionary* in a project such as this.

The word project, and my individual goals for freshmen students, has a definite place in both my heart and my classroom. Instilling a love for research and inquiry in students should be what college is all about. Thank goodness we at Coastal Carolina University have as our primary resource in achieving this goal our excellent library staff and professors like Sara [Sanders], who had the vision to create this amazing project.

Does It Work?

The original word study project serves as a course assessment for the Introduction to the Study of Language and Modern Grammar. Successful completion of each assignment is necessary for students to be able to complete the next assignment. The structure of the project asks not just for the results of the research but also for reflective pieces where students are asked to evaluate how the structure and organization of the resources used impact the information located. An analysis of grades over seven semesters shows that the students who do well on the word study do well on the final exam and in the final grade for the course. Grasping the underlying theoretical concepts of the project is the determining factor in a student's success rate in the linguistics course. In addition to providing a context for the theoretical information, the word study project invites habits of investigation that allow students to develop scaffolding for each new concept in the course. It has been interesting to note that students who do well with the project continue to exhibit much higher levels of information-seeking skills in their ensuing contacts with Fain and other librarians. Students in this class spend a lot of time working in the library and become well known to the librarians. Subsequent interactions with the librarian often begin with the phrase "you helped me with the word study."

In the first-year class, students learn that the patterns of behavior required to complete the assignment successfully are the same skills that they must use for the entire class. These include attention to detail, following instructions, meeting deadlines, not being afraid to ask questions, and thinking critically about sources. Students must organize data, discern the relative value of sources, compile the information, and present it in an engaging and coherent manner to the class. Based on the grading data for the past several years, students who receive higher project grades receive higher overall grades at the end of the semester. In addition, students who go into the project with a lower class grade but accomplish all the tasks of this project typically receive a final letter grade that is higher than their initial work indicated. This is the first research project encountered by students in the class and lays the groundwork for all the projects that follow.

Another measure of the success of the project with students is that it has led to panel presentations at the 1999 and 2000 Celebration of Inquiry Conferences at Coastal Carolina University. In fall, English 451 students were invited to consider choosing for their Word Study project one of the words in the title of the conference. The 1999 theme was "Conflict and Creativity in the Search for Knowledge." The 2000 Celebration of Inquiry theme was "Truth, Beauty and Imagination in the Academy." During the spring conference, students participated in a panel presentation along with Fain, Sanders, and an education professor. The panel presentations focused on the origins, meanings, and contemporary uses of each word in an interactive presentation that engaged the audience in word study. This was an enriching experience for all participants and demonstrated to the student presenters the broader applications of classroom work.

Conclusion

The collaboration continues to work and leads to new collaborative projects because it has been successful in creating meaningful assignments and because it creates an atmosphere that encourages experimentation. Word of mouth creates more opportunities for collaboration with other faculty, which are sustained and developed because of mutual respect for each other's expertise and appreciation for the rich results of combining perspectives from multiple disciplines. Librarians at Coastal Carolina University assisted in the design of the capstone research course for recreation majors and work with faculty in fields as diverse as psychology, sociology, and business to redesign and develop more effective course assignments.

This word study project has been successful because it was collaboratively designed from the beginning and also in its subsequent variations. Both the librarian and the professor are integral parts of the project, as Martin discovered when she attempted to redesign the project without librarian participation. In her own words: "I crashed and burned." The project works in a broader sense because words are personal to each of us. The pieces of the project are flexible; sections can be moved, deleted, added, and refined depending on the goals of each individual class. The project is adaptable to institutions of all sizes because all academic libraries have access to a variety of linguistic source data or "authentic texts." All that is needed is a working partnership between a librarian and a professor to make the project a reality.

For any project to succeed, it requires all participants—student, professor, and librarian—to collaborate. Together we use the threads of our experiences to create a valid learning space for all involved. Each word becomes a thread that the students follow to gain not only information literacy but also a broader sense of themselves. When students are truly reflective about the connections they are making, their word is woven into a larger tapestry that examines the role of language in constructing our ideas of self and society. This is a real collaboration in which all participants have differing needs and expectations. The word study project allows these needs to intersect in a manner that is engaging for students and accomplishes the objectives of both the professor for content and the librarians for critical thinking skills. Willingness to understand the needs of professors for subject content enables librarians to create a meaningful experience for all involved.

References

Association of College and Research Libraries (ACRL). 2000. *Information Literacy Competency Standards for Higher Education*. Chicago: ALA.

Ayers, William. 1993. *To Teach: The Journey of a Teacher*. New York: Teacher's College Press.

Bicknell-Holmes, Tracy, and Paul Seth Hoffman. 2000. "Elicit, Engage, Experience, Explore: Discovery Learning in Library Instruction." *Reference Services Review* 28, no. 4: 313–322.

Cooperstein, Susan E., and Elizabeth Kocevar-Weidinger. 2004. "Beyond Active Learning: A Constructivist Approach to Learning." *Reference Services Review* 32, no. 2: 141–148.

Escholz, Paul, Alfred Rosa, and Virginia Clark, eds. 2000. *Language Awareness: Readings for College Writers*. 8th ed. Boston: Bedford/St. Martins.

Fromkin, Victoria, and Robert Rodman. 1998. *An Introduction to Language*. 6th ed. New York: Harcourt Brace Jovanovich.

Gilson, Caroline, and Stephanie Michel. 2002. "Fishing for Success: Faculty/Librarian Collaboration Nets Effective Library Assignments." In *Making the Grade: Academic Libraries and Student Success*. Edited by Maurie Caitlin Kelly and Andrea Kross. Chicago: Association of College and Research Libraries: 57–70.

Good, Thomas L, and Jere E. Brophy. 2003. *Looking in Classrooms*. 9th ed. Boston: Allyn and Bacon.

Iannuzzi, Patricia. 1998. "Faculty Development and Information Literacy: Establishing Campus Partnerships." *Reference Services Review* 26, no. 3/4: 97–102.

Lakoff, George, and Mark Johnson. 1980. *Metaphors We Live By*. Chicago: U of Chicago P.

National Council of the Teachers of English (NCTE). 2003. *NCTE/NCATE Program Standards: Program for Initial Preparation of Teachers of Secondary English Language Arts, Grades 7–12*. Urbana, IL: NCTE.

Raspa, Dick, and Dane Ward. 2000. "Listening for Collaboration: Faculty and Librarians Working Together." In *The Collaborative Imperative: Librarians and Faculty Working Together in the Information Universe*. Edited by Dick Raspa and Dane Ward. Chicago: ACRL: 1–17.

Thomas, Jenny, and Mick Short, eds. 1996. *Using Corpora in Language Research*. New York: Addison Wesley.

Tribble, Chris, and Glyn Jones. 1990. *Concordances in the Classroom: A Resource Book for Teachers*. London: Longman Group.

Wichman, Anne, Steven Fligelstone, Tony McEnery, and Gerry Knowles, eds. 1997. *Teaching and Language Corpora*. New York: Addison Wesley.

Appendix 5.1: English 451 An Inquiry-Based Word Study Assignment

English 451

Twenty percent of your course grade will be based on this semester-long word study project and the presentation you give of your findings. The nine assignments in this project are designed to give you an opportunity to conduct basic linguistic research and apply concepts presented in the related chapters of our text: *An Introduction to Language*, 7th ed. edited by Victoria Fromkin, Robert Rodman, and Nina Hyams (Boston: Heinle, 2003).

You will pick one word that has special significance for you to be the hook on which your language study hangs. Collecting data related to your word's history, structure, and use and writing reflectively about your data will bring the principles of linguistic analysis to life for you. "It is possible to learn everything from anything" (William Ayers, *To Teach*), so your word will be the thread you follow to learn all you can about language and the study of language.

Keep your word study assignments and research notes in a loose-leaf notebook with dividers. Date each entry so you will have a record for yourself of the way your ability to think about language grows during the semester.

Overall questions to consider in each reflective entry:

- What have I learned about my word? about language?
- What have I learned about this source of data?
- What have I learned about the world (human beings, organization of thought, history, development of ideas, etc.)?
- **What questions does this research raise for me?** (Identifying your questions and looking for answers to them is a way of "following the thread" that helps anything teach you everything.)

If your word does not show up in a data source, write reflectively about why it isn't there. What is it about the word that keeps it from appearing in the source? Consider whether there is an alternate term (perhaps a more general word) or a synonym you could use to search in the same source. If so, see what the source has to say about your alternate word. Consider whether there is a related source which might include your word.

- *Note: **[Library]** at the end of an entry means library resources are needed.

Assignment 1: Choose your word. [In connection with CH 1 of our text: What Is Language?]

Begin by thinking about words that interest you. The words might be significant to you for some reason, ones that name or relate to something that matters to you—a value or ideal, a passionate cause, a career or hobby. The words might just be ones that sound interesting to you or ones that you are curious about. Some words that have produced excellent studies in the past are **celebrate, saucer, board, smock, jack, academy, knowledge, inquiry,** and **celestial.**

Have a look at *Studies in Words*, 2nd ed., by C. S. Lewis (1967), which is on reserve in the library for this course. As a way of beginning to think about possibilities for your word choice, note the words Lewis chose to study and some of the connections he made to them. **[Library]**

Look up your word in three "good" dictionaries by different publishers. **[Library]** Make a photocopy of the entry from each dictionary and label the entry with the name of the dictionary, name of the publisher, and the date of publication. If the entries seem scant, think about choosing another word. You will also use the copies of these dictionary entries in assignments 2, 3, and 5.

For your project notebook write a response to your perusal of Lewis's book and a reflective entry about your personal connection(s) with the word you've chosen for your study. Why did you choose the word? What do you hope to learn about it?

Assignment 2: The meaningful units in your word. [In connection with CH 3 of our text: Morphology]

How many morphemes does your word have? What types are they? How are they combined? Make some kind of chart or visual representation of the morpheme arrangement in your word.

What other words are structurally related to your word?

For example, *photograph, photographer, photography,* and *photographic* are structurally related words which belong to the same "family" and share common elements. You may need to use the *Oxford English Dictionary* to see whether or not the words you've chosen are in fact related to your word or just SEEM to be related. **[Library or online]**

Make a chart that shows the array of structurally related words. Write reflectively about your work.

Assignment 3: Your word in your mental lexicon. [In connection with CH 4 of our text: Syntax]

Refer to your dictionary entries from assignment 1. Can your word be used as more than one part of speech? Are sample sentences given for different uses of the word in all the dictionaries? What does this research tell you about dictionaries? Does it raise any questions for you about dictionaries?

What would the entry for your word look like in your mental lexicon? Write as complete an "entry" as possible.

How is your entry similar to the dictionary entries? How is it different?

Assignment 4: What your word "means." [In connection with CH 5 of our text: The Meanings of Language]

What words do you associate with your word? What words have a similar meaning? How are the words related to your word? Is your word broader or narrower than the others? Is it more formal or informal? Make your own array of words that are semantically related to your word.

Check 3 thesauruses and make a list of the synonyms or related words they provide for your word. Give the name and publisher of each thesaurus you use. Use a different color of ink to add to your semantic array any words that are related that you hadn't included there. **[Library]**

Do a word-association interview with at least ten people about your word. Consider the sociolinguistic factors related to the respondents. Does gender, age, occupation, and the like, seem to make a difference in your results? Make an array that shows the responses. Write reflectively about your discoveries.

Assignment 5: Your word in phonetic symbols. [In connection with CH 6 of our text: Phonetics]

Write your word in phonetic symbols. Check your dictionary entries from assignment 1. Can your word be pronounced in more than one way? How closely does the pronunciation provided for the word in the dictionaries match your phonetic transcription of it? If there are differences, how do you account for them?

Assignment 6: Your word in translation. [In connection with CH 8 of our text: Language Acquisition]

Look up your word in German/English–English/German, French/English–English/French, Spanish/English–English/Spanish dictionaries and two other foreign languages of your choice. Photocopy (or copy) the word(s) given in the target language to translate your English word. Then look up the target language words to see what English definition is given for each. **[Library]**

Write about what this research tells you about translation, about language, and about the relationship of languages to each other.

Interview someone who is a native speaker of one of the languages you have investigated for this exercise about the meaning and use of your word in that language. If there are multiple translations offered for your word, ask your informant how these words are related to each other. Write a summary of the interview and your response to it.

Assignment 7: Your word in use. [In connection with CH 10 of our text: Language in Society and CH 5: The Meanings of Language]

Explore the ways your word is used in the world by exploring at least **four** of the following options and writing reflectively about your discoveries. In your reflective writing, consider your discoveries about the stylistic and pragmatic features of your word. Who uses the word? Why? What are some connotations of the word?

a. Do "keyword" searches using your word in the computerized library card catalog and relevant periodical indexes. Record the name of the source used, the number of "hits" for your word from each source. Copy sample/representative titles or other contexts in which the word appears. Are there significant differences in the number of times you find your word used in one source compared to another? Do the contexts vary from one source to the next?

b. Try a keyword search in three Internet search engines. Record number of hits for your word in each to get an idea of usage. Copy sample/representative titles or other contexts in which the word appears. Are there significant differences in the number of times you find your word used in one source compared to another? If so, how do you explain this? Do the contexts vary from one source to the next?

c. Look for quotations in books of quotations that contain your word and make copies of what you find. **[Library]**

d. Is your word used in a trade name or brand name? **[Library]** Look for advertisements in which your word is included and put copies of them in your word study notebook.

e. Can this word be jargon, slang, taboo language, a personal name? Does your word have metaphorical associations? Is it euphemistic in any way? **[Library]**

f. What examples of wordplay can you find related to this word? What feature(s) of language make this "play" possible? Look at creative, imaginative uses of language in song lyrics, cartoons, puns, jokes, film and book titles, greeting cards, bumper stickers, games, poetry, advertisements, vanity license plates, and so on.

g. Look at the Library of Congress Subject Headings, commonly referred to as "The Red Book" (Tech Services Z695 .Z5 L524a). What is the subject under which you find your word? What are related subjects? What does this tell you about where your word fits in the web of connected subjects? **[Library]**

Assignment 8: Your word's history. [In connection with CH 11 of our text: Language Change]

Look up your word in the *Oxford English Dictionary* (OED) and make a photocopy of the entry there. What is the origin of your word? How long has it been used in English? Has there been a change of the word's meaning over time? **[Library or online]** Look for all the uses of your word in the online version of the *OED*. How many entries are there? What do they tell you about the journey your word has made in its use in the English language? What are the different spellings of your word? What kinds of documents does it appear in? How frequently does it appear at different times in the history of English? Write about the history of your word and its uses.

Assignment 9: What I've learned about my word and language.

Write reflectively about what you have learned from this word study project.

Word Study Presentation

Prepare a one-page handout with a copy for each class member presenting the "news" about your word. Distribute the handouts during your word study presentation.

This project was developed by Sara Sanders and Margaret Fain.

Appendix 5.2: English 102 First-Year Word Study Assignment

Word study project: English 102

Assignment 1: Word history and you   Due in one week   50 points

Step 1: Begin by thinking about words that interest you. The words might be significant to you for some reason. They may name or relate to something that matters to you—a value or ideal, a passionate cause, a career or hobby. The words might just be ones that sound interesting to you or ones that you are curious about. The word you select must be at least 100 years old.

Some words that have produced excellent studies in the past are **celebrate, knock, saucer, board, smock, jack, academy, kin, kettle, knowledge, inquiry,** and **celestial**. Words that do not work as well include *love, pretty, whore,* and *chauffeur* (which is actually a French word).

Step 2: Look up your word in the *Oxford English Dictionary* (OED) and make 3×5 card showing: the origin of your word, how long it has been used in English, does its original meaning sound like Modern English, has there been a change in the word's meaning over time, how many *OED* entries are there, what do the entries tell you about the journey your word has made in its use in the English language, what are the different spellings of your word, what kinds of documents does it appear in, and how frequently does it appear at different times in the history of English? **[Library]** In 1 1/2 to 2 pages typed, write about the history of your word and its uses.

Write a reflective, 1–2 page typed entry about your personal connection(s) with the word you've chosen for your study. Why did you choose the word? What have you learned about it thus far?

Assignment 2: Words, Words, Words   Due in one week   50 points

Step 1: Look up your word in three "good"—not online—dictionaries by different publishers. **[Library]** Make a 3×5 card from each dictionary and label the entry with the name of the dictionary, name of the publisher and the date of publication. If the entries seem scant, choose another word.

Step 2: Look up your word in two foreign language dictionaries of your choice. Make a 3×5 card that indicates meanings from English to the language of your choice. On the reverse side of the card indicate the way the meaning changes when the foreign language is translated back into English. For example, the word *window* has a meaning that is fairly obvious to us. However, a good French dictionary lists over thirty types of *window* meanings. What does the difference in translations say about the ways language is perceived and used worldwide?

Step 4: Write a one-page paper that explains the journey your word has made through history and how your word has expanded or completely changed meaning.

Assignment 3: Your word in use   Due in one week   50 points

Present your word to the class in a 3–5-minute presentation that is both informative and appealing to the audience. Ideas that have worked well in the past include Jeopardy type games, stories or songs featuring your word, words in crossword puzzles, "lectures" that take your word to unexpected places. For example, the word *court* can be expanded to include offshoot words such as *courtesy, courtroom, courtesan,* and *courtship*. The idea is to give the class an idea how your word has "grown up" over the ages. Please let me know if you will need any special equipment such as PowerPoint.

Appendix 5.3: Word Study Library Orientation Handout

Word Study English 451

"We should constantly use the most common, little, easy words." John Wesley

Dictionaries: [assignment 1, 2]

> *Oxford English Dictionary.* Second Edition (20 volumes). REF PE 1625 .O87 1989. Or online at http://www.coastal.edu/referencesdb.html. Undoubtedly the most comprehensive and widely used dictionary of the English language. Excellent for archaic uses and word origins. "Good Dictionaries": a selection of "good" dictionaries can be found in the REF PE 1675 section of the library.

Lexicons: [assignment 4]

> WordNet: http://www.cogsci.princeton.edu/~wn. Lexical database for English words. Entries provide synonyms, hypernyms, coordinate terms, and familiar uses for nouns, verbs, adjectives, and adverbs.

Thesaurus and Synonym Dictionaries: [assignment 4]

"A synonym is the word you use when you can't spell the word you first thought of." Burt Bacharach

> *Roget's Thesaurus* Dictionary Stand, first floor
> *Random House College Thesaurus* REF PE 1591 .R314 2000
> *Bartlett's Roget's Thesaurus* REF PE 1591 .B35 1996

Foreign Language Dictionaries: [assignment 6]

"He . . . speaks three or four languages word for word without book." Shakespeare, *Twelfth Night*
The English-to-another-language dictionaries are located in the Reference section under the call number for the language.

> PD = Norwegian, Swedish
> PF = Dutch, German
> PJ = Hebrew, Yiddish, Arabic
> PL = Japanese, Chinese, Vietnamese
> PE = English
> PG = Serbo-Croatian, Russian, Polish
> PK = Persian

Quotations: [assignment 7]

"I hate quotations." Ralph Waldo Emerson
The standard and not-so-standard quotation books are all shelved in the **REF PN 6081-6083** section.
(The quotes on this sheet came from the *Oxford Dictionary of Quotations, Macmillan Dictionary of Quotations,* and *Morrow's International Dictionary of Contemporary Quotations.*)
"A proverb is one man's wit and all men's wisdom." Lord John Russell

The proverb, maxims, and motto quotation books are shelved just beyond the quotation books in the **REF PN 6231-6426** section. These are especially useful for older words and older meanings.

Trade Names: [assignment 7]

Brands and Their Companies (2 vol.) REF T 223 .V4 A25 1996

Slang/Taboo/Jargon: [assignment 7]

"Yesterday's daring metaphors are today's clichés. Yesterday's obscenities are today's banalities." Arthur Koestler

Historical Dictionary of American Slang. REF PE 2846 .H57 1994
A Dictionary of Slang and Unconventional English REF PE 3721 .P3 1984
Other slang/taboo word dictionaries are located in the same call number area.

Etymology/Word Meanings: [assignment 7]

The Barnhart Dictionary of Etymology REF PE 1580 .B35 1988
Webster's Word Histories REF PE 1580 .W35 1989
Other dictionaries of word meanings are located in the REF PE 1580 section.

Phrases: [assignment 7] "I'm tickled pink."

Heavens to Betsy! & Other Curious Sayings. REF PE 1689 .F757
The Facts on File Encyclopedia of Word and Phrase Origins REF PE 1689 .H47 1987
Picturesque Expressions: A Thematic Dictionary REF PE 1689 .P5
Other phrase and expression books are located in the REF PE 1689 section.

6

Semillas de Cambio: The Teaching of Information Competency in Chicano and Latino Studies

Grace Peña Delgado, Assistant Professor of History and Religious Studies, Pennsylvania State University, Formerly Assistant Professor of History, Chicano and Latino Studies Department
Susan C. Luévano, Librarian, Anthropology, Ethnic Studies, and Women's Studies
California State University, Long Beach

When it comes to navigating the labyrinth of online information sources, students in Chicano and Latino studies (CHLS) approach this effort with as much trepidation as other university students. Although scholars have done a fine job in identifying material and social reasons for this condition, few have ventured into the learning experiences of CHLS students or faculty engaged in information literacy.[1] One such place that has tackled this issue is the Chicano and Latino Studies Department at the California State University, Long Beach (CSULB), campus. In the fall semester of 2004, the authors of this article were awarded a grant entitled *Semillas de Cambio* (Seeds of Change) from the California State University Information Competence Initiative. This project was among the first of its kind to address information literacy in the context of curriculum reform while utilizing a collaborative librarian-faculty model in the discipline of Chicano and Latino studies. *Semillas* grew from a strong interpersonal relationship, a shared disciplinary vision, and a desire to integrate library research and computer, new media, and technology literacy into the CHLS curriculum. The contribution of the *Semillas* project demonstrates how faculty, once peer trained, can become the primary facilitators of course-integrated information competency.

Equally, the disciplines of Library and Information Studies and Chicano and Latino studies have experienced colossal shifts over the last ten years in ideology, pedagogy, and purpose. While librarians have attempted to master, manage, and teach information literacy in a continuously evolving technological environment, instructors have rapidly conceptualized courses in new areas of Chicano and Latino studies; at the same time, librarians and faculty continuously experiment with inventive classroom approaches just barely keeping pace with students' needs. Teaching, nonetheless, would be made much easier if librarians and faculty joined efforts in designing information literacy and content-based assignments and assessments. Given the distinct yet complementary perspectives of librarians and faculty, the benefits of their efforts would be immense, but students would be the clear winners here.

Collaborative teaching efforts almost always lend themselves to posing student-centered questions: What are students' race and class backgrounds? What institutionally based barriers impede the acquiring of information literacy? What are students' skills gaps and their skills strengths? Although some of these conversations may conclude that Chicano and Latino university students are at a material or even *cultural* disadvantage when engaging the exotic world of information technology, these suppositions are clearly wrong. In fact, it is precisely the positive life experiences that can connect Chicano and Latino students to the realm of research, writing, critical thinking, and information literacy.

This is not a new idea. Brazilian educator and philosopher Paulo Freire places great emphasis on a "lived-experience" model of educational empowerment (Freire, 1970). Rather than regarding the various experiences of class, caste, and race as liabilities that somehow educators must transcend before molding their students anew, Freire considers the positionality of those on the societal margin (now what postmodernists call "subaltern" groups) a requisite of raising democratic consciousness and, ultimately, freedom. Founders of the Chicano Movement took hold of Freire's theories of popular education and transfigured them into *Chicanismo* (literally, Chicano-ness)—a deep feeling of cultural pride premised on the reaffirmation of culture and identity among Mexicans in the United States (Gómez-Quiñones, 1978; Mariscal, 2005). Chicanos viewed the university as a critical space to develop concrete solutions to combat racism, poverty, and educational marginalization—that is, to make the university work for the Mexican community in the United States. Although Chicanismo is close to forty years old and Central Americans, Puerto Ricans, and South Americans have since expanded the meaning of "brown pride," this notion still resonates in many departments and programs of Chicano studies (CS) and Chicano and Latino studies, particularly those in the Los Angeles–Long Beach region of southern California.

The Local Context

Latinos are the predominant population in the Los Angeles–Long Beach region. While Los Angeles and Long Beach are independent, self-governing entities, Latinos comprise the largest ethnic group in both cities, with a heavy concentration of recently arrived immigrants: Long Beach, 44 percent, and Los Angeles, 47 percent (Marie Jones Consulting, 2005). Between 2000 and 2004, Los Angeles–Long Beach gained over 600,000 new residents, most of whom were immigrants from Mexico, but populations from El Salvador and Guatemala each numbered over 100,000. During this time, Latinos experienced the greatest numerical increase in Los Angeles County, whereas the non-Hispanic white population declined substantially. In 2004, Los Angeles County was home to the highest concentration of Latinos (4.6 million) nationwide (Public Policy Institute, Los Angeles County, 2005). Despite the demographic composition of the Los Angeles–Long Beach region, Latinos are conspicuously under-represented at college and university campuses; California State University, Long Beach, is no exception.[2] Commonly referred to as "The Beach," CSULB is approximately thirty miles south of Los Angeles, and is the second-largest university in the state of California (next to UCLA), with over 33,000 graduate and undergraduate students. Latino students make up 25.1 percent of the total undergraduate student body, whereas Latino professors and librarians comprise only 6 percent of the entire tenured and tenure-track faculty, with seven tenured and tenure-track faculty housed in the Chicano and Latino Studies Department.[3]

Despite these numbers, the interest in studying Latino and Chicano peoples has increased considerably over the past three years. Diverse learning experiences, including creating opportunities to study in Cuba, Puerto Rico, Mexico, and Venezuela, have attracted significantly more students into majoring or minoring in Chicano and Latino studies: from approximately 56 in 2001, to over 200 in 2004. This rate of growth—a pace no other academic department at CSULB has matched—validated pre-existing efforts to strengthen introductory-level courses while prompting efforts to develop new classes in community service learning, transnationalism, public policy, gender, sexuality, and education.

Literature Review

Two models combining student-centered pedagogies with faculty-librarian collaboration in Chicano and Latino studies guided our project. At the California State University, Fullerton, (CSUF) librarian Barbara A. Miller and faculty member Nancy Porras Hein described how students enrolled in a Chicana and Chicano studies class blended their newly acquired skills in information literacy with assignments in family history (Porras Hein and Miller, 2004). The primary assignment required students to document their individual family histories using a "*Familia* History Form" developed by Miller and Porras Hein. Students produced an outline, rough draft, final paper, and bibliography of resources used in researching the genealogical and social aspects of their family history. In addition, two research journal worksheets, reflective writing exercises, formal class presentations on research finding, and class discussions that assisted students in structuring and organizing their research strategies were required to successfully complete the class. Miller and Porras Hein worked collaboratively to develop and assess these active learning assignments. They also jointly created a class-specific research Web site. The librarian attended selected class sessions, offered information literacy instruction at critical points, and met with students for individual consultations. This collaborative structure has been adapted in other Chicana and Chicano studies classes at CSUF. The Porras Hein and Miller model is the most collaborative faculty-librarian effort documented for CHLS to date and provides an engaging model for other social science and humanities disciplines.

The Chicano and Latino Studies (CALS) Information Literacy Competence Program at Sonoma State University developed in 2001 by Raymond E. Castro, CALS department chair, and Paula Hammett, social sciences librarian, is another early example of a discipline approach to information fluency (ACRL, Instruction Section, 2005). In this effort, CALS faculty, with the assistance of the discipline librarian, were oriented during a one-day faculty retreat to information literacy issues and Association of College and Research Libraries (ACRL) standards (ACRL, 2000). Following this information literacy session with department faculty, the curricula of two core research methods classes were retooled (CALS, n.d.). The grant provided release time for the discipline librarian to prepare for the training and funding for the retreat. Although the long-term project outcomes have yet to be published, the CALS project accomplished a great deal: the integration of information literacy skills into two courses (CALS 458, Latino Studies Research Issues and Information Literacy, and CALS 480, Chicano and Latino

Studies Senior Seminar); and the integration of faculty-librarian collaboration (Hammett, 2006).

Aside from Miller and Porras Hein and CALS, collaborative information literacy projects of CHLS students, faculty, and librarians have not been recorded in the extensive literature on information literacy. Researchers, however, will find numerous articles about the need for information fluency among Latino students in higher education (Ayala et al., 2000; Garcha and Baldwin, 1997; Hinojosa, 2000; McCook, 1999; Mestre, 2000; Moore and Ivory, 2003). This body of literature not only elaborates the need for information literate Latino students but also describes specialized Latino studies information competency programs conceptualized and implemented by librarians and university staff.

Laskin, for example, writes about interesting faculty-librarian collaborations for a campus-wide program at Hostos College, a community college in New York City (Laskin, 2002). The librarians worked with the counseling faculty in establishing a curriculum-integrated information literacy component for their college orientation class, a one-semester course that reviews subjects required by the City University of New York. The faculty counselors and library faculty determined that three information literacy workshops taught by the library faculty would be mandatory to pass the course. While the Hostos College model addresses Latino students, their efforts did not integrate the information literacy component into Chicano and Latino studies or any other academic discipline. Instruction was conducted by the library faculty, not by the instructor of record, and no information literacy training was provided for faculty counselors.

Evolution of *Semillas de Cambio*

Over the course of three years, ethnic studies librarian Luévano frequently offered research methods lectures in Peña Delgado's CHLS classes. These classes and faculty-librarian interactions with CHLS students were the basis for an ongoing discussion about student learning outcomes and information competence that blossomed into a full-fledged department-level endeavor. In addition to the shared commitment to student success, the faculty-librarian team maintained a common understanding of Chicano and Latino studies and the discipline's theories of student-centered learning and teaching. A common vision about the place of Chicano and Latino studies in the struggle for equal rights, also expressed in the work of Ochoa and Ochoa (2004) and Córdova (2005), guided the goals and objectives of the *Semillas* project. It was understood that the development of information literacy within the CHLS curriculum would provide discipline majors and minors with a needed skills base to affect community change. Consider the case of Hector Flores, a recent CHLS graduate. As a community organizer, Flores was quick to relate his effectiveness in advocating for East Los Angeles residents to his mastery of information competency. Applying finely honed skills in research, writing, and critical thinking, Flores believed he was able to thoroughly grasp the complexities of Latino politics and therefore better able to assist residents (Flores, 2006).

Beyond the disciplinary philosophy and pedagogical bases of *Semillas*, the project offered a practical solution to instruct an ever-increasing CHLS student population in information literacy skills. With the popularity of the CHLS major and minor placing heavy demands for lectures and individual student consultations on the discipline librarian, it became clear that any substantive instruction in information competency warranted fuller participation from faculty. At the center of the *Semillas* model, then, was a focused training of faculty in information literacy skills, assignment development, learning outcomes, and assessments. *Semillas* faculty not only would be proficient in teaching information literacy tenets to students without the assistance of the librarian but also would eventually embed information competency into other CHLS courses. In this manner, the *Semillas* project answers the challenge of Samson and Millet (2003) and Conteh-Morgan (2001) who advocate for faculty and teaching assistants as the primary facilitators of information literacy development.

The project co-directors spent nine months preparing for the six-session project workshop, beginning with the writing of the successful grant proposal to the California State University (CSU). Each component of the project was discussed, revised, and jointly approved. In addition to the collaborative planning efforts, each co-director took the lead in her areas of expertise. Susan Luévano was responsible for designing the general structure of the workshop sessions, determining the order of specific topics by adapting a pre-existing online training tutorial to the *Semillas* project that originated from a similarly faculty-focused, CSU-award project in CSULB's Black Studies Department; Luévano was also a co-director for that project (Luévano, Travis, and Wakiji, 2003).[4] Luévano also created a project Web site (*Semillas de Cambio* / Seeds of Change, 2005), and selected and compiled readings, resources, and sample information literacy assignments. Her suggestions to create a more integrated approach to information literacy in Chicano and Latino studies were apparent throughout the project. Luévano, for example, urged faculty to carefully weigh adopting information competency skills appropriate to course content area and pedagogical approach.

Grace Peña Delgado served as the lead person in all aspects of curriculum design and assessment. In this key role, Peña Delgado facilitated faculty-librarian workshops and, at times, guided faculty through the unfamiliar terrain of information competency. Her extensive background in information competency pedagogy and expertise in higher education instruction made for perceptive discussions about evidence-based, inquiry learning. Because Peña Delgado had been the chair of the CHLS curriculum committee, she also encouraged faculty to consider fundamental changes in the instruction of CHLS majors and minors. She shared her opinion that any changes in CHLS education are most appropriately made at the level of a "learning environment" where reform initiatives must be undertaken with an eye to what students learn instead of what they are taught. This alternative framework advocates for assessments and the embeddedness of information competency in all CHLS courses. Together, Peña Delgado and Luévano agreed to target four core courses in the CHLS major and minor that are most frequently taken before students enter advanced-level studies: CHLS 101, An Introduction to Chicano Life; CHLS 104, Bilingual Communication Skills; CHLS 150, Introduction to Chicano Literary Studies; and CHLS 300, Chicano History. Through a course-integrated approach to information literacy, the project co-directors believe CHLS students will develop as independent and self-directed learners equipped to excel in research-intensive learning environments, especially CHLS 498, Senior Colloquium.

Faculty-Librarian Training

In a spirit of cross-discipline collaboration, the participants commenced an intensive six-session training workshop in the pedagogy and application of information competency. These meetings took place over an eleven-week period in spring 2005 that also included an introductory meeting and the administration of pre- and post-tests to faculty participants. Preparation for each session took place before the day of the workshop. Faculty prepared themselves by reading and analyzing content information from five teaching modules, each meticulously conceptualized to orient faculty to the areas of information competency, search strategies, assessment, and student-centered instructional strategies. The *Semillas* online tutorial included five modules starting with an "Introduction" and pre-test. These were followed by modules entitled "Find Information," "Evaluate Information," and "Apply Information." The last module, "Future Considerations," concluded with a post-test (Luévano and Peña Delgado, 2005a).

The "Introduction" provided a detailed definition of information literacy and why it is important. A framework for teaching information literacy in a collaborative faculty-librarian environment was also explored. The "Find Information" module presented skills that an information literate student should master. Issues to consider when creating an assignment were outlined. In "Evaluate Information" participants were presented with critical thinking skills related to the evaluation of Web sites. "Apply Information" covered copyright and plagiarism issues. "Future Consideration" raised issues related to future department curricular changes and national information literacy standards for the discipline of Chicano and Latino studies.

Each module in the tutorial was structured in a similar format. First the conceptual issue was presented. For example, "Find Information" included a discussion of information literacy skills. Sample student assignments, both research and community service learning activities, were then provided. In addition, each module listed required readings as well as links to supplemental articles, books, and Web sites. The modules also required development of an assignment, learning outcomes, and a suitable assessment tool; written reflections on the module content and activities were submitted electronically to the project co-directors.

Reflections disclosed faculty perspectives that, in many cases, were poignant and candid. Professor Julie M. Rivera, for example, reminded us that students remained quite inhibited about asking for assistance: "I was amazed that 68 percent of faculty expected students to ask for help when doing research; but on second thought, I realized that this assumption flows from our work habits and our prior educational experiences. The culture in K–12 education does not lend itself to encouraging students to seek help, lest they confess ignorance and lower their self-esteem."[5] On several occasions, faculty contemplated their own in-classroom practices while identifying both strengths and weaknesses in their teaching. Dr. Luis Arroyo, who shared his approach on the research process in history, disclosed, "The problem is that I do not systematically teach students all the steps involved in producing a research paper. I do model . . . how to devise a research topic, develop a set of questions to govern the research, and then develop a preliminary working hypothesis that serves as a basis for a research strategy."[6] Learning took place through reflection and disclosure, prompting faculty to contemplate their classroom experiences and critically evaluate them. Reflection activities not only resulted in a deeper understanding of the professor-student dynamic but also underscored the construction of information competency assignments and assessments.

From the beginning, the CHLS faculty recognized and wholly supported the teaching of information literacy as a viable means of instructing students in writing and research. Three factors explain why CHLS faculty welcomed the *Semillas* project: faculty use of information literacy in their own research endeavors; the widespread adoption of the university's e-learning classroom environment, Beachboard (this is how we have branded Blackboard applications on our campus; CSULB is known as "The Beach"); and the early adoption of technology-based learning by university librarians. Faculty members drew on a variety of previous experiences using technology that deepened the level of discussion about the opportunities and drawbacks of emphasizing information competency in the classroom: Would faculty become overly dependent on information literacy to the exclusion of building basic skills in writing and reading? Or, conversely, would information competency provide an entrée to reinforce content-area themes? Although faculty recognized both the pitfalls and possibilities of information competency, there was consensus that assignments and assessments inspire students to become self-directed, lifelong learners.

Assignments

Instructors designed learning outcomes to assess student progress toward mastering information competency but, in doing so, were keen on developing skills that graduated from lower-order thinking skills to higher-order thinking skills. This approach was in keeping with the philosophy of the Association of College and Research Libraries (ACRL, 2000) and the mission of librarians at California State University, Long Beach (Information Literacy Minimum Standards, 1998). Learning outcomes in introductory-level assignments, for example, stressed that students were able to define and articulate the need for information, identify the most appropriate and effective search methods, and design and execute a strategic research plan. The lone upper-division course built on the introductory-level assignments, focusing on the evaluation of source material, analyses of the cultural contexts in which the information was created, and the understanding and use of interdisciplinary source material in the research project. In their effort to maintain a coherent and consistent educational mission, the faculty reviewed the department's goals statement to determine how information competency could be embedded throughout the CHLS curriculum.

Peña Delgado and Professor Julie M. Rivera developed three assignments that equally applied to CHLS 101 (An Introduction to Chicano Life) and CHLS 104 (Bilingual Communication Skills). Together, these three "step" assignments eased students into the research-writing process. For example, in "How to Write a Winning Research Paper: Information Competency and the Pre-Writing Process," Rivera and Peña Delgado outlined prewriting steps that students often do not undertake. The purpose here was to encourage students to make deliberate and manageable decisions about the research and writing process. The redesigned assignments had students pose research questions, create keywords, apply Boolean operators, and generate preliminary thesis statements.

The titles of the two other assignments are "Evaluating a Website in Chicano and Latino Studies" and "Boolean Searches."

Professor Anna Sandoval's student assignments in CHLS 150, Introduction to Chicano Literary Studies, included the analysis of central conventions of literary discourse through technology and research. In "The Critical Research Paper," Dr. Sandoval required students to select a particular methodology that guides a critical analysis of a literary text. Information competency skills are integrated into the project when students design and implement an Internet-based search strategy. As part of their search strategy, students must use appropriate commands in retrieving information; they must also summarize the main ideas of their findings in preparation for writing an annotated bibliography.

Professor Arroyo's upper-division course (CHLS 300, Chicano History) attracts many transfer students who often lack university-level research skills. Dr. Arroyo designed a series of assignments to ensure proficiency in the research and writing process. In "Choosing and Focusing Your Topic," Dr. Arroyo's course in Chicano history fused information literacy skills with the 300-level research paper process. Dr. Arroyo guided students in choosing their topic (e.g., biography of a Mexican American) while encouraging them to design a question that best expressed their research focus. He continued this deliberate approach, integrating university electronic resources and academic databases into the research process. His assessment of the assignment included evaluating students on their ability to list subtopics, pose clearly stated research questions, and provide relevant keywords.

Assessment

Although the *Semillas* project was reconceptualized to include learning outcomes and rubrics for each targeted course, the following narrative chronicles the assessment journey of Peña Delgado's course, CHLS 101, The Introduction to Chicano Life. CHLS 101 is a general introductory course that addresses themes of national and international import in the shaping of the Chicano experience in the United States. Peña Delgado teaches CHLS 101 twice a semester, offered in both fall and spring. This course stresses writing and the acquisition of information competency skills through several assignments throughout the semester, but most deliberately in the prewriting process of the final research paper. After the midterm examination, it is the usual practice of Peña Delgado to encourage students to begin thinking about a research topic, one that is of great intrigue and personal interest. Peña Delgado urges students to conceptualize the topic without the actual retrieval of source material. The purpose here is to encourage students' creative processes without imposing restrictions on topic choice. After a week of free-flowing musings, however, students are asked to transform their ruminations into a preliminary research question, the first of many steps they follow in "How to Write a Winning Research Paper: Information Competency and the Pre-Writing Process." The handout (see appendix 6.1) is designed to guide the step-by-step process of writing and research; student progress is monitored by the professor after each incremental step of the writing-research process.

Following these pre-research steps, students receive a lecture in research strategies and library resources by university librarian Luévano. The class, which usually enrolls forty students, meets in the library's technology-ready classroom, where Luévano presents various research strategies, including defining and using Boolean operators and defining and using effective keyword searches. Luévano also details the library's vast electronic resource database and provides an overview of CHLS reference material located in the university library. With the hands-on guidance of Luévano and Peña Delgado, students apply just-introduced search techniques to using various keywords, which in almost all cases need alteration after the initial search. Luévano and Peña Delgado constantly assist students in the research process until they can successfully engage the next set of research steps independently.

Once students are prepared to engage the research process outside of the classroom, Peña Delgado encourages them to identify a second, more precise set of keywords. What new keywords did students learn from their initial searching? After some time mining the university databases, students are required to record articles and books (full citations) most relevant to their preliminary topic. They also document the specific names of databases used to glean articles and books. Students are then asked if this new source material encouraged them to *refine* their topics. Peña Delgado provides written feedback after students complete this step in the process to ensure the use of effective keywords and appropriate databases. At this point, Peña Delgado reminds students that they must voraciously read the scholarly material they have culled to master the subject at hand; this last step is a crucial one, since students often overlook that they must read before they can generate a second, more manageable research question and later design a successful thesis statement.

At this juncture, students begin interpreting and synthesizing material guided by a revised research question. Assessments indicate that students can more effectively negotiate a morass of information when consciously guided by a research question to discern between "what is important" and what is tangential. At the same time, students are prepared to read actively, that is, to read while keeping in mind what themes, topics, and arguments may be viable to their research. If any conceptual adjustments are to be made, they may be reflected in the drafting of a working thesis statement, the next step of the prewriting process.

By adopting a writing, research, and information competency model for CHLS 101, we engaged students in a multi-staged process of conceptualization, practice, and execution of the research-writing process. Efforts to engage the research-writing endeavor as a progression of incremental steps were similarly woven into the information competency instructional assignments of CHLS 104 (Bilingual Communication Skills), CHLS 150 (Introduction to Chicano Literary Studies), and CHLS 300 (Chicano History). Together, these classes will counter the strong tendency to approach writing and research as an abbreviated exercise in which students research, outline, write, and revise over the span of one or two days.

Innovations

The *Semillas* project is inventive because it shifted the discipline librarian's instructional role from one of cooperation to one of collaboration. Instead of waiting to be asked to conduct a student-oriented skill-building lecture, the librarian became part of a group process to achieve curricular reform. The librarian's identity as an occasional lecturer on research methods evolved into that of a team player working toward improved instructional delivery, thus dissolving the librarian's traditional role as the sole deliverer of and expert on information literacy. This realignment allowed the discipline librarian to address internal concerns and conflicts, share in proposed innovations, become more keenly aware of department instruction and service priorities, and find strength and validation through the commonality of the CHLS Department. Faculty also benefited from the re-drafting of student assignments because the assignments resulted in improved student research. This research was reflected in the increased quality of the required research paper or essay, indicating that the skill set had been successfully modeled and applied.

Furthermore, the CSULB faculty-librarian collaboration afforded both parties the opportunity to share teaching and learning strategies that may have otherwise remained unexplored. Both the faculty and the ethnic studies librarian learned new disciplinary methodologies. This cross-fertilization prompted faculty to seek other grant opportunities to integrate information literacy in the CHLS curriculum. Peña Delgado, with the assistance of Professors Luis Arroyo and Anna Sandoval, applied for and was awarded an Enhancing Educational Effectiveness (EEE) Grant through the Center for Faculty Development at CSULB. The immediate objective of the EEE project is to develop five new courses advancing the department's long-term goal of becoming a leader in information competency, service learning, and community-based approaches to teaching.

Conclusion

The *Semillas de Cambio* project presents a model of genuine collaborative work bridging two entities of the university: CHLS faculty and a librarian. The value of the *Semillas* model showed how an informal but solid working relationship between a librarian and professor was successfully transformed into a grant-funded, multi-faculty initiative that embedded information competency skills into the CHLS curriculum. The effort required a significant investment of time and trust among colleagues, but nevertheless, demonstrated how collaboration can yield information literate CHLS majors and minors. What is more, teaching students to access, analyze, and evaluate a wide variety of communication technologies is one full-proof way to ensure students receive the necessary tools to engage information critically and reflectively. Embedding information literacy into CHLS courses invariably enriches the lives of students as they wrestle to make sense out of an academic world in constant flux.

Notes

1. We understand the term "information competency" to mean the ability of the student to recognize the need for information, possess the knowledge and skills to obtain the information, choose the proper sources and successfully retrieve appropriate information, and organize, analyze, and synthesize information. We therefore interchange the term "information literacy" with "information competency." See Illene F. Rockman, "Introduction: The Importance of Information Literacy," in Rockman, ed., *Integrating Information Literacy in Higher Education Curriculum: Practical Models for Transformation* (San Francisco: Jossey-Bass, 2004, 1–28); and M. B. Eisenberg, C. A. Lowe,

and K. L. Spitzer, "Defining Information Literacy," in Eisenberg, Lowe, and Spitzer eds., *Information Literacy: Essential Skills for the Information Age* (Westport: Libraries Unlimited, 2004, 4–11).

2. In the late months of 2005, CHLS faculty, staff, students, and university administrators began formulating a proposal to Hispanic Association of Colleges and Universities (HACU) predicting that in 2005, Latino undergraduate student enrollment will meet or exceed one-quarter of the total undergraduate enrollment. "Hispanic-Serving Institutions: Statistical Trends, 1990–1999" (National Center for Education Statistics, U.S. Department of Education, 2002: 1).

3. The California State University system assigns librarians the status of faculty. For other facts and figures mentioned, see "CSULB University Facts, 2004," 1.

4. An information competency literature search related to departments of ethnic studies including black, American Indian, or Asian American studies revealed limited published scholarship. However, Luévano, Travis, and Wakiji (2003) cite Information Competence for the Disciplines of Black Studies at California State University, Long Beach, as an example of a collaborative librarian-faculty project in ethnic studies. The effort was conceived and originally directed by a team of librarians. However, it developed organically into a collaborative learning experience for all involved parties. The project, which targeted black studies faculty, used an online tutorial and focus groups to enhance faculty knowledge of information literacy and allowed faculty to incorporate assignments into class assignments in cooperation with library faculty. The project inspired participant faculty and librarians to address issues of national information literacy standards for the discipline at the National Council of Black Studies conference in 2002. This recognition of the need for national information competency standards for the discipline of black studies was the most significant project outcome (Luévano, 2003).

5. Julie Rivera, WWW Form Submission, reflection, March 15, 2005.

6. Luis Arroyo, WWW Form Submission, reflection, March 23, 2005.

References

Association of College and Research Libraries (ACRL). 2000. "Information Literacy Competency Standards for Higher Education." American Library Association. Retrieved January 2006, from www.ala.org/ala/acrl/acrlstandards/informationliteracycompetency.htm.

———. Instruction Section. 2005. "Information Literacy in the Disciplines: Hispanic-American, Puerto Rican and Mexican-American." American Library Association. Retrieved January 25, 2006, from www.ala.org/ala/acrlbucket/is/projectsacrl/infolitdisciplines/hispanic.htm.

Ayala, John, Luis Chaparro, Ana María Cobos, and Ron Rodríguez. 2000. "Serving the Hispanic Student in the Community College." In *Library Services to Latinos: An Anthology*. Edited by Salvador Güereña. Jefferson, NC: McFarland.

"CALS Information Literacy Competence Proposal to CSU." Sonoma State University. Retrieved January 25, 2006, from www.sonoma.edu/cals/informlitercy.html.

Conteh-Morgan, Miriam E. 2001. "Empowering ESL Students: A New Model for Information Literacy Instruction," *Research Strategies* 18: 29–38.

Córdova, Teresa. 2005. "Agency, Commitment and Connection: Embracing the Roots of Chicano and Chicana Studies." *International Journal of Qualitative Studies in Education* 18, no. 2 (May–June): 221–233.

Espinal, Isabel. "What Do Latino Students Know Anyway about Information Literacy?" American Library Association. Office for Diversity. Retrieved January 25, 2006, from www.ala.org/ala/diversity/versed/versedbackissues/backissjan2004/latinostudents.htm.

Flores, Hector. 2006. Personal communication, February 4.

Freire, Paulo. 1970. *Pedagogy of the Oppressed*. New York: Seabury.

Garcha, Rajinder, and Julia Baldwin. 1997. "Bibliographic Instruction for the Upward Bound Residential Students." *Reference Librarian*, no. 58: 135–141.

García, Ignacio M. 1997. *Chicanismo*. Tucson: University of Arizona.

Gómez-Quiñones, Juan. 1978. *Mexican Students por La Raza: The Chicano Student Movement in Southern California, 1967–1977*. Santa Barbara, CA: Editorial La Causa.

Hammett, Paula. 2006. Personal communication, January 25.

Hinojosa, Susana. 2000. "Libraries in the New Millennium—and What about the Students?" In *Library Services to Latinos*. Edited by Salvador Güereña. Jefferson, NC: McFarland.

"Information Literacy Minimum Standards." 1998. University Library, California State University Long Beach. Retrieved January 25, 2006, from www.csulb.edu/library/guide/infocomp.html.

Laskin, Miriam. 2002. "Bilingual Information Literacy and Academic Readiness: Reading, Writing and Retention." *Academic Exchange* 6, no. 4: 41–46.

Luévano, Susan C, Tiffini Travis, and Eileen Wakiji. 2003. "Information Competence for the Discipline of Black Studies, PRIMO: Peer-Reviewed Instructional Materials Online, June 2003, Site of the Month." Association of College and Research Libraries, Emerging Technologies Committee. Retrieved March 9, 2006, from www.ala.org/ala/acrlbucket/is/iscommittees/webpages/emergingtech/site/june2003.htm.

Luévano, Susan C, and Grace Peña Delgado. 2005a. "Seeds of Change / *Semillas de Cambio*: Information Competence for the Discipline of Chicano and Latino Studies." California State University, Long Beach. Retrieved January15, 2006, from www.csulb.edu~sluevano.chls/.

———. 2005b. "*Semillas de Cambio* / Seeds of Change: Information Competence in Chicano and Latino Studies." California State University, Long Beach. Retrieved December 12, 2005, from www.csulb.edu/~sluevano/seeds/.

Marie Jones Consulting. 2005. "Long Beach Economic and Market Analysis." vol. 3: 13–15.

Mariscal, George. 2005. *Brown-Eyed Children of the Sun: Lessons from the Chicano Movement, 1965–1975*. Albuquerque: University of New Mexico.

McCook, Kathleen de la Pena. 1999. "*Punto Final!*: Empowerment of Hispanics through Information Literacy." *Hispanic Outlook in Higher Education* 9, no. 13 (March 12): 62. Retrieved December 6, 2004, from proquest.umi.com.mcc1.library.csulb.edu/.

Mestre, Lori. 2000. "Improving Computer-Use Success for Students of Diverse Backgrounds." *Knowledge Quest* 28, no. 5 (May/June): 20–28.

Moore, Anne C, and Gary Ivory. 2003. "Do Hispanic Institutions Have What It Takes to Foster Information Literacy? One Case." *Journal of Latinos and Education* 2, no. 4: 217–231.

Ochoa, Gilda Laura, and Enrique C. Ochoa. 2004. "Education for Social Transformation: Chicana/o and Latin American Studies and Community Struggles." *Latin American Perspectives* 31, no. 1 (January): 59–80.

Porras Hein, Nancy, and Barbara A. Miller. 2004. "*¿Quién Soy?* Finding My Place in History: Personalizing Learning through Faculty/Librarian Collaboration." *Journal of Hispanic Higher Education* 3, no. 4 (October): 307–321.

Public Policy Institute, Los Angeles County. 2005. "Just the Facts." 1.

Samson, Sue, and Michelle S. Millet. 2003. "The Learning Environment: First-Year Students, Teaching Assistants, and Information Literacy," *Research Strategies* 19: 84–98.

Shor, Ira. 1996. *When Students Have Power: Negotiating Authority in a Critical Pedagogy*. Chicago: University of Chicago.

U.S. Census Bureau. 2002. "United States Census 2000." Retrieved January 25, 2006, from www.census.gov/main/www/cen2000.html.

Appendix 6.1: How to Write a Winning Research Paper Assignment

Please read this handout very carefully and thoroughly before you begin internet research. Follow the instruction and advice provided by Ms. Susan Luevano in our library instruction class; reference her research website on our Beachboard platform if you need a "refresher."

INTEREST: Choose a topic that interests you. You will have to spend a lot of time and energy on it, and there is more chance you will do a good job if it is something you want to know more about.

IDEAS: You can get some ideas by browsing among current periodicals (*Newsweek*, *Time*, *La Opinion*), or by browsing through

SCOPE: Your topic must be manageable. Avoid choosing a topic that is too broad or too narrow. If it is too broad, you will be overwhelmed by too much information (e.g. Latino education). If it is too narrow, too specialized, too new, too limited in appeal, you may not find enough material (e.g. ethnic Latino-Africanos migration from Cuba to Eau Claire, Wisconsin in the 1940s). Refine the subject by focusing on a broader/narrower time span, a larger/smaller place, a broad/specific group of people, or a general/specific event.

TIME: Choose a project that can be finished in the time you have. If it is a busy semester, choose a topic you know something about and that is common enough to be found easily. It is better to do a smaller project well than to do a sloppy job on a more elaborate project. You will run into snags: you need Interlibrary Loan, you need to recall a book, you need to visit other libraries, etc. Allow time for the frustrations of using a busy library: lines at the copy machines, books not on shelves. Then plan for enough time to read the material and THINK about it before writing your paper. It is important to find information. It is more important the way you use it.

APPROACH: There are different approaches that can be taken with a topic. For example, you can analyze or explain, narrate events or developments, argue pro or con, or be rhetorical or serious.

ASPECTS: Most topics have many different aspects you can research. Each aspect requires different sources of information so it is important to establish what aspect of the topic interests you most from the beginning. For example, take the subject of trucking. You could look at the engineering aspects of trucks, energy and environmental issues related to trucking, government regulation of the trucking industry, truck driving music, women truck drivers, or the language of trucking.

CLARITY: Be clear about what topic you are researching. It is true that a topic needs to be adjusted as the information is gathered, but you should always know what topic you are searching. Not having a clear idea of what you are looking for is dangerous because you are likely to get off track and waste time you cannot afford.

II. What is your preliminary research question?

What are your keywords?

III. Researching: This means going to the CSULB databases and/or University Library home page. What did you find? Cite at least five articles and their titles:

What University databases were most useful to you and why?

How did specific resources make you rethink your topic?

Turn in handout.
IV. What is your *refined* research question?

What are your new keywords?

V. Working thesis that will guide your research.

Turn in handout.

VI. Working Bibliography: 15–20 key sources that may be useful for your final research project. Use MLA style.

7
Reconstructing the Research Project: A Case Study of Collaborative Instruction

James B. Tuttle, Assistant Professor of Education, Shepherd University, Formerly
  Assistant Professor of Education
Steve McKinzie, Director of Catawba College Library, Catawba College,
  Formerly Collection and Research Services Librarian, Library and
  Information Services
Dickinson College

Many courses at the collegiate level include a research paper assignment; in fact, the research paper could be said to be a hallmark and staple output of postsecondary courses. In turn, helping students with research papers has been a standard practice for college library staff members. However, course instructors and librarians do not typically develop structures for designing and delivering integrated, planned instruction and mentoring in ways that link the environment and resources of the classroom to those of the library. Course instructors often are unsure of the specific context of the library or do not have time to consult before the unit starts with library staff, so it has become standard practice for teachers to turn teaching over to the librarian at the library door. Sometimes course time is built into the syllabus for library orientation; often it is not.

Meanwhile, librarians are typically not made aware of the specific protocols for research and writing in a particular course, nor are they necessarily aware of the exact content presented by an instructor in a given course. As a result, they must restrict their information sessions to more generic, universal introductions to the library's resources and how to use them. The resulting disconnection between coursework related to the research paper and the process of writing it often frustrates course instructors, librarians, and many students. This lack of coherence is also difficult to defend as a teaching practice, since research has long shown the importance of prior planning and clear communication in team teaching. One impact is that the organic process of research that informs university culture is broken-backed in its delivery to students, who are meant to learn precisely how to analyze and appreciate this research and the various processes of conducting it. Another result is that, especially for students whose research and writing skills lag behind those of their peers or their instructors' expectations, research and writing are perceived as onerous scholastic tasks rather than opportunities to deepen their own understanding. Further, most students rarely perceive the research project as a vehicle for student empowerment to contribute to the evolving dialogue in a given discipline. The impact for pre-service teachers is that they may become less, rather than more, prepared and equipped to teach the research process to their own students. The following excerpt from a pre-service education student course evaluation captures and conveys this dissatisfaction with disconnected, but typical, instruction and evaluation of the research paper process and products.

> The syllabus told us there would be a research paper for this class. I dread every aspect of them, and I imagined it would play out in this class just as it has in the other classes I've taken where research papers are required. I knew I'd be confused and bored to death by the inevitable rote orientation to the library. I knew that the paper would be due months away, near the end of the semester, that a host of other activities would seem more pressing and would push the paper from my mind, and that the day before it was due I'd rush to the library, get whatever research done that I could, and stay up all night writing the paper to turn it in the next morning. I didn't expect to learn much from the process, and I didn't expect a good grade on the paper. I'm not a great writer, and although I knew I'd see many of my classmates in the library the day before the paper was due, I never seem to be able to compete with their writing skills. That's all these papers usually are to me, a writing contest—we have three months to do the work, but all we ever hand in is the final paper. I don't like doing research papers or going to the library, and I wasn't happy when I saw a paper included for this course.

Because the research project is a vital pedagogical process, it is important to try to engineer better scholastic dispositions, habits, and outcomes than those reflected in this student anecdote. Research on programs that address these traditional shortcomings of research instruction lies at the intersection of several branches of educational study because the instruction of research embeds many pedagogical and epistemological components that are each complex and differently interpreted by various instructors and disciplinary protocols. One of these pedagogical elements is the process of student learning and writing, both in effective standard written English and in the development of propositional, evidence-based logic. Enhancing the quality of the scholarly conversations between students and instructor and ways of recording the engaged student voice, improving research and writing in disciplines across the curriculum, and developing librarian-instructor collaboration are all key features of the instructional program whose need is documented and whose feasibility is presented in the model described in this chapter. There is warrant in educational research for each of these practices and for their continued development and study.

A Review of Related Literature

It has been established that curriculum can be aptly characterized as an extended series of conversations within students' minds and between students and others, including their instructors, and that these conversations are integral traditions, products, and engines of learning (Applebee, 1993; Bereiter, 1994; Gabella, 1994; Greene, 2000; Heath, 1983; Ryken, 2004; Shulman, 1987; Vygotsky, 1962). Applebee (1996) notes the critical importance for instructors of framing relevant conversations that constitute instruction and enhance student achievement: "The problem for curriculum and instruction is to ensure that those traditions are constituted as systems of knowledge-in-action, available as tools to guide present and future behavior, rather than systems of knowledge-out-of-context, stripped of the constructive and constitutive potential" (36). One goal of educators, then, is to design instruction that facilitates and captures salient scholarly conversation in ways that are appropriate to the discipline and that reflect student scholarship.

Over the past three decades, writing as a process has developed among instructional methods as a means of capturing and directing student conversation in literature and language arts courses and, more recently, across the curriculum (Langer and Allington, 1992; Ochsner and Fowler, 2004). A comprehensive study by Langer and Applebee (1987) concluded that writing in content areas across the curriculum had a marked positive effect on student content mastery. While the merits of any given instructional methodology continue to be debated, it is clear that engaging teachers and students in the process of discipline-based writing yields student products that are intrinsically valuable, give instructors another basis for genuine assessment, and deepen the student-produced contribution to the conversation of enacted curriculum. Bazerman (2005) notes the impact of student-generated discipline-based writing in the postsecondary curriculum as a means of identity discovery as well as scholarly achievement. Exploring means to develop student writing in content areas at all levels of education continues to be a concern of curriculum designers and instructors.

Collaborations between instructors and librarians connect the content discipline to the research engines and the scholarship in disciplines across the curriculum, but electronic structures for these collaborations have evolved rapidly and require evolving instructional and research methods. Because these associations vary widely in form and effectiveness, a research base that studies instructor-librarian collaborations has been needed and is beginning to emerge, identifying effective elements and structures for team instruction, including Web-based and online elements (Bhavnagri and Bielat, 2005; Cook-Sather, 2001; Cox and Housewright, 2001; Cudiner and Harmon, 2000; Kaplowitz and Yamamoto, 2001). Despite this increased emphasis on collaboration, some librarians have been hampered in their efforts to work closely with faculty. At times, the specific discipline of a faculty member has been a problem (Badke, 2005). To some degree, this issue holds true for the field of education. Even though almost everyone recognizes the importance of research in the areas of pedagogy and the widespread availability of bibliographic databases such as ERIC and Educational Abstracts in most academic libraries, faculty and library collaboration in the area of education seems to be rare. Except for some salient, fascinating exceptions, as in the case of the University of British Columbia and Wesleyan University of Illinois, faculty-librarian collaboration in the area of teacher education has received only scant attention within the professional literature (Naslund, Asselin, and Filipenko, 2005; Witt and Dickinson, 2003).

Montiel-Overall (2005) contends that teacher-librarian collaboration is considered critical to support the changing population of students, complexity of educational issues, and increased information that characterize today's classrooms. The article discusses four models of teacher and librarian collaboration: coordination, cooperation, integrated instruction, and integrated curriculum. It also identifies five elements of the models that can be used to evaluate the effect of each model on students' academic achievement: interest, level of involvement, improved learning, innovation, and integration. In suggesting that high levels of these five constructs in teacher-librarian collaboration may have the greatest effect on students' academic achievement, Montiel-Overall provides both a model for collaborations and a paradigm for assessment of their effectiveness. These five criteria are applied later as one basis for assessment of the collaborative model described in this chapter.

Recent instructor-librarian collaboration research has also identified other means of assessing the effectiveness of collaboration through examination of student-generated products. Malenfant and Demers (2004) noted that in their structure for assessment of student work generated after collaborative instruction, points were awarded not only for final research products but also for information literacy assignments themselves. This study reveals the usefulness of incorporating research-as-process assessments into course design to complement the assessment of final research papers. To date, there is little research on the specific collaborations between librarians and instructors of pre-service teachers, although the warrant is clear. Because teachers typically model their own practice after models of instruction they have learned, there is a premium in schools, colleges, and departments of education to help pre-service teachers develop their own abilities to conduct and to assess research by providing models of integrated, synthetic instruction. The collaboration described as a case study as the focus of this chapter was intentionally designed, conducted, and assessed as a model for the integration of research writing across the curriculum. It presents a model of librarian-education faculty collaboration and a model for the instruction of the discipline-based research process to pre-service teachers. It was conceived to empower pre-service teachers and their instructors with enhanced access to the tools of scholarly production, assessment, and self-assessment of the research paper and process by requiring students to create not only a final product but also a formal record of their experience in the research process. The combination of librarian and instructor, of paper and process, and the development of collaborative structures for assessing both the completed work and the process of research give this instructional model for teaching the research process to pre-service teachers its uniqueness.

Institutional Background and Context

To a large degree, the institutional context in which we found ourselves helped offset barriers to effective collaboration between librarian and instructor in the Education Department. Dickinson College is a nationally recognized, highly selective liberal arts college in south-central Pennsylvania. Enrollment hovers around 2,300 and student-faculty ratios are relatively low. The school encourages interdisciplinary approaches to research and promotes innovative uses of technology in the classroom. This rather forward-looking approach enabled Dickinson to pioneer creative approaches to pedagogy, such as the development of revolutionary bench physics courses that won national recognition in the last decade as well as an in-house faculty group called Teaching without Walls, which explored issues exclusively related to cutting-edge pedagogy (Johnson, 1996; Stearman, 1990). Dickinson College has also had a Library Department with a rich tradition of class-specific library instruction, beginning with first-year seminars and culminating in senior research capstone experiences. These traditions, combined with a thoroughgoing liaison program, meant that librarians were expected to work as closely as possible with faculty (McKinzie, 1997; Stachacz and Brennan, 1990). The library and the college fostered an environment that naturally encouraged collaboration. They created, in a sense, a natural synergy between individual librarians and the faculty with whom they worked.

Development of the Course and Instructional Context

At the time the course design described in this chapter was delivered, the Education Department consisted of three full-time faculty and offered a secondary education licensure program in the core disciplines. EDUC 231, Development and Diversity, was the second course in a sequenced curriculum and featured topics in human development, diversity and equity issues, and an introduction to educational psychology. Students in the course completed an intensive field practicum in addition to classroom instruction and wrote a research paper interpreting their experiences and observations in the field in terms of educational theory as presented in the text and ancillary instructional materials and media. Developing, executing, and assessing the research component of the course became a focus of instructional preparation and is the subject of this chapter.

An Overview of the Collaboration

The course instructor approached the research librarian responsible for coordinating with the Education Department before the semester began, explained rationale and vision for integrating instruction of the research component of the course, and introduced the librarian to the specific course content about which students would research and write. This began a dialogue between the two instructors (course instructor and librarian) that continued throughout the semester. The course instructor learned invaluable information about navigating the library's resources for his own research and for guiding the research of his students, and the librarian instructor learned specifically what topics the students would study and what forms of research the course instructor preferred for the specific course. Because so much of the environment for research has shifted from print text to online sources, within the library's larger site the librarian designed and built a Web page that was dedicated to the course (see figure 7.1). The link was accessible from the library page, and it was loaded with database access links to information sources pre-approved and targeted toward, for example, refereed scholarship. In this way, the foundation was established for integrated instruction of the class-based and library-based instructional cycles of the course, and this process.

Case Study Model

The specific Web-based guide that we designed for this class was customized to the particular needs and assignments of the course. This was not an all-encompassing discipline-specific guide designed to teach students everything they need to know about educational research or everything they might need to understand about the field of

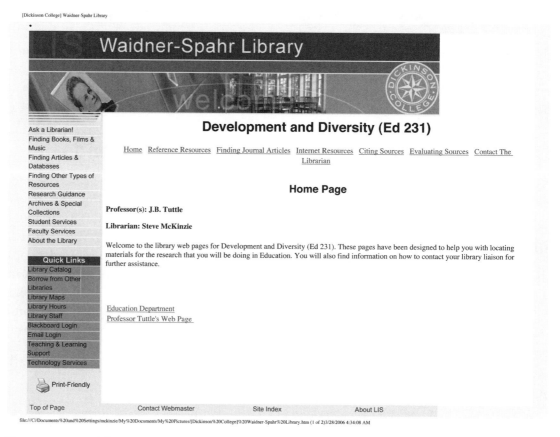

Figure 7.1   Development and Diversity (ED 231) Course Web Page

pedagogy. The Dickinson College library system does have such a generic guide for education, as well as a host of other subject guides for all the fields taught at the college. However, course guides such as the one we developed for this class are custom-made. They are specific, designed to teach students a command of specialized course-related tools. They allow students to get immediately engaged in research for the course based on the assignment at hand.

For Dickinson's Education 231 class, our customized site came with some advantages. Most important, it enabled us to cluster all relevant search data at a single virtual location. Students had a single place to begin their research. The homepage featured a navigation bar and links to additional pages on appropriate databases, reference sources, recommended Internet sites, information on evaluating sources, citation data, and library contact detail. Conversely, the course guide also gave us classroom instructors a point of reference in our classroom research sessions. Even if we did not cover everything or if we failed to mention something important, the Web page served as a way to orient us—a means of keeping track of which research elements the session had covered and which ones it had not.

After discussing the class needs and projects, we decided that the Web course guide needed to include additional features and pages. The following list and our reasons for including them go to the heart of what we wanted the course to accomplish.

Reference Sources

One of our pages listed major relevant subject encyclopedia and reference sources. Our reasons for this were straightforward. We wanted students to understand at the onset of the course that the Internet could not answer everything. Sometimes print resources were useful, especially if they saved a researcher time. A source such as Macmillan's eight-volume *Encyclopedia of Education* could give students a succinct, scholarly, and authoritative overview of a subject—an overview that might also include a useful bibliography. Such outlines and abbreviated bibliographies saved time and energy—valuable commodities in any student's life. As researchers, students had to understand they needed to work critically and actively, not just hard.

Finding Articles

The Finding Articles page listed relevant bibliographic databases and full-text sources. We included ERIC and Educational Abstracts, Project Muse, ProQuest, and JSTOR, as well as any database that might be particularly relevant. Each link was dynamically linked to our Web database editor page so any changes in the URL addresses would be updated immediately on our database page without specific page editing. The links also included brief explanations of the databases, since some of the databases may have been entirely new to class members. The brief descriptions helped students know what they were searching and why.

In our class explanations about locating articles, we used student topics (already identified in the classroom) to conduct sample searches on the large classroom screen to exemplify the respective features of ERIC and Educational Abstracts as subject-specific databases. We then moved on to ProQuest to illustrate the aggregate's multidisciplinary dimensions. At that juncture, we pointed out some of ProQuest's narrowing features to good advantage. We showed how one could configure ProQuest searches to retrieve only editorials or reviews. We then employed ProQuest's scholarly journal–limiting feature to eliminate everything from the search results except referred periodicals. The former search enabled us to introduce a discussion on the value of book reviews in scholarly analysis and the place of editorials in getting a handle on popular opinions about educational policy. The latter allowed us to engage students in a dialogue about the differences between scholarly and popular sources—distinctions that would have an enormous bearing on the success of their class research projects.

Internet Resources

Most of our students were tech savvy but all-too-often undiscerning users of Web resources. To counter this, we made sure that our Internet page listed some of the best and most reliable educational sites: the U.S. Department of Education site, the Educator's Reference Desk, the Yale University Educational Association Listing, and others.

Citation Assistance, Evaluating Resources, and Contact the Librarian Pages

Citation Assistance, Evaluating Resources, and Contact the Librarian Pages were each valuable, although we sometimes ran out of classroom time to discuss all three. Our citations page helped students cite properly. It contained links to major online citation guides. The evaluation page included major online evaluation sites, which equipped students to understand the varieties of Internet sites—their dangers and potentials. The Contact the Librarian page unabashedly promoted librarian consultation and expertise. As a secondary goal of our course, we wanted students to view librarians as consultants, professionals to whom they could turn in a research clutch or data quandary.

In planning the course, it was important to the course instructor to include a research component to enhance the academic rigor of the course and to serve as a foundation for the students' field experiences. Stymied by negative personal experiences as a student and teacher and the anecdotes of the vast majority of students (and instructors), the course instructor decided that the construction of this unit required reconceptualization. For many students, research paper writing consisted of negative experiences like the vignette that opens this chapter. It became an instructional goal to provide structures for the research paper, in instructional delivery as well as assessment, which would address the issues of student disengagement and lack of sustained interest and effort, instructor conflation of content assessment with assessment of writing skills, and the fragmentation of library orientation from content instruction.

Course Evaluation

To encourage student interest and engagement, the course instructor decided to design a rubric for evaluation of the research project that reinforced maximum effort on both the writing of the final paper and the process of research itself (see appendix 7.1). Students were assigned to create two products: a final paper and a record of research. This record of research consisted of all the artifacts from the student's research, including library search results, abstracts, full-text printouts, notes and citations, and a narrative describing the student's quest for timely, relevant, refereed sources of information on the educational topic of his or her selection (from a list distributed to the class by the instructor). At the deadline for submission of the papers and research records, students were allowed to weight the respective documents according to their own assessments of the relative success of each. Specifically, students were allowed to weight their records of research between 10 and 40 percent of the final project grades. For students who believed their methods and effort were superior to the final work, the opportunity to weight the research record more heavily was a welcome alternative to the paper-only evaluation model. However, this structure did not penalize students who write well, since it was determined by each student: those who perceived their papers to be stronger than their records of research were welcome to weight the paper as 90 percent of their final project grades. Not only was assessment differentiated in this way, but instruction was differentiated in a similar way. Since each student worked on a topic of individual selection and interest, each was mentored individually on that topic and its attendant research challenges.

In order to integrate the library instruction into the course, the instructor provided the librarian with a list of topics and the names of students. These topics were chosen on the basis of their timeliness, their relevance, and the existence of a relatively well defined and accessible research base. In turn, the librarian was able to mentor the instructor on the research engines available through the Dickinson library network and to prepare a Web site as part of the library Web that targeted refereed journals and other authoritative source guides on these topics.

The course instructor knew well the content of many of the journals and the conventions for research in education, so the course library page the librarian set up was easy for the instructor to understand and instruct—it was familiar academic ground. The nature of the library Web page gave the instructor the opportunity to help conduct the library orientation and research methods lessons, usually the province of the librarian alone. During the actual classroom instructional periods, we did everything we could to avoid the classic librarian or faculty monologue or lecture. We encouraged dialogue. We provoked interaction. We often asked students to define their research strategies or to articulate how and where they might find the best and most reliable information. As instructors, we also approached our sessions like seasoned broadcasters or tag team wrestlers, reluctant to take the mike or the mat for too long. We interrupted each other in our presentations, interjecting comments when it seemed helpful, and offering reflections when it seemed appropriate. This technique of using alternating voices, an old broadcast journalist's trick, helped students to gain more from the sessions than they might otherwise have. The structure was planned and coordinated, but the delivery facilitated spontaneity. Rather than being absent from the room or silent in a corner, the course instructor actively connected students to their topics, and students were able to engage research on their topics and begin asking targeted questions immediately. This gave the research process a living context, as each student actively engaged research techniques taught in the library classroom using their topics. The librarian answered questions and corrected errors of library engine usage, while the course instructor engaged students on content implications of research as they read it.

Three weeks and again six weeks after the initial orientation period, classes were scheduled in the library, where follow-up research workshops were conducted. Both of these workshops were directed at individual paper advisement and mentoring; and in both workshops, the librarian fielded questions about procedure and access while the instructor handled issues of content comprehension, writing strategy, argument construction, and support. After students submitted their research records and final papers, each presented his or her own research to the class, and the final examination incorporated this body of information.

Student Assessment and Feedback

When the students submitted their papers and records of progress, they were also asked to write summary assessments of the process and to rate their success and experience. To prevent the possibility that reading these students' process and product self-assessments would affect instructor grading, these were collected anonymously and were not read until after the papers and research records were scored and returned. Of twenty-two students in the course, all twenty-two returned self-assessments. Of these, nineteen stated that they liked the dual process of keeping and submitting their research records as well as the papers. The following response typified student assessment of this element of the instructional model: "I could not find all the articles I needed, or evidence for all the arguments I wanted to make in my paper, but I was able to show that I worked hard and did all the library searches, and used everything I could find." The other three student assessments did not address this element. Twenty of twenty-two students said that they liked the co-ownership and weighting of the grades; one student's response revealed that the timing of the decision was important to her: "At the beginning, I didn't like the idea of keeping the research record, because I wouldn't expect anyone to be able to tell what my system is. But, I had to be more organized, which at the end made me realize the record came out at least as well as the final paper." Two students reported that keeping the research record was cumbersome and took longer than their own systems of research. All twenty-two student assessments of the instructional model indicated a satisfaction with the tandem instructional model: most reported reactions similar to the following: "The best part was it wasn't boring, and we really started researching our topics right away and got results. I feel that both [the professor] and [the librarian] knew what they were talking about." The vignette used as the beginning of the chapter concluded in this way:

> But this turned out to be a way different research paper than I'd expected in every sense: the way it was introduced and taught, the products that mattered, and the way it was graded made the experience more valuable to me than I imagined on that first Tuesday in September.

Overall, these qualitative data indicate strong patterns of positive response to the instructional model as compared to traditional instruction and evaluation of the research process and products generated from it.

The assessment of student work as represented in the research records and the final papers can also be described in terms supplied earlier by Montiel-Overall, although these categories had not yet been identified at the time of the instruction. Student evaluations for the course can be used to assess student interest, level of involvement, learning, assessment of innovation, and assessment of integration of instruction and student processes and products. Of twenty-two students in the course, seventeen submitted course evaluations. These student course evaluations take the form of Likert scale ratings from strongly disagree (0) to strongly agree (6); numeric conversions have been used to compute mean ratings presented here, so mean ratings reported have a maximum of 6.0. Student evaluations feature ratings of course materials, instruction, and assessment: twelve items from these evaluations have been selected and presented here as the most relevant indicators of students' perceptions of instructor materials (2 items), instruction (5), and evaluation (2), and of student performance (3) in the course.

For the two items rating the selection of materials and instructor preparation, the student mean ratings were 5.24 and 5.86. Among items rating quality of instruction, student mean ratings for lectures was 5.8; they rated class discussions 5.47, other instructional methods 5.14, instructor interest 5.93, and student rating of whether the course was intellectually challenging 5.06. Among items rating student performance, one item asked for students' perceptions of whether the course helped them improve their own abilities to reason; students' mean rating for this item was 5.23. For the item "Now that I have taken this course, I have a better understanding of the subject matter," students' mean rating was 5.35, and on "I have a better understanding of the methods used in this field of study" a 5.53. No item was rated lower than a 4 by any student.

Findings

Overall, these data support the instructional program designed and implemented in this course. The findings show high levels of student interest, involvement, and learning. In addition, the actual quality of the students' final papers was, on balance, slightly better than usual, and the records of progress were highly valuable to the course instructor in assessing the effort and relative quality of students' research methods, data collection, and analysis. Further, while some students' weighting of their work showed acute self-assessment abilities, there was a range here that provided a teachable moment for many students in developing and using structured criteria as the basis for scoring evaluation. These results indicate a probable association between high levels of student interest, engagement, and learning and innovations used in the collaborative instructional model designed and delivered in the course, and they are also likely to be related to the structure for assessment of the research paper and process.

Most of the advantages of this model of research instruction are functions of innovations for instruction and assessment of the research project and process. By creating a course-specific (discipline-specific) library page using a topics list, the librarian was able to transform his presentation by giving it living, immediate context, and the instructor was able to help students evaluate actual search results during classroom whole-group instruction. The advantage here was not just for the students, who were able to engage discipline-appropriate reasoning skills to analyze and evaluate actual search results and secondary materials immediately, but also for the instructor, who learned through this process the exact research holdings and patterns of access for many topics in his or her discipline at the particular institution. Since institutional protocols for access and research engines vary, sometimes widely, from each other, this collaboration and tutorial from the librarian facilitates for the instructor informed, targeted instruction and the instructor's own research.

Conclusion

By requiring a record of research and accompanying narrative, making it part of the research project grade, and allowing students to weight their process and product grades at time of submission, the instructional model gained several advantages. Having the students organize and present their own research narratives gave them a voice in the scholarly conversation and helped make clear the quality of their work for the instructor in unique ways. Not only did the research record provide another platform for sustained scholarly student conversation, but it also made the student's research process transparent, susceptible to instruction and guidance, and creditable by the instructor, who otherwise would know little of the unique research experiences of his or her students.

Although it was not a conscious part of the design, this model also eliminated the possibility of plagiarism: each student's work was monitored individually throughout the process, so substituting a different document at the end of the process would have been impossible. The record of process would not have matched the final paper, nor would the reference lists or arguments. Sharing the responsibility for assessment applied democratic teaching practice in the classroom, dignified the research process in addition to the product, and forced students to evaluate their own work carefully. They could then triangulate their own assessments using the instructor's evaluation (as did the instructor). Because students selected their own topics, and because they weighted their own work, this instructional model also applied principles for differentiation of instruction and assessment. Students used their own research to instruct their peers, and these research-based student presentations became part of the basis for the final examination, showing students a model of integrated instruction. This model was considered particularly beneficial to pre-service teachers, who themselves will be teaching and evaluating writing and research as a large part of their professional responsibilities. Finally, this model took several innovative elements and synthesized them into an integrated, knowledge-in-context means of teaching and evaluating research projects in any given discipline.

References

Applebee, Arthur. 1993. *Beyond the Lesson: Reconstructing Curriculum as a Domain for Culturally Significant Conversations.* Urbana, IL: National Council of Teachers of English.

———. 1996. *Curriculum as Conversation.* Chicago: U of Chicago P.

Badke, William. 2005. "Can't Get No Respect: Helping Faculty to Understand the Educational Power of Information Literacy." *Reference Librarian* 89/90: 63–80.

Bazerman, Charles. 2005. "A Response to Anthony Fleury's 'Liberal Education and Communication against the Disciplines': A View from the World of Writing." *Communication Education* 54, no. 1: 86–91.

Bereiter, Carl. 1994. "Implications of Postmodernism for Science, or, Science as Progressive Discourse." *Educational Psychologist* 29: 3–12.

Bhavnagri, Navaz P., and Veronica Bielat. 2005. "Faculty-Librarian Collaboration to Teach Research Skills: Electronic Symbiosis." *Reference Librarian* 89/90: 121–138.

Cook-Sather, Alison. 2001. "Unrolling Roles in Techno-pedagogy: Toward New Forms of Collaboration in Traditional College Settings." *Innovative Higher Education* 26, no. 2: 121–139.

Cox, Suellen, and Elizabeth Housewright. 2001. "Teaching from the Web: Constructing a Library Learning Environment Where Connections Can Be Made." *Library Trends* 50, no. 1: 28–46.

Cudiner, Shelley, and Oskar R. Harmon. 2000. "An Active Learning Approach to Teaching Effective Online Search Strategies: A Librarian/Faculty Collaboration." *T.H.E. Journal* 28, no. 5: 52–57.

D'Angelo, B., and B. Maid. 2004. "Moving beyond Definitions: Implementing Information Literacy across the Curriculum." *Journal of Academic Librarianship* 30, no. 3: 212–217.

Gabella, Marcy S. 1994. "Beyond the Looking Glass: Bringing Students into the Conversation of Historical Inquiry." *Theory and Research in Social Education* 22, no. 3: 340–363.

Gorman, Michael, and Mark Y. Herring. 2003. "Do Librarians with Tenure Get More Respect?" *American Libraries* 34, no. 6: 70–72.

Greene, Maxine. 2000. "Imagining Futures: the Public School and Possibility." *Journal of Curriculum Studies* 32, no. 2: 267–280.

Heath, Shirley B. 1983. *Ways with Words*. New York: Cambridge University Press.

Johnson, Karen L. 1996. "1996 Robert A. Millikan Medal: Priscilla W. Laws, American Association of Physics Teachers." *The Physics Teacher* 4: 470.

Kaplowitz, Joan R., and David O. Yamamoto. 2001. "Web-Based Library Instruction for a Changing Medical School Curriculum." *Library Trends* 50, no. 1: 47–57.

Langer, Judith, and Richard Allington. 1992. "Curriculum Research in Writing and Reading." In *Handbook of Research on Curriculum*. Edited by Philip W. Jackson. New York: Macmillan: 687–725.

Langer, Judith, and Arthur Applebee. 1987. *How Writing Shapes Thinking: Studies of Teaching and Learning.* Urbana, IL: National Council of Teachers of English.

Malenfant, Chuck, and Nora Egan Demers. 2004. Collaboration for Point-of-need Library Instruction. *Reference Services Review* 32, no. 3: 264–273.

McKinzie, Steve. 1997. "Librarians and Faculty in Tandem: Taking our Cue from the Evening News." *Reference & Users Services Quarterly* 37, no. 1: 19–21.

Montiel-Overall, P. 2005. "A Theoretical Understanding of Teacher and Librarian Collaboration (TLC)." *School Libraries Worldwide* 11, no. 2: 24–48.

Naslund, Jo-Anne, Marlene Asselin, and Margot M. Filipenko. 2005. "Blueprint for Collaboration: An Information Literacy Project at the University of British Columbia." *PNLA Quarterly* 69, no. 3 (Spring): 10, 29–32.

Ochsner, Robert, and Judy Fowler. 2004. "Playing Devil's Advocate: Evaluating the Literature of the WAC/WID Movement." *Review of Educational Research* 74, no. 2 (Summer): 117–140.

Ryken, Ann. 2004. A Spider and a Fly In a Web: Seeing Myself in the Details of Praxis. *Reflective Practice* 5 (February, 2004): 111–123.

Stachacz, John, and Thomas Brennan. 1990. "Bibliographic Instruction in an Undergraduate Biology Course: Faculty-Library Liaison at Dickinson College." *Research Strategies* 8 (Winter): 14–21.

Stearman, David M. 1990. "Dickinson College: Studying Physics in Depth by Learning to Think." *Liberal Education* 76 (September/October): 38–40.

Shulman, Lee. 1987. "Knowledge and Teaching: Foundations of the New Reform." *Harvard Educational Review* 57: 1–22.

Vygotsky, Lev S. 1962. *Thought and Language*. Cambridge, MA: M.I.T. Press.

Witt, Steve W., and Julie B. Dickinson. 2003. "Teaching Teachers to Teach: Collaborating with a University Education Department to Teach Skills in Information Literacy Pedagogy." *Behavioral & Social Sciences Librarian* 22, no. 1: 75–95.

Appendix 7.1: Assessment Rubric for Research Project

This research assignment has been designed to help you and the instructor assess both the quality of your final paper and your research journey. The following rubric will serve as a basis for the evaluation of your work in the research component of the course. Please construct two separate notebooks for submission on or before the syllabus deadline, as described below.

I. Process (x% of final grade: minimum 10%, maximum 40%)

    A. Documented attempts to access sources not appearing in paper reference list (include list of sources with hard copy of library search strategies employed).

    B. Self-Assessment of research narrative: record your experiences, including successes, frustrations, and failures, in conducting research for this assignment. This should be converted to coherent essay form and proofread for mechanics and accuracy before submission.

    C. Self-Assessment of writing narrative: record your experiences, including successes, frustrations, and failures, in writing the research paper. This should be converted to coherent essay form and proofread for mechanics and accuracy before submission.

II. Paper (x% of final grade: minimum 60%, maximum 90%)

    A. Content and scholarly quality of secondary sources selected for use (15%)

    B. Number of secondary sources used (15%)

    C. Quality of argument/content (30%)

    D. Quality of evidentiation (30%)

    E. Mechanics (10%)

III. Student weighting

    You have completed two documents: one details the quality of your effort, while the other demonstrates the quality of your final product. On which, in your view, did you perform better? After reflection (which should take the form of a mental comparative analysis and evaluation), replace the "x's" above with the percentage of your final grade for this project you wish to be assigned to each.

8

The Politics of Information Literacy: Integrating Information Literacy into the Political Science Curriculum

Christy R. Stevens, Humanities Librarian, California State University, Sacramento, Formerly Assistant Professor, Ingram Library Instructional Services
Patricia J. Campbell, Professor of Political Science
University of West Georgia

For academic librarians, the idea that effective information literacy (IL) instruction involves both integration into the academic curriculum and collaboration with teaching faculty has become axiomatic. Indeed, library literature abounds with articles propounding the dual "integration" and "collaboration" imperatives. This is generally not the case, however, in the teaching literature of other disciplines. Although faculty across the disciplinary spectrum may teach components of what librarians refer to as information literacy in their courses and perhaps write about them in their pedagogical scholarship, they remain largely unfamiliar with the vast body of library literature focusing upon information literacy and the many ways that librarians can work with them in enhancing the learning experiences of their students. And while many librarians view integrating IL competencies across disciplines and academic levels as a best practice, many faculty assume that students should have mastered these competencies prior to arriving in their classrooms and that it is simply not their job to embed IL instruction into their courses. "Integration," then, does not hold the same sway for most teaching faculty, nor are they lining up outside the library doors to collaborate with librarians on IL initiatives.

Such is the case at the University of West Georgia (UWG), where instructional services librarians have evinced their commitment to information literacy instruction through the development of a liaison program, a bibliographic instruction program that offers a series of one-shot sessions geared toward lower-division students and a two-credit course—LIBR 1101, Academic Research and the Library—that fulfills a general education requirement, but where fewer strides have been made in terms of actively collaborating with faculty to integrate IL instruction into the fabric of disciplinary courses and curricula. Because the library already had a strong independent instruction program in place, however, the instructional librarian in this study was able to begin exploring ways that the program could be enhanced through collaborative and integrative initiatives, which the Association of College and Research Libraries (ACRL) has included among its list of best practices for IL programs (ACRL, 2003). According to former ACRL president Larry Hardesty, most successful collaborative instructional programs have been and will continue to be accomplished through "one-on-one informal contacts between librarians and faculty members" (1995: 362). Similarly, Booth and Fabian assert that IL integration is a "relationship-based evolutionary" process rather than a "task-based, end-product activity (2002: 140). Both assertions are consistent with the development of the collaborative partnership that is the basis of this chapter. Indeed, informal, ongoing discussions between an instructional services librarian and a political science professor regarding what information literacy is, what instruction librarians do, and how they can complement faculty efforts to ensure that student learning preceded and laid the groundwork for our collaborative endeavor. Over time, "shared goals, a shared vision, and a climate of trust and respect" (Sonntag and Meulemans, 2003: 10) emerged (the foundational elements of successful collaborative endeavors), and our discussions shifted to exploring ways we could work together to enhance student learning by integrating IL instruction into political science courses. We agreed that the best way to proceed was to cast aside traditional models of librarian involvement in course instruction, which tend to position the librarian as a helpful resource for finding "stuff," but an outsider nonetheless, tangential to the real work of the course (class content, assignments, and grades). Instead, we decided to work together fully, from initial curriculum development to the final assignment of grades.

This case study examines the results of that pilot collaboration, including the development, implementation, and assessment of a semester-long instructional initiative that involved three different political science courses (Introduction to American Government, a lower-level course; Comparative Politics, a mid-level course; and African Politics, an upper-level course), reaching undergraduate students ranging from freshmen to seniors. We begin with a brief review of library and political science literature that focuses on IL instruction in the political science context followed by a description of the institutional context at the University of West Georgia. The remaining sections focus on the case study itself. We describe the goals of the collaboration and the development of learning outcomes, pedagogical strategies, and assignments. We then discuss the development and deployment of assessment tools, including a questionnaire, pre- and post-tests, and research assignments with their corresponding rubrics. We conclude with a discussion of our results, an evaluation of the success of our collaboration, and directions for future instruction and research.

IL Instruction in the Political Science Classroom: A Review of the Literature

Although texts focusing on IL instruction in various disciplinary contexts are abundant in the library literature, very few of these publications focus specifically on the discipline of political science. Hutchins's description of a grant-funded project at St. Olaf College to integrate and assess IL competencies in the courses Latin American Politics and Analyzing Politics and Policy is a notable exception, though brief in length and limited in scope. In collaboration with two political science professors, Hutchins helped develop an annotated bibliography assignment and a corresponding rubric, concluding that the rubric helped faculty articulate their criteria, which in turn empowered students, enabling them to understand the expectations for the assignment. Appended to the article is an example of a "citation skeleton," a useful tool for helping students analyze and evaluate sources in order to produce effective annotations for their bibliographies (2003).

Although the library literature contains a number of other texts that focus on political science, such as those that introduce and promote the use of specific political science sources and access tools,[1] the majority of these texts are not explicitly about IL instruction. Texts that do position IL instruction in the political science context as their primary focus tend not to be formal, scholarly publications. For example, the "Political Science and Government" page on the ACRL Instruction Section's "Information Literacy in the Disciplines" Web site only lists a series of political science–related IL grant proposals from the Five Colleges of Ohio under the heading "Curricula, Articles, and Presentations."[2] Conference papers and the proceedings of relevant panel discussions are also occasionally published online and elsewhere, such as the 2003 American Library Association (ALA) GODORT International Documents Task Force (IDTF) panel entitled "Promoting IGO Information Resources to Scholars and Citizens," which focuses on the panelists' experiences teaching courses on government information (ALA. GODORT-IDTF, 2004). Finally, February 2005 saw the publication of a draft of ACRL's Law and Political Science Section's (LPSS) "Political Science Research Competency Guidelines" (ALA. LPSS Education Task Force, 2005). The document lists standards adapted from the core ACRL Information Literacy Competency Standards (2005) accompanied by examples of how they might be applied in political science and related disciplines. It remains to be seen, however, whether the document will have much impact on classroom practices and library scholarship.

A cursory review of the political science teaching literature suggests that the intersection of information literacy and political science is not a popular site of research for political scientists either. Part of this is a nomenclature issue, however, since "information literacy" is a term that is used predominantly by librarians. While many political scientists attempt to teach students how to conduct political science research and use the information they find effectively and responsibly in the production of political science research papers and presentations, very few would use the term "information literacy" to describe their efforts. For example, Kuzma (1998) argues that because of the explosive growth of information technology, students need to be taught "new thinking skills . . . that allow them to select from a varied array of information" and to sort and use "problem-relevant information" (581). Instructors, Kuzma maintains, must "develop students' 'critical literacy,'" helping them to become "information managers" who know how to "access, organize, and present information," rather than "information regurgitaters" who passively accept and spit back information that is given to them (1998: 581). Instead of "information literacy," Kuzma refers to "critical literacy," while other political science articles use terms like "eliteracy" and "critical thinking" to get at concepts that librarians would generally discuss within an IL framework. The political science–teaching literature focusing on strategies for teaching the research methods course can also prove relevant to IL discussions in that it often deals with issues like developing a topic, finding relevant literature, and producing a literature review.[3] Although these articles tend not to use the term "information literacy," they too are clearly dealing with competencies that are outlined in ACRL's Standards.

Academic articles that make the connection between information literacy and political science explicit, discussing strategies for integrating information literacy into the fabric of political science courses, are decidedly rare. In an unusual reversal, the two recent examples that do make the connection are written by political scientists rather than librarians. In "Information Literacy and the Undergraduate Methods Curriculum," Marfleet and Dille test the hypothesis that undergraduate political science methods courses are "particularly fertile ground for the targeted enhancement of ACRL targeted competencies" (2005: 175). The case study describes the integration of IL competencies into two undergraduate methods courses and two non-methods political science courses. Findings indicate that IL-oriented courses can improve student performance on standardized competency tests, although that improvement is not linked to the methods course. The article also makes the important connection between student experience and IL competency, observing that "information literacy skills accumulate as students progress through their collegiate studies" (2005: 187).

Stephen Thornton's 2005 Political Science Association (PSA) conference presentation, "Information Literacy and Politics," is another recent text that makes the link between political science and IL instruction. Thornton defines information literacy for an uninitiated UK audience of political scientists and describes a pilot study that integrated information literacy into a third-year politics course. Student feedback on the various aspects of the IL project was positive, and Thornton maintained that integrating information literacy does not take too much time, provided faculty are willing to work with library staff. Finally, he concludes that a long-term, discipline-integrated approach to information literacy is the most sensible form of instruction (Thornton, 2005).

The collaboration that is the subject of this chapter shares Thornton's assumption that long-term discipline integration is the best form of IL instruction as well as Marfleet and Dille's assertion that the correspondence between information competency and academic experience "might be accentuated" if information literacy were integrated throughout the curriculum rather than marginalized as a peculiar feature of the library (2005: 187). It also relies upon the assumption that faculty-librarian collaboration is key to the successful implementation of information literacy initiatives, although we take "the collaborative imperative"[4] a step further than these studies, including librarian input and participation in every step of the process.

Institutional Context: About the University of West Georgia

The University of West Georgia is a co-educational, residential, liberal arts institution located in Carrollton, Georgia, approximately fifty miles west of Atlanta. Carrollton is a growing area that is currently transitioning from a small town to a burgeoning city on the outskirts of the Atlanta metropolitan area. Ninety-seven percent of the 10,154 students enrolled at the university are Georgia residents, the majority of whom come from within a 100-mile radius of the campus. Undergraduates make up 81 percent of student enrollment, and the university accepts just over 60 percent of applicants, whose average scores on the verbal and math sections of the SAT are approximately 500. The remaining are graduate students studying toward the master's degree in over two dozen areas. Recently, the first doctoral program was established at the university in School Improvement in the Department of Education. Other doctoral programs are under review.

As is the case at many state colleges and universities, student retention has emerged as a major institutional concern at the University of West Georgia. On average, 32 percent (1995–2003) of incoming students do not persist to the second year (Shooks, 2005: 36), a figure that falls between the average rate of first- to second-year attrition at four-year public colleges that primarily accept students who graduated in the top 50 percent of their high school classes (28% attrition rate) and those that admit primarily from the bottom 50 percent of high school classes (37% attrition rate) (ACT Institutional Data File, 2005: Table 3). Over a span of five years, student persistence continues to decline at the university, culminating in a graduation rate that hovers around 24 percent (Shooks, 2005: 36). This figure is five points lower than the average persistence to degree rate for four-year state institutions that admit primarily from the bottom 50 percent of high school classes (ACT Institutional Data File, 2005: Table 7). As a result, the university has made increasing retention a major institutional goal.

Goals for the Collaboration

The overarching goals of the collaboration were multiple. First, we wanted to begin the process of integrating IL competencies into the political science curriculum. Second, in order to lay the groundwork for obtaining "buy-in" by other members of the department in the future, we wanted to establish that IL instruction is needed across courses and levels of academic experience, but that IL competencies nevertheless improve with academic experience. Third, we wanted to show that course-integrated IL instruction leads to learning, including improved performance on standardized competency tests and satisfactory demonstration of pre-defined IL competencies in meaningful research contexts. Finally, we wanted to use the results of the study to identify the IL competencies that are most difficult for students and where additional IL instruction is needed.

Development

Learning Outcomes

We began developing the curriculum for the courses by outlining the IL student learning outcomes that we wanted all three courses to emphasize, aligning ACRL Standards and Performance Indicators with general learning outcomes for all three classes as well as narrower course and assignment-specific objectives. The ACRL Standards functioned as a generative framework for us, rather than as a set of rigid prescriptions, helping us to isolate key competencies and then contextualize them within the political science context. After much discussion, we narrowed our desired general learning outcomes for all three courses to seven that focused on areas with which we both knew, from our years of teaching experience, students tend to have difficulty. We also attempted to make these outcomes broad enough to allow for flexibility in their implementation in the different courses. More specific instructional objectives tailored to course content and course level were then developed in conjunction with specific assignments and their corresponding grading rubrics. Figure 8.1 illustrates the ACRL Standards and Performance Indicators that correspond with both our general learning outcomes and course-specific objectives.

Pedagogical Assumptions and Strategies

Assignment development was influenced by our belief that teaching can perhaps best be defined as "arranging the conditions for learning" (Chickering, 2000: 25). In this framework, assignments are an integral part of instruction, providing students with the opportunity to learn both through active engagement in various stages of the research process and through feedback on their performances. Writing instructors have long found that a process approach to teaching writing, which involves steps and drafts, providing opportunities for feedback and improvement, is a more effective way to enhance student learning than a product-oriented approach, characterized by the assignment of a final grade without feedback, the opportunity for revision, and the learning that takes place in and through the revision process. The process approach is also ideal for instruction in information literacy, providing students with the opportunity to receive feedback on their work, to incorporate that feedback into their knowledge-base, and to revise their process as they proceed to the next step of the assignment. Without the process approach, we would simply be grading students on what they knew coming into the course, or what they were able to remember from lectures and demonstrations, rather than providing them with hands-on meaningful contexts in which to experiment and learn. We decided to create assignments, then, that were not simply indicators of student success or failure but, rather, integral parts of the instructional-learning process.

We also decided that our assignments should be writing intensive, emphasizing analysis, synthesis, and evaluation (Bloom's "higher-order thinking skills").[5] Rather than simply asking students to "find stuff" or to recall and transcribe correct answers, we decided to design assignments that asked students to use information in meaningful ways and to demonstrate their understanding of key IL concepts. For example, we developed annotated bibliography assignments that asked students to summarize, assess, and reflect. Specifically, students were asked to provide a summary of the key points the author made to support the thesis. After the summary, students were required to assess the source, evaluating its reliability, authority, and underlying assumptions and biases. The last part of the annotation was a reflection that required students to explain how the source was helpful, how it supported and shaped their argument, and how it affected the way they thought about the topic.

Assignments

We tailored general learning outcomes to the specific courses and constructed objectives and assignments around them. In the lower-level introductory American Government course, we placed greater emphasis on the importance of developing a clear thesis statement because students at this level are often unfamiliar with what constitutes an appropriate political science argument. As such, we developed a research proposal assignment that asked students to identify a general research focus from a list of approved topics, to

Standards	Performance Indicators	Learning Outcomes	Course Specific Learning Objectives
S 1: The information literate student determines the nature and extent of the information needed.	**PI 1:** The information literate student defines and articulates the need for information.	1. Students will develop a clear and appropriately narrow research focus that is in accordance with the requirements of the assignment.	**Lower Level:** After selecting a general topic from a list of pre-approved issues, American Government students will construct a clear and arguable thesis statement in their final research projects that connects their topic to a specific and relevant point of law or clause in the constitution. **Mid Level:** After selecting a reaction statement from a pre-approved list, Comparative Politics students will construct an arguable thesis statement in their final research paper that clearly states their position on the issue. **Upper Level:** African Politics students will develop a clear, focused, and correctly formatted resolution that is relevant to their assigned country (Ethiopia or Eritrea) and the AU committee of which they are a delegate.
S 1: The information literate student determines the nature and extent of the information needed. **S 2:** The information literate student accesses needed information effectively and efficiently.	**PI 2:** The information literate student identifies a variety of types and formats of potential sources for information. **PI 3:** The information literate student retrieves information online or in person using a variety of methods.	2. Students will identify, distinguish among, and locate a variety of types of sources relevant to political science research.	**Lower Level:** In their Annotated Bibliographies, American Government students will include accurate and relevant entries for at least seven out of the following ten required types of sources: two books, five scholarly journal articles, one magazine article, one website, one print government document. **Mid Level:** Comparative Politics students will use at least five scholarly sources (academic journals or books) to support the thesis of their final research paper. **Upper Level:** In their Annotated Bibliographies, African Government students will include accurate and relevant entries for at least seven out of the following ten required types of sources: five organizational sources, two news sources, one reference source, and two books.
S 3: The information literate student evaluates information	**PI 1:** The information literate student summarizes the main ideas to	3. Students will accurately identify the main ideas and arguments in the texts	**Lower Level:** In their Annotated Bibliographies, American Government students will summarize at least

Figure 8.1   ACRL Standards and Performance Indicators Corresponding to Learning Outcomes and Course Objectives

and its sources critically and incorporates selected information into his or her knowledge base and value system.	be extracted from the information gathered.	they have selected for use in their research projects, restating them in their own words.	seven out of ten sources, clearly and accurately stating each author's thesis and main supporting points. **Mid Level:** In their final research papers, Comparative Politics students will accurately and clearly discuss the arguments from sources they use to support their own points. **Upper Level:** In their final research projects, African Politics students will provide an accurate and thorough overview of both the African Union and their assigned committee, paraphrasing source material appropriately.
S 3: The information literate student evaluates information and its sources critically and incorporates selected information into his or her knowledge base and value system.	**PI 2:** The information literate student articulates and applies initial criteria for evaluating both the information and its sources.	4. Students will articulate why the sources they have selected for use in their research projects are authoritative and reliable.	**Lower Level:** In their Annotated Bibliographies, American Government students will evaluate at least seven out of ten sources, explaining why each is a useful and reliable source to consult. **Mid Level:** In their Annotated Bibliographies, Comparative Politics students will evaluate at least seven out of ten sources, explaining why each is a useful and reliable source to consult. **Upper Level:** In their Annotated Bibliographies, African Government students will evaluate at least seven out of ten sources, explaining why each is a useful and reliable source to consult.
S 4: The information literate student, individually or as a member of a group, uses information effectively to accomplish a specific purpose.	**PI 1:** The information literate student applies new and prior information to the planning and creation of a particular product or performance.	5. Students will effectively integrate specific information from the texts they have located into their research projects in the form of quotations and paraphrases to support their main points.	**Lower Level:** In their Final Research Projects, American Government students will logically and smoothly integrate three sources into their discussion of their reasons for holding their particular position on their selected issue. **Mid Level:** In their Research Papers, Comparative Politics students will provide accurate, specific, and relevant information in the form of quotations and paraphrases to support the thesis. **Upper Level:** In their Final Research Projects, African Politics students will provide accurate, specific, and relevant information in the form of quotations and paraphrases to support their main points.

Figure 8.1   (*continued*)

S 4: The information literate student, individually or as a member of a group, uses information effectively to accomplish a specific purpose.	PI 3: The information literate student communicates the product or performance effectively to others.	6. Students will communicate their research findings clearly and coherently in writing, using academically appropriate language and style.	**Lower Level:** In their Annotated Bibliographies, American Government students will write their entries using the following format: Author's name and qualifications and the thesis. This is followed by a summary, an assessment, and a reflection. **Mid Level:** Comparative Politics students will write research papers that are organized, logical, consistent, clear, grammatically correct, and easy to follow. **Upper Level:** African Politics students will write final research projects that are organized, logical, consistent, clear, grammatically correct, and easy to follow.
S 2: The information literate student accesses needed information effectively and efficiently. S 5: The information literate student understands many of the economic, legal, and social issues surrounding the use of information and accesses and uses information ethically and legally.	PI 5: The information literate student extracts, records, and manages the information and its sources. PI 3: The information literate student acknowledges the use of information sources in communicating the product or performance.	7. Students will cite sources correctly using the APSA format.	**Lower Level:** In their Annotated Bibliographies, American Government students will cite at least seven out of ten sources correctly using the APSA format. **Mid Level:** In their Research Papers, Comparative Politics students will cite at least five sources correctly using the APSA format. **Upper Level:** In their Annotated Bibliographies, African Government students will cite at least seven out of ten sources correctly using the APSA format.

describe different positions individuals and organizations take on the issue, to identify a specific point of law or clause in the Constitution that is relevant to the topic, to frame their specific issue as a researchable question, and then to construct a clear and narrowly defined thesis in response to their research question.

Although we expected students in the mid-level Comparative Politics course to be more advanced than those in American Government, we had them complete a similar assignment designed to reinforce the importance of narrowing to a specific and appropriate argument. They too completed a research proposal assignment, although they selected a reaction statement from a pre-approved list that invoked a general comparative political controversy, such as "Democracy fosters peace." Students investigated different positions that political science scholars tend to take on the issue and then developed their own position in the form of a thesis statement. For both the Comparative and the American courses, the research proposal provided students with feedback that was designed to point out problems and offer suggestions that would provide appropriate direction for their evolving research process.

In contrast, we did not require the 4000-level African Politics students to complete a research proposal. This decision was based on the content and focus of the course itself, which revolved around preparing students to participate in the Southeastern Model African Union (AU). The Model AU is a simulation similar in form and format to the Model UN, but with a state-centered focus on Africa. As such, we geared our research assignments and IL objectives specifically to this active learning experience, which required students to steep themselves in their assigned country. Rather than conducting research in order to write traditional research papers, students researched their assigned countries (Ethiopia or Eritrea), the AU, the specific AU committees on which they would serve as delegates, and the types of issues they would need to be familiar with in order to vote in the character of their country and to construct and successfully pass an appropriate resolution.

In all courses, students constructed an annotated bibliography that consisted of ten sources. The types of sources students were required to include in their bibliographies varied among the classes, given the course content and course level. Students in the lower-level American Government course, for example, were required to locate books, scholarly journal articles, magazine articles, Internet Web sites, and a print government document in order to introduce them to various types of sources, facilitating their ability to identify and distinguish among them. The mid-level Comparative Politics class culminated in a research paper, so the annotated bibliographies were to consist primarily of scholarly journal articles. In contrast, students in the African Politics class were required to locate reputable organizational sources (e.g., the AU or the UN), news sources, and general historical and reference texts dealing with Ethiopia or Eritrea, as these were more appropriate sources of current information for their specific tasks.

Each course culminated with a final research project, although the projects for each course differed significantly. The lower-level American Government course ended with an assignment that took them through the steps they would need to go through if they were to write a research paper. In short, it consisted of a description of their research issue, a discussion of their current position on the issue followed by reasons for holding this position, an annotated bibliography, and a reflection upon the research process. The final assignment for the mid-level Comparative Politics course was a research paper that took a position on a comparative political issue. The African Politics course culminated in a ten-page paper analyzing the intersection of students' research in preparation for and their actual experience participating in the Southeastern Model AU. Specifically, the paper consisted of a written overview of the AU, the specific AU committee to which the students were assigned, a discussion of the resolution they developed and their experience presenting that resolution at the Model AU, and a reflection on how they went about their research and how it contributed to or affected their experience at the AU.

Despite the differences among assignments and specific objectives across the courses, the more broadly defined learning outcomes were consistent in all three classes, allowing us to measure students' performance of IL skills.

Implementation

At the beginning and end of the semester, we administered a standardized IL competency multiple-choice pre- and post-test. A series of scaffolded assignments, with the latter assignments building on the concepts and skills introduced in the earlier ones, were all introduced and discussed early in the semester. Due dates were staggered throughout the course of the semester to provide opportunities for feedback and to enhance student learning. In each of the upper-division classes, the librarian provided assignment-driven instructional sessions early in the semester that emphasized how to find and evaluate relevant information. These point-of-need sessions discussed various types of sources and access tools as well as provided hands-on demonstrations on how to search for and retrieve appropriate sources of information. Further follow-up sessions involved the librarian returning to the classes to discuss the assignments as well as the assessment rubrics used for each assignment. We used the return of assignments as a "teachable moment," pulling out examples of successful and less-successful responses for group discussion and analysis.

The lower-division course required students to sign up for an instructional session at the library entitled "Introduction to Library Research." These one-shot sessions are taught by instructional services librarians at Ingram Library and are part of the library's instruction program for lower-division undergraduate students. Students in all classes had the opportunity to receive one-on-one instruction while working on their assignments. Many students received this instruction by visiting the professor or the librarian during their respective office hours or asking the reference librarian for assistance. Reference librarians are available during the library's hours of operation, and copies of the students' assignments were kept at the desk.

All feedback and grading was conducted collaboratively using jointly designed grading and feedback rubrics. For an example of a rubric, please see the American Government Research Proposal Rubric appended to this chapter (appendix 8.1).

Assessment

We used multiple instruments and strategies to try to capture learning from different dimensions, all of which were developed in and through the process of constructing overarching collaborative goals and student learning outcomes, objectives, and assignments. In other words, assessment was an integral part of our process, rather than an afterthought appended to the end of our project. In order to establish that IL instruction is needed in introductory, mid-level, and upper-level political science classes, we developed and administered a standardized, multiple-choice pre-test, which tested competencies under ACRL Standards 1 through 3. Because Standards 3, 4, and 5 are particularly difficult to assess through standardized, multiple-choice tests, we also relied upon research and writing assignments completed early in the semester to establish the need for IL instruction in all five competency areas. To show that course-integrated IL instruction leads to learning, we administered a post-test to determine whether our methods of IL instruction led to improved IL competencies. Course-embedded performance-based assignments and corresponding rubrics, consisting of specific pre-established performance criteria, were designed to evaluate students' performance of IL competencies in a meaningful research context. Post-test scores in addition to analytic rubrics designed for scoring individual parts of students' research projects were designed to help us determine which IL competencies were most difficult for students and therefore called for additional IL instruction.

Assignments were a particularly critical component of our assessment plan because students' scores on them constituted a significant part of their final course grades. In contrast, scores on the pre- and post-tests did not count toward students' grades, which increased the possibility that some students might not take them seriously. The assignments, then, were likely to give us a more accurate and in-depth look at students' IL competencies, while the strength of the pre- and post-tests was that results were easier to quantify.

Student feedback was another important assessment strategy that we relied upon in our study. Reflective sections of research project assignments, for example, were designed to elicit student feedback on aspects of the research process that they found difficult and areas where they felt additional instruction would have been helpful. Their comments helped us to make immediate adjustments in the courses when needed and will assist us in the development of courses, assignments, and in-class instruction for future students.

Hypothesis

Early in the process we also outlined three specific hypotheses that we wanted our case study to test:

- H1—On average, students who are further along in their college careers (i.e., seniors) will score higher on the pre-test and perform better on the assignments (as measured by the rubrics) than students with significantly less academic experience (i.e., freshmen), indicating that they have already developed some IL competencies in other courses.[6]
- H2—On average, students in the lower-level course will not perform as well as upper-level students on the standardized tests and research assignments because (1) lower-level students have not had as much exposure to IL because of their lack of academic experience; (2) the lower-level course is a general education requirement that all students have to take, regardless of their interests and academic major and, as a result, lower-level required courses often elicit corresponding lower levels of student motivation, commitment, effort, satisfaction, and performance; and (3) more lower-level students (freshmen) are unprepared or unwilling to fully engage in academic work (as evidenced by high freshman attrition rates at the university in general) than students in upper-level classes, whose very enrollment in an upper-level course indicates their ability or willingness to fulfill academic requirements.
- H3—Students across academic levels will have more difficulty successfully completing tasks that target higher-order thinking skills.

Methodology and Results

At the beginning and end of the semester, we administered our standardized, twenty-item pre- and post-test, which contained four response options per question and targeted the first three ACRL Standards. A total of forty-eight students completed both the pre- and post-tests. Of these, twenty-three were registered for a lower-level Introduction to American Government class; nineteen were in a mid-level Comparative Politics course; and six were in an upper-level African Politics seminar. In all, sixteen freshman, thirteen sophomores, eight juniors, and eleven seniors participated in the survey.

The lower-level class yielded the lowest scores on the pre-test, averaging just below 60 percent correct answers. Students in the mid-level course averaged 71 percent correct, and the upper-level students' average neared 80 percent correct. Students' post-test scores improved in all three classes. The lower-level and mid-level courses produced the greatest improvement, increasing by 10 and 12 percentage points respectively, while the upper-level course showed the least improvement, increasing by 2 percentage points.

When distributed specifically by academic experience, freshmen averaged 64 percent on the pre-test and 67 percent on the post, for an improvement of 3 percent; sophomores averaged 74 percent on the pre-test and 84 percent on the post, for an improvement of 10 percent; juniors averaged 74 percent on the pre-test and 86 percent on the post, for an improvement of 12 percent; and seniors averaged 79 percent on the pre-test and 87 percent on the post, for an improvement of 8 percent. Across age groups, political science majors averaged 73 on the pre-test and 84 on the post, for an improvement of 11 percent. Senior political science majors averaged 79 on the pre-test and 86 on the post, for an improvement of 7 percent.

Assessment for all ACRL Standards, but particularly for Standards 4 and 5, was conducted using grading rubrics designed for each individual assignment. Students' ability to meet specific learning objectives as identified by these assignments is summarized and charted in figure 8.2.

In each class, students were assigned a research proposal designed to assist them in defining and narrowing their topics. Developing a thesis statement was an important part of this assignment, and students received feedback on their initial attempt to formulate a political science argument. This proved critical, as their final assignment demonstrated a high rate of success in achieving learning outcome 1, developing a narrow research focus. As one might expect, the success rate for learning outcome 2, which required students be able to identify, distinguish among, and locate a variety of types of sources, was higher for those students in the mid- and upper-level classes, as most were political science majors, thus demonstrating not only general interest in and commitment to the subject but also at least some previous exposure to political science research and scholarship. As the chart demonstrates, mid- and upper-level students had a high success rate on learning outcome 3 (identifying the main ideas and arguments in the source material), but it posed a problem for the lower-level students, who clearly struggled with this task. The low score for this outcome in the lower-level class reflected a phenomenon not anticipated by the professors: students who chose not to complete this part the assignment. Many students in the lower-level course simply did not complete ten entries in their bibliographies. For learning outcome 4, which required students to articulate why their sources were authoritative and reliable, students were assigned a specific task of developing an annotated bibliography. For those who did complete the requisite number of bibliography entries, this learning objective still proved to be very difficult for students to achieve.

Learning Outcomes	Specific Objectives	Percent Success
1. Students will develop a clear and appropriately narrow research focus that is in accordance with the requirements of the assignment.	**Lower Level Class:** After selecting a general topic from a list of pre-approved issues, students will construct a clear and arguable thesis statement in their final research projects that connects their topic to a specific and relevant point of law or clause in the constitution.	89
	Mid Level Class: After selecting a reaction statement from a pre-approved list, students will construct an arguable thesis statement in their final research paper that clearly states their position on the issue.	85
	Upper Level Class: Students will develop a clear, focused, and correctly formatted resolution that is relevant to their assigned country and the AU committee of which they are a delegate.	100
2. Students will identify, distinguish among, and locate a variety of types of sources relevant to political science research.	**Lower Level Class:** In their annotated bibliographies, students will include accurate and relevant entries for at least seven out of the ten required types of sources.	50
	Mid Level Class: Students will use at least five scholarly sources to support the thesis of their final research paper.	65
	Upper Level Class: In their annotated bibliographies, students will include accurate and relevant entries for at least seven out of the ten required types of sources.	88
3. Students will accurately identify the main ideas and arguments in the texts they have selected for use in their research projects, restating them in their own words.	**Lower Level Class:** In their annotated bibliographies, students will summarize at least seven out of ten sources, clearly and accurately stating each author's thesis and main supporting points.	23
	Mid Level Class: In their final research papers, students will accurately and clearly discuss the arguments from the sources they use to support their own points.	81
	Upper Level Class: In their final research projects, students will provide an accurate and thorough overview of both the AU and their assigned committee, paraphrasing source material appropriately.	100
4. Students will articulate why the sources they have selected for use in their research projects are authoritative and reliable.	**Lower Level Class:** In their annotated bibliographies, students will evaluate at least seven out of ten sources, explaining why each is a useful and reliable source to consult.	31
	Mid Level Class: In their annotated bibliographies, students will evaluate at least seven out of ten sources, explaining why each is a useful and reliable source to consult.	29
	Upper Level Class: In their annotated bibliographies, students will evaluate at least seven out of ten sources, explaining why each is a useful and reliable source to consult.	38

Figure 8.2   Students' Ability to Meet Specific Learning Objectives

5. Students will effectively integrate specific information from the texts they have located into their research projects in the form of quotations and paraphrases to support their main points.	**Lower Level Class:** In their final research projects, students will logically and smoothly integrate three sources into their discussion of their reasons for holding their particular position on their selected issue.	**69**
	Mid Level Class: In their research papers, students will provide accurate, specific, and relevant information in the form of quotations and paraphrases to support the thesis.	**65**
	Upper Level Class: In their final research projects, students will provide accurate, specific, and relevant information in the form of quotations and paraphrases to support their main points.	**75**
6. Students will communicate their research findings clearly and coherently in writing, using academically appropriate language and style.	**Lower Level Class:** In their annotated bibliographies, students will write their entries using the following format: Author's name and qualifications and the thesis. This is followed by a summary, an assessment, and a reflection.	**58**
	Mid Level Class: Students will write research papers that are organized, logical, consistent, clear, grammatically correct, and easy to follow.	**77**
	Upper Level Class: Students will write final research projects that are organized, logical, consistent, clear, grammatically correct, and easy to follow.	**100**
7. Students will cite sources correctly using the APSA format.	**Lower Level Class:** In their annotated bibliographies, students will cite at least seven out of ten sources correctly using the APSA format.	**38**
	Mid Level Class: In their research papers, students will cite at least five sources correctly using the APSA format.	**54**
	Upper Level Class: In their annotated bibliographies, students will cite at least seven out of ten sources correctly using the APSA format.	**86**

Discussion

Returning to our overarching goals for the collaboration, our first goal was to begin integrating IL instruction into the political science curriculum. This study marks the beginning of that ongoing process. Our second goal was to demonstrate that IL instruction is needed across academic experience levels, although IL competencies do improve with academic experience. The low pre-test scores at all levels support our assertion that this need exists, as do the students' gradually improving performances on the various stages of their research projects. Moreover, students with more academic experience performed better on the pre-test, as evidenced in seniors scoring 15 percent higher than freshmen. Upper-level students consistently scored higher on their final research projects as well.

Our third goal was to show that integrated IL instruction leads to learning. One way this goal was accomplished was through the post-test; students at all academic levels demonstrated improvement on the standardized competency test. In the lower-level course, however, which contained freshmen and sophomores, freshmen showed the least improvement, gaining only 3 percentage points. At first glance this might suggest that the lower-level class as a whole did not receive adequate instruction, but when we factor the scores of the sophomores back into the composite, the score for the class increases by 10 percent. It is unclear why freshmen improved so little, though several factors may be at work here, which we will discuss shortly. In contrast with the freshmen, students at all other academic levels showed substantial increases, with seniors averaging a score of 87 percent. Political science majors also showed significant improvement (11%), suggesting that students' IL competencies may improve at increased levels when instruction is embedded in a context that is meaningful to them (i.e., a course within their major). We also attempted to show that IL instruction leads to learning by measuring students' IL competencies in meaningful research contexts. Overall, students in the mid- and upper-level courses benefited from IL instruction the most, as seen in their successful performance of IL competencies related to learning outcomes 1, 2, 3, and 6 in the research assignments. Lower-level students again struggled, performing well only on outcomes 1 and 5.

Goal 4 was to identify the IL competencies that posed the most difficulties for students. Across academic levels, all students struggled with learning outcome number 4, which called on them to assess and evaluate sources. Questions on the standardized competency test targeting students' analytical and evaluative skills were also answered incorrectly by the majority of participants on both the pre- and post-tests. These results speak to our third hypothesis, which suggested that higher-order thinking skills would prove more difficult for students, no matter their academic level, thus indicating that more instruction and practice should be integrated into future courses. This also appears to be supported.

This study also supports our first hypothesis, that students who are further along in their college careers will already have developed some IL skills and thus will perform better than their lower-level counterparts. Upper-level African Politics students did indeed outperform students in other courses, whereas freshmen students exhibited the lowest levels of IL competency. Although freshman scores and performances did increase, they did not increase to the extent that we see with more experienced students. Juniors and seniors also exhibited significant IL weaknesses, but their performances indicated an increased ability to apply the feedback they received and to achieve specified learning objectives in authentic research contexts. This is consistent with the UK's Society of College, National and University Libraries (SCONUL) "seven pillars" IL model, which illustrates an ongoing "iterative process whereby information users progress through competency to expertise by practising the skills" (Advisory Committee on Information Literacy, 1999: 7). According to SCONUL, "First year undergraduates will largely be at the bottom of the arrow, perhaps only practising the first four skills" (1. recognizing an information need, 2. addressing an information "gap," 3. constructing research strategies, 4. locating and accessing information), whereas "postgraduate and research students will aim to be towards the expert end, and will be aspiring to the seventh," which involves synthesizing and building upon existing information (8).

Finally, we also hypothesized in H2 that lower-level students would not perform as highly because (1) they would not have had as much exposure to IL because of their lack of academic experience; (2) American Government is a required class that most students do not take because they want to but, rather, because they are forced to; and (3) more lower-level students (freshmen) are unprepared or unwilling to fully engage in academic work (as evidenced by high freshman dropout rates at the university in general) than upper-level students. H2 also appears to be supported. Freshmen scored lowest on the pre- and post-tests and consistently scored lower on research assignments that asked them to perform IL competencies. In contrast, students with the most academic experience (juniors and seniors), were more likely to perform higher on assignments.

One of the reasons why some lower-level students scored poorly on the research assignments was that they simply failed to do all or parts of the assignments. Students' failure to attempt to complete the requirements for the assignments was unique to the lower-level course and speaks to larger issues that fall outside the scope of this study, including student preparedness, commitment, accountability, goals, and responsibility, as well as university retention efforts, admission standards, the nature and purpose of the core curriculum, and general education requirements. And yet it is important to point out that all these issues were at play in this lower-level course, particularly when considering the distribution of final grades. Of the three groups of students, the lower-level American Government students were the least likely to ask for assistance outside of class. By all accounts, however, they were the ones who needed it the most, given that a startling and dispiriting 47 percent of students enrolled in the lower-level course (or 15 out of 32) earned an F for the course. That number is deceptive, however, and should be adjusted to account for a number of factors. Of the fifteen who failed, six stopped attending the class early in the semester but, oddly, did not drop it. Adjusting the numbers accordingly brings the failure rate for those who continued attending class down to 35 percent (9 out of 26). Of the remaining nine failing students, three would have passed the course had they internalized ACRL's IL Standard 5, which focuses on the ethical and legal use of information, and refrained from copying from each other and the book on an exam. If nothing else, failing the course may have driven home the point to both these particular students and their classmates that cheating and other forms of academic dishonesty are serious offenses with real consequences. The remaining six students (26 percent, or 6 out of 23) who failed earned failing grades not only on IL assignments but also on content exams. These students also tended to skip major sections on assignments and exams, in some cases turning in products that did not fulfill enough of the requirements for the assignments to earn anything higher than an F.

Although a 26 percent failure rate is lamentable, it is far from atypical in lower-division required courses at a university like ours that loses 32 percent of admitted students during their first year. Of the fifteen total who earned an F for various reasons, one did not return to the university, six were on probation, three were suspended, and only five remained enrolled "in good standing" at the university the semester following the study. Of those five, the highest GPA among them was a 2.18, with the average GPA resting at 1.96. Clearly, these students' records point to larger issues impeding their academic success that are unrelated to our IL initiative. And while we believe that successful IL integration into disciplinary courses can contribute to university retention efforts by helping students develop IL competencies that are critical to academic success in all disciplines, the success of these initiatives will inevitably be affected by students' willingness to put forth the effort to complete assignments, to ask for help from any number of people and institutional resources available to them, and to be active participants in their own learning. While these characteristics are also IL skills that are critical to the process of lifelong learning, they are decidedly difficult to teach. At issue here is student motivation. Students entering our classrooms who are neither extrinsically motivated by grades nor intrinsically motivated by curiosity and the desire to learn the material that is being taught may simply need more time and experience to view working for a college degree as something they want for themselves. A future challenge for us as instructors will be to find ways of inciting student motivation while also encouraging students to take responsibility for their own education. This is a difficult balance to achieve and an ongoing challenge that is simply part of the educational enterprise.

Conclusion

Measuring Success

Definitions of success are contingent upon a number of factors, including pre-defined goals and disciplinary perspectives. As such, we count our collaboration as a success in part because it produced results consistent with our goals and hypotheses, indicating, for example, that IL instruction is needed across academic levels and that IL competencies improve with academic experience. Our study also indicates that instruction can improve student performance of IL competencies and facilitate the performance of them in authentic learning contexts.

But we count our collaboration as a success not only because we saw improvement in students' IL competencies but also because of what *we* learned through the process. To begin with, we both gained an increased appreciation for the other's discipline, perspective, and pedagogical approach. Furthermore, the collaboration was successful for both of us because the learning experiences we developed for the students, including the assignments, activities, and assessment tools, were superior to what either of us would have been able to produce independently. As we developed the curriculum, we found that we each brought specific strengths and perspectives to the project that provided us with a more holistic approach to instruction. The political science instructor had vast content knowledge, including key journals, authors, and arguments circulating in the discipline. As such, she shaped the specific content focus of the assignments. She also had knowledge of and concerns about typical student strengths and weaknesses, including poor choice of sources, tendency to summarize rather than evaluate and analyze sources, inappropriate use of the copy and paste functions, and failure to credit sources. The librarian, on the other hand, contributed her extensive knowledge of information literacy as well as strategies for teaching IL competencies. This knowledge helped the team to devise instructional strategies for meeting the weaknesses in student work that the political scientist identified. Moreover, the librarian also advocated for the use of rubrics as both a feedback and a grading tool, which provided students with useful feedback and the instructors with an important tool for grading and assessing students' IL strengths and weaknesses. In addition, the librarian's experience at the reference desk made her aware of areas in the research process where students have particular difficulties as well as assignment-related problems that elicit student frustration, including unclear expectations and the absence of steps and procedural guides for completing the assignment. This contributed to the development of assignment sequences with more opportunities for feedback as well as the inclusion of more explanatory text and examples than the political science professor would have otherwise provided.

What counts as success is also related to one's disciplinary perspective and position within the academic community. For this librarian, our pilot collaboration was a success because the assignments led to high use of library resources. As the result of instruction, the majority of students used library databases and the catalog to find relevant and authoritative sources instead of simply turning to the Web. When students were specifically asked to use the Web, however, most located relevant and authoritative organizational Web sites. The collaboration was also a success from the librarian's point of view because it functioned as a springboard for future collaborations. Our sustained commitment to infusing information literacy into lower-, mid-, and upper-level political science courses ensures that political science students will be exposed to long-term, discipline-specific IL instruction throughout their academic careers at UWG.

Our collaboration has also been successful in that it has contributed to the integration of information literacy into other areas of the political science curriculum. Specifically, as the result of our collaboration and Dr. Campbell's growing exposure and commitment to information literacy, when the topic of revising the department's curriculum arose in a departmental meeting, she suggested that the department should develop a required methods course for majors with a strong IL emphasis. This course will be implemented in the 2006–07 academic year and will be taught by other members of the department. We have also expanded our focus to include integrating IL instruction into the interdisciplinary global studies program. This project involves collaborating with a History Department colleague and head of the global studies program. Our work has also caught the attention of administrators, who have invited us to share our finding and experience at university-wide symposia. In short, our collaboration was successful because it is not only ongoing but also expanding to include additional courses, academic programs, and faculty collaborators. It is gratifying indeed to experience firsthand how IL faculty and librarian collaborations can have far-ranging positive curricular impacts that extend beyond the immediate participants, specified goals, and anticipated outcomes.

For the political scientist, the collaboration was a success because it highlighted areas where students were lacking basic research skills and provided instruction that successfully enabled students to perform them. In more than ten years of teaching political science at the university level, the political science instructor had tried a variety of methods to engage students in the research process, with mostly disappointing and frustrating results. But this time, rather than feeling frustrated by students' lack of prior academic preparation and poor performances, the collaboration provided the political scientist with productive, concrete strategies for identifying and addressing student IL weaknesses. The quality of work turned in by the participating students evidenced remarkable improvement over the work that had been submitted in previous years without the benefit of IL instruction. Students selected and appropriately used key journals, referenced scholars in the field, and grappled with complex concepts and arguments. In the mid-level course, for example, many students selected the reaction statement "Democracy fosters peace." Rather than the usual passionate defense of democracy as an inherent good that "naturally" produces good results, students wrestled with definitions of both democracy and peace, and the often inverse relationship between the two. They were confronted with dilemmas such as the tendency of democracies to be peaceful toward one another but aggressive in spreading their values and ideals and in securing their interests in the international arena, thus causing conflict and strife elsewhere that can and does become circular. Many students, in their reflections, noted that they had never thought about the complexities involved in such a statement until they began to read the academic literature that wrestled with this issue. Not only were students' ideas challenged, but in many cases their opinions changed from reactionary to informed.

For students in the upper-division class, the opportunity to apply the IL knowledge they had gained proved motivating. In fact, during the Model AU session, one of our students was overheard chiding another student from a different university about the sources for their information, specifically admonishing the student for using less-than-credible sources. The debate that followed led to the students seeking out computers and databases to compare their sources.

Overall, students rated the IL instruction highly. For the first time in the political science instructor's career, she heard many students praise a research assignment, some going so far as to say that they really enjoyed the process.

Directions for Future Instruction and Research

The high percentage of students who failed the lower-level American Government course opens up a number of directions for future instruction and research revolving around the relationship between IL and university retention efforts. Certainly we did not expect that integrating IL instruction into a freshman-level required course would magically solve the problems that are endemic to such a course. And yet in this pilot study, there is no evidence to suggest that IL integration worked to further university retention efforts either. As a result, there remain questions to consider: How do we reach freshman students whose response to assignments that may be difficult or time-consuming is simply not to complete them or to stop attending class? At what point might we intervene to assist such students, and what would that intervention look like? Conversely, at what point should the responsibility for completion of assignments, course persistence, and seeking out help be laid at the feet of students, who must become responsible for their own learning in order for the academic enterprise to succeed? How might IL and retention efforts best be joined to successfully meet the needs of at-risk freshmen while also maintaining high expectations and standards?

Furthermore, student performance on assignments indicates a need for more hands-on instruction in how to evaluate the authority and reliability of sources and how to integrate specific information into their research projects to support their main points. Student reflections also point to a great deal of anxiety around APSA citation practices. Providing students with models and reference sources was not enough for many students, who found it difficult to make connections between the provided examples and the specific sources they located. In the future, additional hands-on instruction is needed.

In future projects, we will also revise our standardized pre- and post-tests, omitting less effective questions, for example, and adding a questionnaire that gets at library use patterns and library instruction experience. This will allow us to correlate degrees of library use with degrees of improvement on the post-test as well as library instruction experience with score levels on pre- and post-tests. In addition, we will further examine the correlation between student grade point averages and IL skills. Finally, we will continue to seek out avenues for further collaboration with other interested faculty, "politicking" for IL integration into other areas of the University of Georgia's academic curriculum.

Notes

1. See, for example, Thomas Schaeffer's, "Databases and Political Science Research" (2001). Schaeffer compares the coverage, content, and retrieval methods for nine databases, providing recommendations for matching databases with specific political science research needs.

2. Description based on material last accessed on January 21, 2006, at http://www.ala.org/ala/acrlbucket/is/projectsacrl/infolitdisciplines/political.htm.

3. See, for example, Larry Hubbell, "Teaching Research Methods: An Experiential and Heterodoxical Approach," PS: Political Science & Politics 27, no. 1 (March 1994): 60–64. Hubbell argues that the research methods course should "roughly mirror the research process itself" and should approximate it "by providing students with practice in formulating a research question; conducting a literature search; collecting data and information; and analyzing political phenomena" (60); Allan McBride, "Teaching Research Methods Using Appropriate Technology," PS: Political Science & Politics 27, no. 3 (September 1994): 553–557. McBride argues for a "hands-on" approach to research in the political science methods course and discusses strategies for teaching topic development, literature reviews, and research design.

4. The phrase "the collaborative imperative" is also part of the title of a book. See Dick Raspa and Dane Ward, The Collaborative Imperative: Librarians and Faculty Working Together in the Information Universe (Chicago: ACRL, 2000).

5. See Benjamin Samuel Bloom, Taxonomy of Educational Objectives: The Classification of Educational Goals by a Committee of College and University Examiners (New York: D. McKay, 1956).

6. See B. Gregory Marfleet and Brian J. Dille, "Information Literacy and the Undergraduate Research Methods Curriculum." Journal of Political Science Education 1, no. 2 (May–August 2005): 175–190. Marfleet and Dille hypothesize that "since virtually all courses incorporate some information literacy relevant components, more senior students who have had more opportunity to develop information literacy competencies should score higher on the test than less senior students." Their results indicate that "information literacy skills accumulate as students progress through their collegiate studies."

References

ACRL. 2000. "Information Literacy Competency Standards for Higher Education." American Library Association Retrieved Octobert 28, 2005, from http://www.ala.org/ala/acrl/acrlstandards/informationliteracycompetency.htm.

————. 2003. "Characteristics of Programs of Information Literacy That Illustrate Best Practices: A Guideline." Retrieved November 30, 2005, from http://www.ala.org/ala/acrl/acrlstandards/characteristics.htm.

ACT Institutional Data File. 2005. "National Collegiate Retention and Persistence to Degree Rates." Information for Policy Makers. ACT. Retrieved December 5, 2005, from http://www.act.org/path/policy/reports/retain.html.

Advisory Committee on Information Literacy. 1999. "The Seven Pillars of Information Literacy." Retrieved November 30, 2005, from http://www.sconul.ac.uk/activities/inf_lit/papers/Seven_pillars2.pdf.

ALA. GODORT-IDTF. 2004. "Promoting IGO Information Resources to Scholars and Citizens." *Dttp: Documents to the People* 32, no. 1 (Spring): 24–25, 28–34.

ALA. LPSS Education Task Force. 2005. "Political Science Research Competency Guidelines: Draft." Political Science and Government. Information Literacy in the Disciplines. Instruction Section. Association of College and Research Libraries. American Library Association. Retrieved December 12, 2005, from http://www.ala.org/ala/acrlbucket/lpss/PoliticalScienceStandardsDraftRevisionFeb2005.doc.

Bloom, Benjamin Samuel. 1956. *Taxonomy of Educational Objectives: The Classification of Educational Goals by a Committee of College and University Examiners.* New York: D. McKay.

Booth, Austin, and Carole Fabian. 2002. "Collaborating to Advance Curriculum-Based Information Literacy Initiatives." *Journal of Library Administration* 36, no. 1/2: 123–142.

Chickering, Arthur W. 2000. "Creating Community within Individual Carses." New Directions for Higher Education 2000, no. 109 (December): 23–32.

Hardesty, Larry. 1995. "Faculty Culture and Bibliographic Instruction: An Exploratory Analysis." *Library Trends* 44, no. 2 (Fall): 339–367.

Hubbell, Larry. 1994. "Teaching Research Methods: An Experiential and Heterodoxical Approach." *PS: Political Science & Politics* 27, no. 1 (March): 60–64.

Hutchins, Elizabeth O. 2003. "Assessing Student Learning Outcomes in Political Science Classes." In *Assessing Student Learning Outcomes for Information Literacy Instruction in Academic Institutions.* Edited by Elizabeth Fuseler Avery. Chicago: Association of College and Research Libraries.

Kuzma, Lynn M. 1998. "The World Wide Web and Active Learning in the International Relations Classroom." *PS: Political Science & Politics* 31, no. 3 (September): 578–584.

Marfleet, B. Gregory, and Brian J. Dille. 2005. "Information Literacy and the Undergraduate Research Methods Curriculum." *Journal of Political Science Education* 1, no. 2 (May–August): 175–190.

McBride, Allan. 1994. "Teaching Research Methods Using Appropriate Technology." *PS: Political Science & Politics* 27, no. 3 (September): 553–557.

Nimon, Maureen. 2001. "The Role of Academic Libraries in the Development of the Information Literate Student: The Interface between Librarian, Academic and Other Stakeholders," *Australian Academic and Research Libraries* 32, no. 1 (March): 43–52.

"Political Science and Government." 2005. Information Literacy in the Disciplines. Instruction Section. Association of College and Research Libraries. American Library Association. Retrieved January 7, 2006, from http://www.ala.org/ala/acrlbucket/is/projectsacrl/infolit disciplines/political.htm.

Raspa, Dick, and Dane Ward. 2000. *The Collaborative Imperative: Librarians and Faculty Working Together in the Information Universe.* Chicago: Association of College and Research Libraries.

Schaeffer, Thomas. 2001. "Databases and Political Science Research." *Online Information Review* 25, no. 1: 47–53.

Shooks, Erma, and Tara Panter Pearson. 2005. *University of West Georgia Fact Book: 2004–2005.* Department of Institutional Research and Planning. University of West Georgia. Retrieved January 17, 2006, from http://www.westga.edu/~irp/Factbooks/FB_FY2005.pdf.

Sonntag, Gabriela, and Yvonne Meulemans. 2003. "Planning for Assessment." In *Assessing Student Learning Outcomes for Information Literacy Instruction in Academic Institutions.* Edited by Elizabeth Fuseler Avery. Chicago: Association of College and Research Libraries.

Thornton, Stephen. 2005. "Information Literacy and Politics." Paper presented at the Annual Political Science Association Conference, Leeds University, April 6.

Appendix 8.1: American Government Research Proposal Rubric

I. *General Topic*	+, √, −

Identified an appropriate and approved topic:
- Abortion
- Affirmative Action
- Death Penalty
- Evolution vs. Intelligent Design
- Flag Burning
- Gay Marriage
- Gun Control
- Right to Die
- Prayer in Schools

II. *Keyword Search Terms*	+, √, −

A. Identified the major key terms that relate to the topic.

B. Constructed a thorough list of synonyms for these major key terms.

C. Constructed at least three different and potentially fruitful search queries.

III. *The Constitutional Issue*	+, √, −

A. Identified a constitutional issue that is relevant to the general topic.

B. Located two articles from reputable online news sources or organizations that focus on both the general topic and the specific constitutional issue.

Article 1

   i. Listed the author, article title, name of the organization/news source, and the URL.

   ii. Explained why the source is reputable, backing up responses with evidence.

Article 2

   i. Listed the author, article title, name of the organization/news source, and the URL.

   ii. Explained why the source is reputable, backing up responses with evidence.

C. Defined the constitutional issue and explained how it relates to the topic.

   Described the controversy (i.e., the opposing arguments).

IV. *Research Question*	+, √, −

A. Constructed a specific research *question*.

B. Question points to an issue about which reasonable people disagree.

C. Question addressed the general research topic.

D. Question specifically addressed a relevant constitutional issue/point of law.

9

Integrating Information Literacy into the First-Year Biology Course: The Poster Project

Elsa E. Winch, Associate Professor and Instruction Coordinator
Shonah A. Hunter, Professor, Department of Biological Sciences
Lock Haven University

Writing to understand biological concepts is at the heart of many introductory biology classes, and much has been written about the importance of writing in the content area (Moore 1992, 1994, 1997; Steglich 2000; Trombulak and Sheldon 1989; Zeegers and Giles 1996). The instructors of the introductory biology classes, Principles of Biology I and II (PoB), at Lock Haven University (LHU) of Pennsylvania experimented with various writing assignments to provide first-year students with meaningful writing instruction that requires them to demonstrate their understanding of the process and content of science. As is typical of many introductory biology classes, the traditional laboratory report was included as a major writing assignment for PoB I and II students. Inherent in teaching writing in the content area was teaching discipline-specific information literacy strategies to augment research assignments. Through trial and error, and numerous changes to the assignments, the traditional experimental-based laboratory report was abandoned for the first semester and was replaced with a semester-long poster project. This successful project is the result of many years of collaboration between Shonah Hunter, Principles of Biology lead instructor, and Elsa Winch, library instruction coordinator.

Literature Review

Significant literature exists about library instruction within the context of introductory undergraduate biology courses, especially instruction conjoined with laboratory research assignments (Bowden and DiBenedetto, 2001; Martin, 1986; Orians and Sabol, 1999; Souchek and Meier, 1997; Stachaez and Brennon, 1990). Although many of these reports outline collaboration between lead instructor and librarian, Bowden and DiBenedetto (2001) and Orians and Sabol (1999) provide examples of the biologist and the librarian teaching as partners over the course of a semester. Smith and Chang (2005) used a modified collaborative learning model to incorporate an information literacy component into an undergraduate community ecology course.

Although pedagogical components of the aforementioned collaborations vary, they generally include the librarian partnering with the course instructor to develop an instruction session or Web page to teach course-specific information access to the students. To reinforce information literacy skills, these collaborations usually included follow-up assignments such as a library exercise, workshop, review article assignment, or research lab report. Although a variety of approaches have been reported, the main point that has emerged is the shared vision, or belief, of the biologist and librarian that the mastery of library research skills is key to creating the self-sufficient (budding) scientist. This mastery is accomplished within the context of meaningful research assignments that make possible a synthesis of new information into existing knowledge.

Souchek and Meier (1997) report on a collaborative model that integrates biological investigations with information literacy activities. They include search strategy development, discussion of print and electronic resources, and a summary of scientific literature. Key to their collaborative success was the opportunity for students to develop sound scientific process and information literacy skills in separate lab sessions scheduled early in the semester. Students then practiced those skills in subsequent lab research assignments and applied them to new situations. Extensive and repeated feedback between the biology instructor and students was an important teaching methodology used in this collaboration.

Huerta and McMillan (2004) successfully integrated information literacy into first-year and upper-division undergraduate science writing courses to address students' recurring problems of topic development, recognition of the relevance of research databases as opposed to the Internet, development of background knowledge, and use of primary sources, as well as grammar and composition. They used intensive individual conferences, peer workshops, and accumulated assignment portfolio activities to accomplish their goals. Their approach was impressive. However, the issue for us still remained: how to integrate information literacy into a first-year biology content course, as opposed to a science writing course.

It is apparent that successful collaborations involve significant feedback to students, incremental or multiple assignments, and a commitment of time by the librarian and the biology professor. The faculty and librarian teams addressed the need to teach students to become competent in the techniques of online searching and to understand the scope and nature of electronic resources particular to the institution—both skills necessary to achieve success within a specific biological research assignment. Improvement of student proficiencies in applied scientific skills and information research drives these collaborations.

It is in this context that we strove to develop information literacy skills at the introductory biology level. Our approach was not unique, but the poster project is novel in that it meshes with the introductory biology curriculum, with the general education goals of LHU, and most important, with our students. This chapter describes the collaboration as a process of developing successful information literacy pedagogy based largely on a process of trial and error or give and take. The success of this project depends on the instructor's ability to communicate her pedagogical philosophy and approach and on the responsiveness of librarians to the assignment goals and objectives.

The History of the Poster Project

Lock Haven University is one of the fourteen public universities of the Pennsylvania State System of Higher Education. From its early beginnings as a Normal School with the mission to prepare teachers for the Commonwealth, LHU has grown into a comprehensive, primarily undergraduate institution of about 5,000 students. As is true of many universities, LHU is committed to providing students with an effective liberal arts education as well as preparing students for productive careers, especially through focused programs (www.lhup.edu).

The general education requirements at LHU were designed "to reflect on-going advances in technology, rapidly expanding sources of information . . . and revised conceptions of the nature of knowledge" (www.lhup.edu). Students are encouraged to explore topics from different points of view and to integrate new knowledge with existing knowledge to synthesize and form new perspectives (www.lhup.edu). In addition to specific discipline and distribution requirements, LHU has created a unique feature that incorporates writing and information literacy skills and multicultural experiences embedded in courses across the curriculum. An existing course in any discipline may acquire an "overlay" when it is modified to address learning outcomes based on criteria established by the faculty and approved through the university curricular process. In order to graduate, students must have three "writing emphasis" courses, two courses that integrate information literacy skills, and two courses incorporating multicultural experiences.

Inclusion of information literacy as an overlay allows it to be integrated into discipline-specific curricula. The purpose of this requirement is to help students develop critical thinking and technical skills that enable them to access, evaluate, and use information to solve problems, answer questions, and meet informational needs. Its inclusion in general education reflects the faculty's belief that these capabilities are important for success in academics and for lifelong learning. This integration of information literacy and discipline-orientated instruction enables students to learn, test, and apply information literacy skills within the context of their coursework. We believe this carries the greatest potential for long-term impact because it gives students a specific goal in the form of a relevant, content-based assignment for recognizing when information is needed and how to find it.

Principles of Biology I and II are the two introductory biology courses for science and health science majors that meet the general education natural sciences requirement. In addition to the discipline content, science courses designated as meeting the general education requirements emphasize practicing scientific methodologies, understanding concepts within and among scientific disciplines, understanding how someone is personally affected by science, and critically evaluating the scientific information provided by the mass media (www.lhup.edu). The library instruction coordinator (Elsa Winch) and Principles of Biology lead instructor (Shonah Hunter) were directly involved in developing the rationale and criteria for the general education program and both continue as members of the General Education Subcommittee of the University Curriculum Committee. This close involvement in general education was important in the development and testing of various pedagogical approaches in these introductory biology classes. Developing the PoB poster project that integrates the natural sciences and information literacy requirements of general education was a natural extension of the authors' involvement in general education curricula, and we believe it results in increased student learning.

The Poster Project

The poster project is embedded in the course's laboratory component, where it is easier to manage assignments and evaluation. Each fall semester, PoB I has ten laboratory sections with an average of 26 students per section for a total of approximately 260 students. Logistics of any assignment related to this number of students is of immediate concern. The lead instructor teaches the lecture component as well as two lab sections, and typically three or four other biology faculty members are assigned to teach the remaining lab sections. Because PoB labs are permanent in-load teaching assignments for many of our veteran faculty, we are able to maintain continuity of teaching from one semester to another. Three or four library faculty members serve to complete the project team. In addition to Elsa Winch, the instruction coordinator and Biology Department liaison, the team includes the health sciences liaison and the chemistry liaison; other librarians are included as needed or available. A full-team meeting of librarians and lab instructors at the beginning of the semester includes discussion of objectives of the poster project and the organization, content, timing, and logistics of the library presentation. All assignments are available to the librarians at the reference desk, and all handouts, presentation materials, and assignments are placed in the study guide section of the library Web page and are linked from the PoB I course Web page. We have found this explicit and clear communication among team members to be essential to ensure a clear understanding of the intent and direction of the project.

The poster project requires students to transform a traditional review paper into a poster format. Students are expected to present valid scientific content in a visually creative way. For example, they might include photographs, maps, figures, and lists; they might use arrows and colors to show stages of a process, or they might juxtapose sections of the poster for dramatic effect. This is a very different approach to a text-based format and challenges students to think about the visual organization of information and the relationship to content. The poster has four content sections: Introduction, Current Research, Future Considerations, and Literature Cited. The finished project is the result of five cumulative activities or assignments spaced throughout the semester: (1) selecting a topic and examining information-seeking strategies, (2) developing the Introduction, (3) developing the Current Research and Future Considerations sections, (4) drafting a poster layout, and (5) engaging in the scientific-style poster session to which the campus community is invited.

The project is introduced the first week of the semester when students are provided with a list of topics developed from news headlines, including those related to public health issues, environmental issues, and emerging technologies. Topics are worded in the form of a research question and are reviewed each year by the biology and library faculty to ensure their currency and relevance. In addition, topics are initially researched by the librarian and lead instructor prior to inclusion on the list to ensure the availability of adequate information to develop the project. Students also have the option of selecting their own topic, with instructor approval.

During the second week, students in each lab section are randomly assigned a number and topics are chosen in rank order. In each laboratory session, the library faculty presents an instruction program that introduces students to the library Web page, basic search strategy skills, and information-seeking strategies, defining key concepts and compiling keywords from the topic question, critically evaluating Web sites, and using and locating background research materials. A library exercise developed by Winch and Shonah Hunter, with input from other team members, requires the students to practice the information literacy skills outlined by the librarian during the presentation, using their topic. The library assignment encourages students to use information literacy skills and guides students logically through the process of defining the research or topic question, conducting background research, using appropriate computer operators and library databases, and critically evaluating search strategies and the research results. In addition, students are required to document and justify the databases, keywords, and operations they used. Students must identify and cite in correct format five sources related to their topic from popular literature, scholarly literature, and the Internet. These citations become the preliminary bibliography for their posters. The lab instructors provide students with evaluative feedback regarding additional materials or information. Students are encouraged to consult a librarian at the reference desk if they have difficulty at any point on the assignment. Critique of the research strategy by the instructor is one of the focuses of this assignment, more so than the actual bibliography. If necessary, students are instructed to return to the assignment for revision.

The second assignment, the Introduction, is scheduled to be turned in three weeks later and builds upon the skills learned from the library exercise. It assumes students understand the need to continue searching for relevant information to revise their existing bibliography. The Introduction includes the definition of the topic, an explanation of any technical terms, a historical perspective of the topic, and a statement of the focus of the rest of the poster. Background literature is the key component that supports the Introduction section of the project. Winch has developed the reference collection over the years to include handbooks and encyclopedias that specifically address the topics most often used in PoB. Lab instructors again provide evaluation and feedback to the students and, if necessary, encourage them to re-evaluate resources to support the introductory information of the topic. It is once again assumed students will keep working on the project components. Throughout the project, frequent communication between librarians and laboratory instructors ensures that any unforeseen problems are addressed in a timely manner.

Approximately three weeks later, the students are assigned the final content portion of the poster project. They are required to research Current Information and Future Considerations for the topic. At this time, students will have collected government reports, statistics, scholarly articles, and calls for action from advocacy groups, depending on their topic. They now have to cull through the materials and select the most appropriate information from a variety of sources to produce a cohesive, well-organized, and comprehensive document. This assignment gives the students the opportunity to again practice their information-seeking skills and to engage in critical thinking. It is an initial step in developing critical thinking and the ability to synthesize and communicate information in a relatively sophisticated and scientific way.

The PoB poster project assignments are based on active learning principles that challenge students to examine the range and scope of our library's scholarly and popular literature, to make critical decisions about finding information and using information, and ultimately, to synthesize new knowledge with existing knowledge. The written sections are drafts that students are expected to revise prior to the final poster. The instructors submit the students' draft electronic documents to an online, plagiarism-detection service to which LHU subscribes. This service scans the submitted documents and compares them to billions of electronic and print documents (www.turnitin.com). The results of the scan of each document are returned to the instructor in the form of a report that identifies sections of the draft with a high percent match, indicating potential plagiarism problems. This data is then used by the instructor to identify sections of the draft that require revision and to review with the student ways to avoid plagiarism. This, of course, reinforces the ethical use of information, a topic addressed in the library presentation at the beginning of the semester.

Posters are created using the Microsoft Publisher program. Students learn the basics of this software during a laboratory session at the time the Current Research and Future Considerations is assigned. Using poster samples as models, lab instructors illustrate the visual elements of layout, composition, and graphics within the context of a scientific report. Students have the opportunity to practice using the software on laptops during the lab session while instructors provide feedback on specific questions that arise. A draft "mini-poster" is submitted the following week to allow instructors to provide feedback to the student on the design and layout. Peer evaluation and collaborations on design and layout are encouraged as students develop the final poster. Two weeks are allotted for printing, during which time each student schedules a fifteen-minute printing session, facilitated by trained student assistants.

Final posters are presented during the ten individual laboratory sessions in a typical poster presentation format. In two forty-minute blocks of time, half the students (the presenters) stand at their posters and the other half (the visitors) circulate around the room and ask questions. The presenters must summarize their topic to visitors, include a statement of the most important thing they learned from their project, and answer questions posed by the visitors. Students convey their pride in their work by dressing up for the occasion, inviting friends to the session, and confidently displaying their work and discussing it. The LHU community is invited, and often students have the opportunity to interact with vice presidents, deans, faculty, librarians, and their peers outside of their laboratory section. This project provides first-year students the opportunity to make an initial presentation in the discipline as an expert on the topic. Visitors have often expressed their delight upon viewing students' final projects and engaging with them about their research. This forum provides students with the opportunity to refute, extend, and, we hope, synthesize information based on their knowledge of the poster topic. The energy and excitement (the buzz!) in the lab during this session is tangible. Students are actively engaged in asking and answering questions, demonstrating that learning is occurring. At the beginning of the semester many students had doubts

Week	Activities and Assignments
1	Introduce poster project. Provide models of previous posters. Provide list of possible research topics.
2	Library presentation. Students choose topics from the list or their own. Library exercise and preliminary bibliography assigned.
3	Turn in library exercise and preliminary bibliography.
4	Graded assignment with feedback returned to students.
5	Communicating Scientific Information–Poster Project I. Instruction session on poster content, composition and using the software. Title and Introduction assigned.
6	Title and Introduction assignment due.
7	Graded assignment with feedback returned to students. Communicating Scientific Information–Poster Project II. Current Information, Future Considerations, Literature Cited assigned. Mini-poster for layout evaluation assigned.
8	Current Information, Future Considerations, Literature Cited assignment due. Content checked for plagiarism using Turn-it-in services online. Peer evaluation and feedback on Mini poster content, composition, and layout.
9	Graded assignment with feedback returned to students. Students are expected to revise work.
10	Scheduled printing times for all students.
11	Scheduled printing times for all students.
12	Poster Session during each laboratory session.

Figure 9.1   Timeline of Poster Project during the Fifteen-Week Semester of Principles of Biology I

that they could complete the project, but the final poster product is evidence of their accomplishment. By incorporating numerous small assignments over several weeks, the seemingly insurmountable project became manageable and students felt successful. Many visitors comment that they would never have guessed that scientific posters such as these could have been produced by first-year students. It is reaffirming to PoB students that they are capable of understanding and explaining often complex biological information in an exceptional manner.

Figure 9.1 presents an overview of the poster project, week by week.

The Collaboration

The collaboration between library faculty and PoB instructors began in 1992. It involved a library tour to familiarize students with the location of the reference collection, show them the location and the various types of periodicals, and examine the scientific journal format. For a follow-up assignment, students were asked to analyze the components of a journal article to understand the format so they would be prepared to write a traditional lab report later in the semester. Students were provided with a list of journal titles believed to reflect the varied interests of the students (i.e., from pre–physical therapy to marine biology). In addition, specific titles were selected because of their adherence to the format we wanted to teach. The objective was to give students a model for writing the formal laboratory report. Research for the lab report later in the semester was limited to resource materials selected and made available by the instructor. The purpose of the assignment was to teach students how to conduct an experiment and then to write it in the specific format of the discipline.

Formal information literacy instruction in the introductory class took place midway through the second semester during PoB II. Database research was required to support the results of an extensive experimental exercise and lab report completed during the last part of the semester. A follow-up library exercise reinforcing searching principles completed the instruction. This library instruction was provided in a timely manner for the purpose of integrating library and biology assignments. Students were asked to immediately practice the concepts they learned to conduct the research and write the lab report. Despite this planning, faculty and librarians were dissatisfied with the quality of the support literature used by the students for the lab report.

One issue that continued to concern us was the purpose of the library instruction session and its relevance to the lab assignment. The librarian was interested in fostering research in the undergraduate curriculum, and the biologist was interested in fostering the first-year students' use of research. In spite of the enhancement and fine-tuning of the traditional lab and library research session that focused on information retrieval tools, most students could not employ efficient searching skills by analyzing keywords or identifying and conducting or replicating computer operations to find needed information. Similarly, students were less than enthusiastic about the research assignments. They perceived the library exercise as a drill or a demonstration of their ability to follow instructions. They found the experimental topics uninteresting, and, regardless of the instructors' best efforts, failed to see that the assignments had any relevance to their lives. There was general dissatisfaction among all parties.

It was in this context that the PoB poster project evolved. Winch and Hunter continued to grapple with ways to develop an engaging format to teach information literacy and the scientific process at the introductory biology level. As we were struggling with assignments, outcomes, and our dissatisfaction with the library research exercise, the opportunity arose to create posters as a potential presentation format. Using readily available software and a wide-carriage printer purchased by the Biology Department, we created a pilot poster project for 20 students in PoB II in an effort to determine the feasibility of introducing it to 260 students in PoB I. Upper-level students familiar with Microsoft Publisher were recruited to assist the first-year students in the project. After receiving training in some of the subtleties of the software and in visual composition, they mentored the first-year students through the research and presentation process for the entire semester.

The pilot was a resounding success, and in fall 2002, the full poster project was implemented into PoB I. It provided introductory science students with a vehicle to explore current topics in biology so they could understand the relevance and importance of biological research. Essentially, the poster project was a "hook" to attract first-year students' attention and to maintain their interest in subject matter that does not always have obvious application to students' specific areas of interest (e.g., physical therapy or marine biology).

The poster project created an important conceptual shift in our methodology with the realization that in the first semester it could be our primary pedagogical tool for teaching PoB students the research process. We maintained the structure of the library assignment, but we opened up the mode of inquiry to include popular literature. This incorporated search strategy development, background information resources for topic explorations, and information access and retrieval. The poster project now reflected the research process we intended it to represent, and it could graphically accommodate the structural components of the review article (i.e., the Introduction, Current Information, and Future Considerations sections). The poster project created a synergy. It became open-ended and creative, exploratory and demonstrative. Because the instruction has to be linked to the assignment in timing and content, the information literacy instruction was moved to the first semester beginning in 2002.

Looking back at our almost-fifteen-year collaboration, the focus of our attention and the basis of our pedagogy was fueled by the perennial problem of "Why don't the students get it?" Using our institution's general education criteria for the natural sciences and information literacy as a guide, we persistently and stubbornly held to the conviction that we wanted students to understand the necessity of information as a component of good scientific process. We also wanted to show the students how books, primary literature, and indeed, the library's collection of knowledge are relevant in their lives. It became obvious to us that teaching information gathering was not teaching analytical skills; we needed to develop assignments that required students to understand the scientific, situational, social, and sometimes illusive nature of facts. This project and the library exercise emphasize broad concepts of knowledge at the introductory level. The assignments are concrete, highly structured, and incremental in nature. The students are provided with models of sound logic, and they have multiple opportunities to practice and to apply their knowledge in several assignments, yet they also integrate higher-level critical thinking skills.

Our collaboration required mutual recognition of differing disciplinary perspectives, points-of-view, and vocabularies that sometimes resulted in communication difficulties and frustrations. Hunter had clear ideas of what she wanted the students to learn and needed to describe the desired outcomes of the assignments clearly. Winch had the flexibility and the perspective of an "outsider" to ask questions relevant to Hunter's learning objectives. She had to apply her knowledge of information literacy outcomes to the objectives of the research assignment, being mindful of the organizational structure of library resources and undergraduates' naïve information-seeking behavior. The poster project reinforced our commitment to developing curriculum that teaches students how biology uses information and why library resources support their particular poster topic. We learned to teach research skills so that the products (i.e., assignments) were of better quality and better matched the expectations of the faculty. Our discussions were honest and open-minded. We deeply respect each other's dedication to our respective disciplines and teaching philosophies. Through negotiation and communication, we improved learning by this successful collaboration.

With continued evaluation and revision, we believe the goals of the project are being met. Students are learning effective information-seeking strategies to support a biological topic, they are engaged in the process of seeking information, and they are ultimately writing better lab reports at a later date. We teach the concepts, structure the presentations and library assignment, and evaluate the quality and relevance of the sources used in the poster. The science and information literacy general education objectives are elegantly integrated in the poster project, and we know it is a major contribution to students' knowledge. We believe this poster project is an excellent example of teaching information literacy within the context of a discipline and exemplifies what can be accomplished when library and course faculty collaborate.

The Follow-up

Sustaining the momentum of writing and information literacy activities in PoB I, the second semester, PoB II, meets the criteria for information literacy and writing emphasis as part of LHU's general education program. In addition to other assignments, students design and conduct an experiment on some aspect of animal behavior. They then write a traditional laboratory report on their project. This requires more sophisticated and extensive research into primary literature to support the hypothesis being tested. This assignment builds on the more descriptive poster project from the first semester in that information-seeking skills are transferred to this more formal and structured research project. We have seen significant improvement in the quality of support literature in the formal written report because students have developed solid information-seeking practices through the poster project. Students are "getting it"! Principles of Biology I and II are the foundation for teaching research skills upon which the rest of the biology curriculum is based. The information literacy curriculum introduces and reinforces critical reading, evaluation, and the use of information, which develops the skills students need to become lifelong learners. Research in subsequent biology classes builds upon the skills learned in PoB.

Assessment

Assessing information literacy within the context of a course has various approaches. Methodologies include self-reporting pre-tests, and post-tests or questionnaires by students. They also include the instructor's or the collaborating librarian's assessment of students' effective information literacy skills (Bowden and DiBenedetto, 2001; Brown and Krumholz, 2002; Orians and Sabol, 1999). In addition to writing a reflective essay at the end of the semester, Huerta and McMillan (2004) report, students completed a Student Evaluation of Teaching form related to the information literacy content. In all cases, students reported positively as to the effectiveness of the information literacy course content.

Effective information literacy outcomes in the PoB poster project are assessed by the instructor in conjunction with the content and composition of the poster. An evaluation checklist developed by the lab instructors assesses the structure and format of the poster, along with the clarity, structure, and grammar of the written information. Because the lab instructors are secure in the knowledge that their students have been prepared to perform basic literature research, the quality of the students' analysis of sources and the use of this information effectively and ethically (i.e., acknowledgment of intellectual property) are reflected in the poster's final grade. Since the poster project has been introduced, Hunter and the PoB instructors report that the students' information literacy skills have improved, as evidenced by the improved lab reports in PoB II. Because the information literacy general education criteria are iterative and cumulative, we intend to use the PoB I poster project as a benchmark for further assessment in PoB II.

Currently, Winch and Hunter serve on the university-wide Outcomes Assessment Subcommittee for information literacy outcomes. This committee expects to develop a holistic rubric meaningful to all research-based curricula that will be used to assess information literacy for all LHU courses designated as meeting information literacy criteria. We volunteered to pilot the assessment rubric officially on the laboratory report in PoB II in the spring 2006 semester. Because the poster project follows information literacy guidelines, we also plan to use this rubric to assess information literacy competencies at the end of the first semester to provide a baseline for further assessment.

Winch and Hunter continually evaluate instruction and assignments. We plan to restructure the library presentation to reinforce use of background information and reference materials. Each lab session will be split into two groups, each with a librarian. The first group will receive research instruction in the library instruction room, rather than in the science laboratory, and the second group will be engaged in an exercise using the reference materials in the library reference area. Then the groups will switch. We believe this is important so that students recognize the importance and relevance of reference materials in addition to online resources. In addition, discussion with other faculty and librarians on the information literacy Outcomes Assessment Committee stimulated Winch and Hunter to revisit the library assignment. They will develop a document, possibly a matrix, that will follow the structure of a logical research strategy. Students will use it as they progress through their preliminary topic research to visually organize and document their research results. We believe this document will help students understand the research process and better meet the expectations of the faculty and the learning outcomes of the poster project assignments. Ideally, with practiced use, this document will be internalized by the student and will be transferable to any research topic and discipline. We are excited about these continued collaboration possibilities.

Conclusions

With this project, students learn how to do research. Initially, they learn by following a very structured model provided by Winch and Hunter. The assignments and presentations are developed and revised by the entire team of lab instructors and library faculty. It is truly a collaboration in which the biology faculty are teaching the scientific process and the library faculty are teaching the intuitive information-seeking behaviors. We

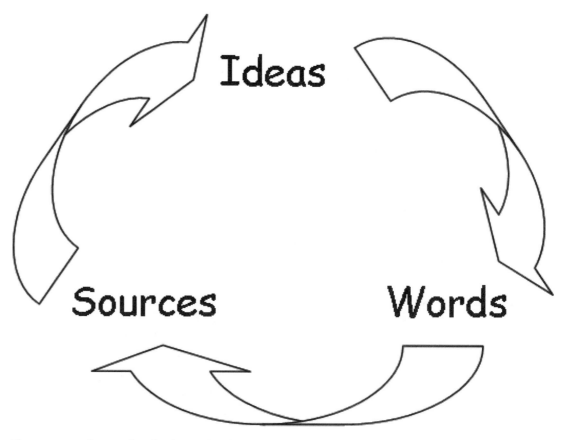

Figure 9.2   The Cycle of Information-Seeking Behavior

believe the actual topic that students research is less important than the fact that they actually complete the research process in a systematic manner. However, the topic is the hook that makes the process more interesting and relevant to the students, who therefore do better work. We have come to the conclusion that because first-year students are still very concrete in their thinking, they need this highly structured, tangible learning environment in which to develop the required skills and to move in the direction required for higher-level thinking skills. The end product is a well-developed poster that reflects their hard work and creativity, a poster they can proudly show to friends and family.

One of the best outcomes of this project is enthusiasm and ownership shown by students in choosing their topics. For example, one student researched athletic head injuries for an athletic training class and then described the biology of athletic head injuries for the poster project, demonstrating transferable skills by approaching a topic from two different points of view. One student researched advances in prosthetic devices because her friend was being fitted for a prosthetic leg. Other students choose topics reflecting a personal interest, such as Crohn's disease, anxiety disorders, or a specific genetic disorder. A student recently told Hunter that her physician, impressed with the information and the graphic quality, is displaying her poster in the waiting room of the office.

As students develop information literacy skills, they understand how to find and use resources to support a topic in the discipline. Recently in the library session for Hunter's upper-level Field Ecology class, we observed that students were very capable of correctly approaching a research assignment. Skills learned in the first year were retained and applied in this upper-level biology course. Students confidently juggled key concepts that revealed the more obscure points of their research problems. The roles of Winch and Hunter changed from instructors to facilitators. Hunter focused on the various approaches of the research problem, and Winch became an information consultant, occasionally interjecting ideas that would elucidate the search strategy. Students left the session knowing what they needed to accomplish.

Teaching information literacy in the first year using the poster project is effective. Students demonstrate continuous improvement of these skills throughout their college career. What we do works. We have developed a theory of information-seeking behavior that can best be illustrated by a cycle (figure 9.2). The topic is comprised of ideas that suggest keywords that, when searched, produce relevant sources. This typifies a continuous cycle of information-seeking behavior that most certainly results in improved student learning.

References

Bowden, Teresa S., and Angela DiBenedetto. 2001. "Information Literacy in Biology Laboratory Session: An Example of Librarian-Faculty Collaboration." *Research Strategies* 18, no. 2: 143–149.

Brown, Cecelia, and Lee R. Krumholz. 2002. "Integrating Information Literacy into the Science Curriculum." *College and Research Libraries* 118, no. 2: 111–123.

Huerta, Deborah, and Victoria McMillan. 2004. "Reflections on Collaborative Teaching of Science Information Literacy and Science Writing: Plans, Processes and Pratfalls." *Resource Sharing & Information Networks* 17, no. 1/2: 19–28.

Lock Haven University of Pennsylvania (LHU). 1999a. "Mission Statement." Retrieved April, 15, 2006, from www.lhup.edu/planning-and-assessment/planning/LHUP%20Mission%20Statement.htm.

———. 1999b. "Rationale and Criteria for General Education Courses." Lock Haven: LHUP. Retrieved April 15, 2006, from www.lhup.edu.

Martin, Rebecca R. 1986. "Library Instruction and the Scientific Method: A Role for Librarians in an Introductory Biology Course." *Research Strategies* 4, no. 3: 108–115.

Moore, Randy. 1992. *Writing to Learn Biology.* Philadelphia: Saunders College Publishing.

———. 1994. "Writing as a Tool for Learning Biology." *BioScience* 44, no. 9: 613–618.

———. 1997. *Writing to Learn Science.* Fort Worth: Saunders College Publishing.

Orians, Collin, and Laurie Sabol. 1999. "Using the Web to Teach Library Research Skills in Introductory Biology: A Collaboration between Faculty and Librarians." *Issues in Science & Technology Librarianship* 23. Retrieved January 5, 2006, from www.library.ucsb.edu/istl/99-summer/article2.html.

Smith, Julia I., and Lena Chang. 2005. "Teaching Community Ecology as a Jigsaw." *American Biology Teacher* 67, no. 1: 31–36.

Stachacz, John C., and Thomas M. Brennan. 1990. "Bibliographic Instruction in an Undergraduate Biology Course." *Research Strategies* 14, no. 1: 14–21.

Steglich, Carolyn S. 2000. "A Writing Assignment That Changes Attitudes in Biology Classes." *American Biology Teacher* 62, no. 2: 98–101.

Souchek, Russell, and Marjorie Meier. 1997. "Teaching Information Literacy and Scientific Process Skills." *College Teaching* 45, no. 4: 128–131.

Summey, Terri P. 1997. "Biological Research and the Library: A Collaboration in Online Research and Library Instruction." Issues *in Science and Technology Librarianship* 16. Retrieved January 5, 2006, from www.library.ucsb.edu/ist1/97-fall/article3.html.

Trombulak, Steve, and Sallie Sheldon. 1989. "The Real Value of Writing to Learning in Biology." *Journal of College Science Teaching.* 18, no. 6: 384–386.

Turnitin. 2006. "Turnitin home page." Retrieved April 28, 2006, from www.turnitin.com/static/index.html.

Zeegers, Petrus, and Lynne Giles. 1996. "Essay Writing in Biology: An Example of Effective Student Learning." *Research in Science Education* 26, no. 4: 437–459.

10

Is It Science or Pseudoscience?
An Inquiry-Based Exploration of Science
Gone Astray

Lori J. Toedter, Professor, Psychology Department
Dorothy F. Glew, Instruction Librarian, Reeves Library
Moravian College

At some time during their education at a liberal arts college, students are exposed to at least a rudimentary discussion of the importance of the use of the scientific method when engaging in a decision-making process. Rarely, however, are students challenged to investigate the consequences to individuals and society when the scientific method is poorly, mistakenly, or incompletely applied. Titled "The Misapplication of Science: Personal Perils and Social Costs," our course was designed as a team-taught, interdisciplinary course for juniors and seniors from any academic discipline. The course was approved by the Moravian College Liberal Education Committee to satisfy the liberal education requirements for an advanced seminar under the "Social Impact of Science" rubric.

Whereas other courses offered to fulfill this liberal arts guideline at the college had tended to explore fairly focused topics (such as the impact of communications technology or genetic testing), our course was designed to be more broad-based, enabling students to explore how science differs from other ways of knowing; to use critical analysis skills to evaluate the quality of evidence; and, most important, to access and use scientific information in making important decisions in their lives. In the process, we helped students to distinguish science from pseudoscience (Wynn and Wiggins, 2001). A pseudoscience (such as astrology) has many of the trappings of a real science (such as astronomy), but without critical features such as falsifiable hypotheses and rigorous, controlled experiments.

Information Literacy at Moravian College

Moravian College is a small, private, liberal arts college in eastern Pennsylvania with a full-time enrollment of nearly 1,800 students. In fall 2000 we began the implementation of a new liberal arts curriculum, which explicitly called for the introduction of writing-intensive and computing-intensive courses across the curriculum. As the curriculum evolved over the next few years, it became clear that there was also a need for public speaking and information literacy courses, although there was no explicit timeline for the integration of the latter two competencies into the curriculum.

In designing our course we found little to assist us from any one disciplinary perspective, since its essence was to be interdisciplinary, multifaceted, and of interest to advanced students from any background or major. The *PESTS: Psychologists Educating Students to Think Skeptically* Web site lists some of the many schools that have offered courses on pseudoscience. (http://www.scottsdalecc.edu/ricker/pests/teaching/teaching_syllabi.html). Among those listed are Plattsburgh State University of New York, Sarah Lawrence College, and Emory University. Some of the courses offered at these institutions resembled ours in that they had similar components. For example, in the course offered at DePaul University, students addressed the question of why people accept questionable beliefs. At Lebanon Valley College and other schools, students critically examined paranormal phenomena. Finally, as was the case with our course, the scientific method was an important course component at Wake Forest University and Southern Methodist University (Ricker, 2006).

While similar to other courses, our course differed from them in that the focus was not only on detecting pseudoscience and understanding its origins and effects but also on building competency, and that was the basis of our collaboration. We used the engaging literature and debate on pseudoscience to help students to achieve important competencies, namely, information literacy and public speaking, in addition to critical thinking. In this respect our course had much more in common with courses team-taught by librarians and faculty at other schools where the focus was also on developing research skills, particularly in science.

Review of the Science Literature

Faculty-Librarian Collaborative Teaching

The library literature is replete with descriptions of courses such as ours. Articles reflect various degrees of faculty-librarian collaboration from whole courses to multiple or single sessions of a course. A good example of an entire course collaboration is the Human Genetics class that Courtois and Handel taught collaboratively (1999). Stachacz and Brennan exemplify the alternative, which incorporates collaboration in multiple or single sessions (1992). They worked together to design and teach the library component of an intermediate-level Biology course at Dickinson College. The instruction took place in the first four-hour laboratory session of the course. The pair introduced students to the science literature and the most effective ways to search it. After completing a follow-up exercise, students selected a topic for a short research paper. Stachacz and Brennan jointly generated the list of topics and graded the papers.

While many collaborative efforts are aimed at preparing students to do the research necessary to write a conventional term paper, others serve a different purpose. For example, at the University of California at Berkeley, students in an introductory biology course were required to apply the scientific method to an ambitious field project. Martin describes the ways that the librarians helped students to develop the investigative skills demanded by the assignment (1986). For example, librarians taught students not only how to search the Biology literature but also how to formulate a research question and hypothesis that could easily be related to the literature. After students had spent several weeks gathering and analyzing data at a site related to their project, the librarians assisted them in finding the multiple sources, including some in the primary literature necessary to substantiate their conclusions. In short, the librarians' skills were employed at various stages to support students engaged in a scientific investigation.

Another project, conducted at Villanova University in 2002, bears notable similarities to our course. At Villanova, several librarians and biology faculty members engaged in a collaborative effort to improve students' ability to find, evaluate, synthesize, and communicate scientific information effectively. After receiving instruction on searching bibliographic databases in the sciences and evaluating Web sites, students were given the opportunity to practice these skills by working collaboratively in groups on a class research project. The research culminated in oral presentations by each group (Bowden and DiBenedetto, 2002). While this project differed in many respects from ours, its objectives and methods of achieving them were strikingly similar.

Over the past several years, librarians have embraced the concept enunciated by the American Library Association of promoting lifelong learning—the ability to find, evaluate, organize, and use information effectively to address a problem or issue. This was the impetus for Pestel and Engeldinger, a faculty member and a librarian who collaborated to promote scientific literacy among non-science majors in a chemistry course (1992). Instruction and follow-up exercises were intended to teach students not only how to find scientific information but also how to read it critically and determine its reliability. The goal was to equip students to deal throughout their lives with scientific issues that have important social significance and to enable them to make sound decisions based on accurate information. Besides the emphasis on the development of skills that would serve them well throughout their lives, this course was similar to ours in that students were given repeated opportunities throughout the semester to practice the skills that they were learning.

Origin of Our Course

The specific idea for our course arose from Professor Toedter's experience teaching her course in abnormal psychology. The history and literature in the field of abnormal psychology are full of examples of great interest to students that illustrate what happens when otherwise well-meaning people improperly apply the scientific method. Blaming parents for making their children autistic (Bettleheim, 1967) and using electroconvulsive therapy to treat schizophrenia (Fink, 2004) are just two illustrations of the suffering that can ensue when bad science is applied to the human experience. Toedter had worked closely for many years with Dr. Glew and other members of the reference staff to improve the quality of her students' bibliographies. Prior to this collaboration, students in abnormal psychology were basing their literature reviews on highly questionable and somewhat randomly selected sources, despite the instructions on their syllabus and extensive handouts on the process. As a result of the faculty-librarian collaboration that developed, students in this course now come to a one-on-one meeting with a member of the reference staff after their topics have been approved. This meeting is tailored to teach each student new skills, regardless of what skills the student brings to the session. For most students, additional training on controlled vocabulary, an introduction to PubMed, more productive use of limiters, and search history evaluation are integral components. Students are also assisted in making preliminary decisions about the quality of sources based on the abstracts produced by the search. As a result, the quality of the students' literature reviews has improved dramatically, as has their satisfaction with the process.

Based on this productive collaboration, in summer 2004 Toedter approached her colleagues on the reference staff with an idea that would include a librarian as a full partner in a course that would help students increase their information literacy and speaking skills. Toedter's invitation was particularly gratifying to the librarians, since the current mode of teaching information skills at Moravian is through course-related instruction with its attendant disadvantages. All our teaching occurs in response to faculty request, and some faculty appreciate the value of research instruction more than others. As a result, some students, depending on the courses they take and the professors they have, get a great deal of instruction, whereas others get little or none. In addition, we never know how much instruction students in a given class have had, so we tend to go over the basics, which is entirely appropriate for some students but repetitious and boring for others. Moreover, the latter group tend to assume that they have learned all there is to know about information skills when, in fact, they need to acquire more advanced skills and have opportunities for supervised practice. This course afforded the chance for students to do both.

Organizing Framework for the Course

Although there was little literature to aid in developing the framework for our course, in early discussions it became apparent that the field of evidence-based medicine (EBM) had much to offer as a model for detecting pseudoscience. In transforming the approach from one practiced by physicians with advanced degrees (Toedter, Thompson, and Rohatgi, 2003) to one used by undergraduates, we renamed it evidence-based decision-making (EBD).

Just as in EBM, this four-step process begins with using the PICO model (for example, see Richardson, Wilson, Nishikawa, et al., 1995) to develop a focused question. Using this approach, students make their questions more specific by specifying the P (person or problem), I (issue or intervention), C (comparison, if any) and O (outcome of interest). (See figure 10.1 for specific, focused examples of this process.) Using PICO to focus questions greatly simplifies the second step of conducting a comprehensive search of the literature. In the third step, students use the information they have learned about assuring validity in research to evaluate the quality of evidence obtained in their search. Finally, through critical thinking and group discussion, students decide whether there is enough information available to answer their question and, if so, what that answer is. As will become apparent in our subsequent case study model, the EBD process provided us the framework for assisting the students in our course to develop competencies that will assist them well beyond their college years.

Case Study Model

Course Overview

The course met weekly over a fifteen-week semester for three hours per week. In addition, students were required to submit homework and participate in online threaded

Step 1: Form a Focused Question using PICO*

Step 2: Conduct a Comprehensive Search of the Literature

Step 3: Critically Evaluate the Literature Obtained

Step 4: Determine Whether There is Enough Evidence to Answer Your Question, and, if so, What That Answer Is

NOTE: AT ANY POINT IN THE PROCESS YOU MAY DECIDE THAT YOUR QUESTION NEEDS TO BE REFORMULATED BASED UPON THE EVIDENCE COLLECTED TO THAT POINT. IN THAT CASE, BEGIN AGAIN AT STEP 1!

PICO and the Focused Question

Questions Prior to Focusing:

Example 1: Do copper bracelets work?

Example 2: Is cold laser therapy effective?

P	is for *"Person"* or *"Problem"*	Example 1: Persons suffering from arthritis Example 2: Getting people to quit smoking
I	is for *"Issue"* or *"Intervention"*	Example 1: Wearing a bracelet made of copper Example 2: Cold laser therapy
C	is for *"Comparison"*	Example 1: Not wearing such a bracelet Example 2: Nicotine gum
O	is for *"Outcome"*	Example 1: Reduction in pain Example 2: Smoking cessation

Focused Questions:

Example 1: In arthritis sufferers, does wearing a copper bracelet lead to a reduction in reported pain intensity?

Example 2: Is the use of cold laser therapy more effective than the use of nicotine gum in smoking cessation treatment?

Figure 10.1   Overview of the Process: Evidence-Based Decision-Making (EBD)

discussions using Blackboard several days prior to the weekly class meeting. As indicated in the syllabus for the course, our main objectives were to help students to understand the proper use of the scientific method in both personal decision making and in service to others; build competencies in both literature-searching skills and critical analysis of the results; work effectively as team members in making interesting, accurate, and informative presentations to peers; and effectively critique the work of peers in an honest, objective, and helpful way.

Given this broad and challenging set of goals, we designed a non-traditional grading scheme. Unlike the traditional college course, exam and papers did not form the primary basis by which students earned their grades. There was one exam, worth only 15 percent of the final grade, to test competencies after the first half of the course. Attendance, homework, and participation (in both Blackboard and class discussions) totaled another 30 percent of the grade. Most of the grade (45%) was based on the quality of each of two presentations, including the required annotated bibliography and group process journals, with the remaining 10 percent based upon the quality and thoroughness of students' evaluations of their peers' presentations.

While attempting to weave course content and research skills together as seamlessly as possible, we were also trying in the process to help students develop useful life skills. An important component of the course was forging effective collaborative working partnerships. The class was divided into six groups of three students for the duration of the semester. Aside from discussions of readings on Blackboard, students worked in their groups both on classroom activities and outside of class in preparing for the two presentations. Group process journals were kept by each group member for each of the presentations. The journals helped us to assess the relative contributions of each group member and to intervene as necessary to assure successful group functioning. We met with each group twice to review journals, bibliographies, and progress.

The class met each week in a computer classroom, giving us maximal flexibility in topic and activity selection. For example, during the latter half of the term the class discussed, on the Blackboard discussion board, an article from *Skeptic* on the Mattoon Phantom Gasser (Smith, 1995). That week in class we considered this World War II vintage case of a town in the grips of a mysterious streak of nocturnal "gassings," which some believed to be the work of a prankster. Townspeople began to report various transitory phenomena, such as weakness in the limbs, sounding much like mass hysteria. The report on the phenomenon reproduced in *Skeptic* was a paper written by a college student at the time. Growing out of our discussion were questions such as "Could this be accounted for by mass hysteria? If so, how is this condition defined?" and "What are the possible signs of someone having been exposed to various gaseous substances? Are the reports from the victims consistent with these symptoms?" Immediate access to computers allowed us to follow this discussion with an online search for answers to these questions. Clever students also found a map of the town of Mattoon with the locations of the reported "gassings" as well as an entire Web site for Mattoon Gasser devotees.

Introduction to EBD and PICO Practice: The Graduate Record Examination as "Fringe Science"

The use of EBD as the framework in our course was introduced at the beginning of the semester and reinforced through a series of activities throughout the term. The first of several readings assigned students was an article in *Skeptic* magazine that questioned the validity of the Graduate Record Examination (GRE) as a predictor of success in graduate school. This reading afforded us one of many opportunities to weave content and research skills together. Students first discussed their responses to the article on Blackboard. During the next class meeting, they used PICO to formulate their focused question. Each student then conducted his or her own database search for journal articles based on the PICO-focused question. In the course of this session Glew reviewed searching strategies, such as generating keywords; using Boolean Operators; using strategies to broaden a search, such as truncation; narrowing a search by imposing limiters; altering a search based on an initial results list; and interpreting citations. While students conducted their searches, Toedter and Glew moved from one group to another providing searching guidance and suggestions where needed. This enabled the instructors to move each student ahead in skill development without holding the more competent students back. In addition, the more advanced group members were able to assist their less advanced peers.

1. EBSCO citations are printed in reverse chronological order. As a general rule, take more recent articles over older ones (particularly if by the same author(s) or research team).

2. Take an article that describes research that **directly answers** your question rather than research where variables of interest to you were of secondary or minor importance in the study.

3. Give articles from well-respected journals priority over those from less well known journals.

4. Evaluate the quality of the study based on class readings and notes. Take studies you deem to have better internal validity over those likely to have confounds.

   - A meta-analysis based on well-controlled, experimental studies is the highest level of evidence
   - Single, well-controlled, experimental studies represent the next highest level
   - Well-controlled quasi-experiments are next in quality
   - See handout on "Evaluating Secondary Sources" for information on how to judge the quality of a review article
   - Uncontrolled or poorly controlled studies should not be used for EBD

5. Choose a study with a sample consisting of subjects most like those to whom you wish to generalize over one with a less similar sample.

6. If two studies appear to be equivalent on the characteristics above, choose a study with a large sample over one with a smaller sample.

7. Watch out for sponsored studies! Independent research and funding sources are preferable to research sponsored by an individual or company to promote its own product.

Figure 10.2   Tips for Reviewing a Set of Abstracts

Prior to this class Glew had created a master search so that students could compare their own results list to determine if their search had yielded the best evidence articles. Then, using Glew's results list, students did an exercise for homework in which they evaluated the results list, and each selected the article that he or she believed represented the "best of the best." During the next class meeting students worked in small groups to compare their individual results. Each group was then asked to reach a consensus about which article from the results list provided the best evidence in answer to the question of the GRE's validity. In the process each group formulated an argument in support of their group's choice.

As a class we then discussed each group's choice of an article. In the process, students learned how to apply the "Tips for Selecting Best Evidence from Abstracts" (figure 10.2) and were able to rule out several choices. For example, some of the articles chosen discussed discipline-specific GRE exams, and one was about minority student performance on the exam, thereby not directly addressing the specific PICO question posed. Another popular choice was a secondary source, giving us the opportunity to teach students the difference between a review article and a meta-analysis, and how to evaluate each. One of the *Users' Guides to the Medical Literature* was helpful to students in understanding the key considerations in deciding if an article is a meta-analysis or a lower level of evidence. (Oxman, Cook, and Guyatt, 1994).

In the end, the class selected a meta-analysis by Kuncel, Hezlett, and Ones as the best article obtained in the search (2001). This exercise enabled students to get other perspectives on the issue of the GRE's validity and, at the same time, get practice searching and thinking critically about the articles in a results list in order to select the most relevant and best-argued response to a question. Its relevance to juniors and seniors considering graduate school made it a good first choice for teaching the process of EBD.

Preparation for the First Presentation
Why Do People Believe What They Do?

Students worked primarily outside of class in their assigned groups on their first presentation. Each group was asked to submit their first and second choice topic for each of the two presentations at the beginning of the term. The first topic, designed to be much easier to research and to present than the second, was on the general question of "Why do people believe the things they do?" It accounted for only 10 percent of the grade and was presented as an opportunity to practice teamwork, literature searching, critical evaluation of results, and evaluation of others' presentations. This presentation was to last ten minutes; it was considered a trial run for the second presentation, more difficult to research and present material on "the misapplication of science." This second presentation was to last twenty to thirty minutes and required students to acquire some historical background on the topic and to incorporate knowledge from several scientific disciplines. In addition, it required them to learn from mistakes made in the first presentation.

Since the presentations demanded that students demonstrate information competence, but many of the students in the class had had little prior research instruction, preparation for the first round of presentations involved a review of basic searching skills and critical evaluation of material, as well as practice exercises. A librarian met with each group to review the research done up to that point and to address any difficulties the group was having. The instruction began with a session on distinguishing between magazines and journals. Each group of three examined a magazine and a journal, and we discussed the differences between the two and the reasons why the former would be unacceptable as sources for their projects.

In addition, like many of their counterparts at other schools, Moravian students tend to use the free Web heavily and indiscriminately when doing research. Accordingly, to prepare students to research their first presentations, Glew did a class on Web evaluation. At the time the course was being offered, the Atkins diet was being widely touted as producing dramatic results while allowing the dieter to eat foods that are normally off limits to someone attempting to lose weight. In addition to having real-world implications, the subject had the added advantage of being of interest to many diet-conscious undergraduates.

In order to prepare them for the class, Glew assigned a section of the library's online research tutorial that covers Web evaluation. The section assigned explains and illustrates the application of seven criteria to Web sites. The class discussed the criteria and then applied them to two sites. One was a commercial site touting the advantages of low-carbohydrate dieting, and the other was an article on low-carbohydrate diets on the Mayo Clinic Web site. Needless to say, the sites were a study in contrasts, and we discussed these at length. One obvious difference was the purpose for which each site had been created. Students became aware of the importance of determining the purpose of a Web site and the ways this can affect content. For example, the first site was clearly intended to sell low-carbohydrate products, and students had to consider the ways this purpose would affect the objectivity of the content. Not surprisingly, the doctor responsible for the material on the Mayo Clinic site was more objective in his treatment of the subject, pointing out the controversial nature of the diet and the fact that it will be some time before anybody can know what, if any, long-term effects it may produce.

Group Process Journals

Preparing for each of the two presentations necessitated that group members meet outside of class to accomplish a series of tasks, including selecting a topic, determining how the work would be divided, finding and evaluating appropriate sources, making decisions regarding the way the material would be presented, preparing PowerPoint slides to organize their presentation, and developing handouts and activities to support their points. Each member of the group was required to keep an independent journal detailing his or her role in the preparation process from the group's first meeting until the presentation. The journals were a great way for us to get a sense of the group dynamic, the relative contributions of each member, and the strategies employed to research the topic. In addition, it provided an opportunity for the students to reflect on what had worked well and what needed to be done differently in preparing for the second round of presentations. We saw the two journals (one for each of the two presentations) as such an important component of the process that together they accounted for 10 percent of the course grade.

Annotated Bibliographies

In addition to submitting a journal record of their presentation-planning process, students in each presentation group were required to submit an annotated bibliography. This revealed a great deal about students' research skills and the areas in which they needed additional work. Shortcomings were particularly apparent in the first set of bibliographies. One major problem was the lack of use of sources from the science literature. Students tended to use Academic Search Elite, the database with which they are most familiar. They were resistant to searching the science databases, such as ScienceDirect, PubMed, and Basic Science Index, to which Moravian subscribes and in which they could find the best material on their topics. Clearly they needed to become more familiar and comfortable with these databases, and this became one of our priorities in preparation for the second round of presentations. Another significant problem was the excessive use of Web sites as sources, requiring a follow-up session on Web evaluation.

Building Critical Analysis Skills: An Exercise in Baloney Detection

The need for skill building in critical analysis of sources was also reviewed both prior to and following the first round of presentations. A chapter in Shermer's book, *Why People Believe Weird Things: Pseudoscience, Superstition and Other Confusions of Our Time* (1997) provides twenty-five tips for detecting pseudoscience. Going beyond the traditional questions about the validity of published scientific research, students are asked to be aware of such issues as over-reliance on authorities and the notion that just because something is unexplained does not mean that it is unexplainable. The exercise we used asked students to evaluate the claims of an advertisement in our local newspaper for a "Thrilling Chinese Diet Pill" (components not given) that was guaranteed to cause instant weight loss. Students did a homework assignment that was followed by a class discussion of which of the twenty-five points raised in the Shermer reading could be applied to this case. Although we used a paid newspaper advertisement, any source making unrealistic claims (e.g., tabloids found at grocery store checkouts) would work as well.

Evaluating Peer Presentations: In-class Search Activity

Another of the many opportunities we had to weave content and skills to serve a very practical purpose was presented by the requirement that students evaluate each group presentation as well as the presentation of each individual in the group. The goals were to sharpen their evaluation skills and provide useful feedback to presenters. We wanted students to go beyond the superficial in their responses to the presentations, and we wanted them to take ownership of the evaluation process, so, working collaboratively, the class created an evaluation form with some assistance from us.

To create the form, students did multiple searches on ERIC to find journal articles with peer evaluation rubrics for oral presentations. As part of the preparation for the course, three librarians had done searches on this topic in order to see if, indeed, there was material on the subject and to get an idea of the most effective search terms. This was fortunate, since finding good articles on the topic demanded repeated searches. Out of this work the librarians found five good articles on the topic. (Freeman, 1995; Hafer, C., and Hafer, H., 2003; Hughes and Large, 1993; Patri, 2002; Quigley, 1998). After students practiced doing guided searching, they studied the five articles containing evaluation rubrics. From these, they selected the criteria that they thought most appropriate and helpful for evaluating each other.

The evaluation form derived from these criteria was six pages long and was divided into two parts. The first part consisted of the criteria by which the group would be judged, and the second part the criteria by which individual members of the group would be judged. For each evaluation criterion, there was a rating scale of 1 (the lowest grade) to 5 (the highest). There was a space below the rating scale for each criterion where students could explain the reasons for their rating and could offer suggestions for improvement. The groups were evaluated by such criteria as creativity, the quality of the content and organization of the presentation, and how concise and persuasive it was. The presentation of each group member was measured by the presenter's level of confidence, enthusiasm, and body language, which included posture and eye contact with the audience, as well as by the quality of the presenter's speech, which included fluency, rate of delivery, grammar, and pronunciation.

After the first round of presentations, students recognized the limitations of the form they had created. Notable was the fact that it was so long and cumbersome to complete that it was difficult to pay attention to the presentation being evaluated. Another concern was that there were categories that sounded independent when the form was created but in actual practice overlapped so much as to be indistinguishable. For example, one question asked how the presenters had engaged the audience while another asked how they had kept the audience interested. As a result, the revised form (see figure 10.3) consolidates evaluative dimensions found to be too similar to each other. Students also found they did not like using so many categories to evaluate each individual presenter, since as with the group ratings each category seemed to overlap with others. This problem was resolved by placing a list of the potentially relevant evaluative dimensions at the top, allowing individual raters to use those they felt to be most relevant in a particular case. Finally, the number of rating points for each item was expanded from 5 to 7, as students found they wished to make the finer discriminations that a five-point scale allows.

All Items Rated on a 7 Point Scale:

Poor	Fair	Average		Good		Excellent
1	2	3	4	5	6	7

Group Criteria:

1. How was the group at ***engaging the audience***? [includes generating discussion, involvement of audience, keeping the audience interested and other forms of interaction]
2. How good a job did the group do in ***integrating science*** into their presentation?
3. How ***creative*** was the group's presentation?
4. How would you rate the quality of the ***content*** of the presentation? [Includes how well researched it appeared, balance between thoroughness and conciseness]
5. How would you rate the ***overall organization*** of the presentation?
6. How would you rate the quality of the ***audio/visual aids*** used by the group?

Criteria for Individuals:

All Items Rated on a 7 Point Scale:

Poor	Fair	Average		Good		Excellent
1	2	3	4	5	6	7

Consider the following in assessing an individual's presentation:

- **Body Language**
- **Eye Contact**
- **Confident**
- **Fluency**
- **Rate of Speech**
- **Posture**
- **Relaxed**
- **Enthusiasm**
- **Loudness**
- **Absence of Distracting Mannerisms**
- **Comfortable with Material**
- **Talking to us/Not Reading**
- **Grammar/Pronunciation**

Figure 10.3   Misapplication of Science Criteria for Evaluating Group Presentations

The Final Presentation: Misapplication of Science

Many of the class sessions following the first presentation were designed to address problems we observed during the planning and execution of this first round. They ranged from unusual and distracting uses of PowerPoint (such as jarring color schemes and lots of literally flipping prose) to lack of integration of science and questionable source evaluation. The PowerPoint problem was relatively easy to fix, involving a workshop session by a member of our instructional technology staff, who was able to advise against using all of the PowerPoint features as well as showing students how to integrate images, moving images, and sound into their presentation.

Another session conducted to improve students' work on the second presentation was a Web evaluation exercise. This time we distributed worksheets with the URLs of three Web sites on the Mozart Effect. Students examined each site to determine if it was an acceptable source for academic research and, if not, which evaluation criterion (criteria) it failed to meet. The Mozart Effect is based on the claim of researchers Dr. Gordon Shaw and Dr. Fran Rauscher that a group of college students who listened to the Mozart Sonata for Two Pianos in D Major for ten minutes experienced a brief improvement in their spatial and temporal reasoning abilities as measured on the Stanford Binet Intelligence Test (Rauscher, Shaw, and Ky, 1993). Since this discovery in 1993, other controversial claims have been made about the positive impact of music on intelligence. The first site that we studied, that of the Child Development Institute, makes no pretense of objectivity in its endorsement of the Mozart Effect (www.childdevelopmentinfo.com/development/Mozart_Effect.htm). This site is intended to educate parents on numerous aspects of childrearing. In many sections of the site there is no indication of who authored the material. Even more disturbing is that woven into the information and advice being offered are what amount to advertisements for games, videos, and other products with contact information for those wishing to make purchases. These products allegedly enhance children's intelligence. Another site that students examined raised questions of authority (http://clearinghouse.missouriwestern.edu/manuscripts/150.asp). The site is a clearinghouse of papers written by students and submitted by them or their professors. The subject of one of the papers was the Mozart Effect. In contrast to this was a site with an article challenging the Mozart Effect that had been published by a college professor in a music journal (www.acs.appstate.edu/dept/psych/Documents/Steele2003.pdf). The discussion of these sites and the worksheets that the students completed reflected a great deal of naiveté on their part and confirmed our belief in the necessity of having this session.

Another class intended to improve students' work on the second presentation was a workshop on integrating science in their material. The goal was to help each group choose the best possible sources by steering them toward the most appropriate databases. Students were resistant not only to searching the science databases on their own but also to getting help searching them. Accordingly, two librarians joined us, and in the course of the session each group received assistance and suggestions from one of the librarians as they began their research. Moreover, their presence afforded students the opportunity to ask questions as they did their online searches.

Assessment

We assessed the success of our course in two ways. One was through the traditional means afforded us by the anonymous evaluations required of all courses offered to fill one of the guidelines within the liberal education curriculum. In this evaluation, students are asked questions specific to the stated goals for the rubric, in our case, the "Social Impact of Science." Students are asked to reflect on the following aspects of the course: if and how it enabled them to better understand scientific principles and technological innovations; if and how it helped them understand the role that science plays in their lives; and if and how it raised their awareness of the impact of science and technology on modern society.

With respect to how it enabled them to better understand scientific principles and technological innovations, students' comments included these:

- "Research skills I learned in the course are a productive scientific tool."
- "Helped me to understand that not all published scientific print is factual."
- "It helped me learn that even if things seem scientific it doesn't mean they are."

On the role of science in their lives, students said such things as these:

- "Helped me realize that there are a lot of articles out there that are playing with the public's opinion with false statements."
- "I never realized how false some of my perceptions actually were."
- "Group presentations eliminated many myths from my head and showed me that science is everywhere."

And finally, with respect to the impact of science on society, students made comments including the following:

- "I now see how society misinterprets science out of their own ignorance."
- "It's important that as a society we let go of our false ideas and learn about the practical applications of science."
- "I have learned that the media plays a huge role in providing the public with misinformation on scientific studies."

In reviewing these comments and others like them, we were pleased to see that students had understood the messages that we were trying to convey. Although the preceding comments reflect only a sampling of those received, comments such as these reflect the virtually unanimous sentiment of our students.

The other approach we took to soliciting feedback on ways to improve the course was to initiate a threaded discussion on Blackboard in which we asked our students to talk with us about the strengths and weaknesses of the course. Since the postings were not anonymous, we initially thought we would have trouble getting our students to give their direct and honest opinions. Our experience was in fact just the opposite: students were far more critical in the Blackboard discussion than in their anonymous course evaluations. For example, some students complained about the amount of class time that was devoted to research skills, feeling they had already mastered the research process.

Their presentation bibliographies, work on in-class exercises, and comments in discussions often belied their assertions regarding their capabilities. Nevertheless, clearly it is absolutely essential that students be aware of their limitations and feel the need for instruction. Only then can teaching the multiple skills that research demands be effective. The problem was compounded by our expectation that students would search the science databases. Some students, believing they could meet their research needs adequately by searching the World Wide Web and a multi-disciplinary database with which they were already familiar, felt the instruction on searching these databases was unnecessary.

On the other hand, a number of students had positive responses to the research component of the course. One student commented that as the semester progressed, "I found myself getting better and better at researching using library databases and the internet [sic]." Speaking of the library search skills, another student noted that these skills would always be of great help to her and "were essential to what we were covering and the research we needed to do." A point made several times was that while library skills are essential, they should be taught to students early on in their college careers and not toward the end. After complaining that she had already known all the research skills that were taught, a senior remarked that incorporating library research skills in a regular class is long overdue. Another component of the course that elicited negative comments was the peer evaluation form. Students disliked being expected to give detailed critiques of their peers' presentations in order to get a good grade on their own evaluations. While students were quite candid about the things they disliked, they also had many positive comments to make. With a few exceptions they liked the assigned readings and the threaded discussions of them on Blackboard, the groupwork on presentations, and the presentations themselves. Moreover, several acknowledged that a course being offered for the first time will almost certainly need some adjustments before it is taught again.

Conclusion

From both a librarian's and a professor's point of view, the course provided optimal conditions for enabling students to become more research savvy. Information needs grew naturally out of the course and were not artificially imposed, for example, by a term paper assignment. As a result, instruction could be provided seamlessly at the point of need, and students could put the skills they had learned to immediate use and appreciate the relationship between good research skills and coursework. Moreover, there were multiple opportunities for supervised searching and evaluating practice. Thus, students could develop the critical thinking skills necessary for effective research over the course of a whole semester. Put another way, they experienced the benefits of course-integrated instruction and strengthened our conviction that this approach, and not course-related instruction, allows students to develop the information skills they need in the most thorough and meaningful way. Moreover, the course not only sharpened the research, presentation, and critical thinking skills of our students but also gave them a deeper appreciation of the importance of the proper use of the scientific method in making personal decisions and in serving others.

References

Bettleheim, Bruno. 1967. *The Empty Fortress: Infantile Autism and the Birth of the Self*. Oxford: Free Press of Glencoe.

Bowden, T., and Angela DiBenedetto. 2002. "Information Literacy in a Biology Laboratory Session: An Example of Librarian-Faculty Collaboration." *Research Strategies* 18, no. 2: 143–149.

Courtois, Martin P., and Mary Ann Handel. 1999. "A Collaborative Approach to Teaching Genetics Information Sources." *Research Strategies* 16, no. 3: 211–220.

Fink, Max. 2004. "Induced Seizures as Psychiatric Therapy: Ladislas Meduna's Contributions in Modern Neuroscience." *Journal of ECT* 20, no. 3 (September): 133–136.

Freeman, Mark. 1995. "Peer Assessment by Groups of Group Work." *Assessment & Evaluation in Higher Education* 20, no. 3 (December): 289–301.

Hafer, C., and M. Hafer. 2003. "Quantitative Analysis of the Rubric as an Assessment Tool: An Empirical Study of Peer-Group Rating." *International Journal of Science Education* 25, no. 12 (December): 1509–1528.

Hughes, I. E., and B. J. Large. 1993. "Staff and Peer-Group Assessment of Oral Communication Skills." *Studies in Higher Education* 18, no. 3 (October): 379–385.

Kuncel, Nathan R., Sarah A. Hezlett, and Deniz S. Ones. 2001. "A Comprehensive Meta-analysis of the Predictive Value of the Graduate Record Examinations." *Psychological Bulletin* 127, no. 1 (January): 162–181.

Martin, Jenna R., and Celesta L. Sword. 2006. "Does Bach Have the Same Effect as Mozart on Spatial Reasoning?" National Undergraduate Research Clearinghouse. Retrieved March 29, 2006, from http://clearinghouse.missouriwestern.edu/manuscripts/150.asp.

Martin, Rebecca R. 1986. "Library Instruction and the Scientific Method: A Role for Librarians in an Introductory Biology Course." *Research Strategies* 4 (Summer): 108–115.

Oldfield, Kenneth. 1998. "The GRE as Fringe Science: The Politics and Economics of the Graduate Record Exam." *Skeptic* 6, no. 1: 68–72.

Oxman, A. D., D. J. Cook, and G. H. Guyatt. 1994. "Users' Guides to the Medical Literature: How to Use an Overview." *Journal of the American Medical Association* 272, no. 17: 1367–1371.

Patri, M. 2002. "The Influence of Peer Feedback on Self- and Peer-Assessment of Oral Skills." *Language Testing* 19, no. 2: 109–131.

Pestel, Beverly C., and Eugene A. Engeldinger. 1992. "Library-Labs-for-Science Literacy Courses: Improving Science Literacy and Critical Thinking Skills of Nonscience Majors—a Success Story from Terre Haute." *Journal of College Science Teaching* 22, no. 1 (September/October): 52–54.

Quigley, Brooke L. 1998. "Designing and Grading Oral Communication Assignments." *New Directions for Teaching and Learning*, no. 74 (Summer): 41–49.

Rauscher, Frances H., Gordon L. Shaw, and Katherine N. Ky. 1993 "Music and Spatial Task Performance." *Nature* 365, no. 6447 (October): 611.

Richardson, W. S., M. C. Wilson, J. Nishikawa, et al. 1995. "The Well-Built Clinical Question." *American College of Physicians' Journal Club* (November/December): A12–A13.

Ricker, Jeffry. 2006. "PESTS: Psychologists Educating Students to Think Skeptically." Retrieved May 19, 2006, from http://www.scottsdalecc.edu/ricker/pests/teaching/teaching_syllabi.html.

Shaw, Gordon L., Amy Graziano, and Matthew Peterson. 2005. "The 'Mozart Effect': How Classical Music Improves Intelligence & Learning." Child Development Institute. Retrieved November 29, 2005, from www.childdevelopmentinfo.com/development/Mozart_Effect.htm.

Shermer, Michael. 1997. *Why People Believe Weird Things: Pseudoscience, Superstition, and Other Confusions of Our Time.* New York: W. H. Freeman.

Smith, Willy. 1995. "The Mattoon Phantom Gasser: Was the Famous Mass Hysteria Really a Hoax?" *Skeptic* 3, no. 1: 33–39.

Stachacz, John C., and Thomas M. Brennan. 1990. "Bibliographic Instruction in an Undergraduate Biology Course." *Research Strategies* 8, no. 1 (Winter): 14–21.

Steele, Kenneth M. 2003. "Do Rats Show a Mozart Effect?" *Music Perception* 21, no. 2 (Winter): 251–265. Retrieved November 29, 2005, from www.acs.appstate.edu/~kms/documents/Steele2003.pdf.

Toedter, Lori J., Lora L. Thompson, and Chand Rohatgi. 2004. "Training Surgeons to Do Evidence-Based Surgery: A Collaborative Approach." *Journal of the American College of Surgeons* 199, no. 2 (August): 293–299.

Wynn, Charles M., and Arthur W. Wiggins. 2001. *Quantum Leaps in the Wrong Direction: Where Real Science Ends–and Pseudoscience Begins.* Washington, D.C.: Joseph Henry Press.

11

Collaborating on the Core Curriculum: Transformation of an Environmental Studies Course

Laurie A. Kutner, Bailey/Howe Library
Cecilia Danks, Environmental Program
University of Vermont

In recent years, librarians and subject faculty have come to recognize that collaboration to incorporate information literacy instruction into individual courses creates a highly meaningful context for teaching information literacy skills. It is rare, however, for information literacy objectives and skills to be fully and collaboratively integrated into the core curriculum of a major. At the University of Vermont, a strong relationship between the library and the Environmental Program has enabled this to happen. Information literacy instruction is purposefully and progressively built into the introductory, intermediate, and advanced core courses in the environmental studies major. The focus of this chapter is on the current model of full collaborative partnership to provide progressive, intensive information literacy instruction as part of the curricula of the intermediate- and advanced-level required courses.

Over time and through continued communication, the library and the Environmental Program at the University of Vermont have developed a close working relationship regarding the best way to teach information literacy skills to Environmental Studies majors. In order to best understand the current relationship between the library and the Environmental Program, we will discuss the evolution of our work together, and our collective thought processes that have taken shape over a period of years. This historical approach provides the perspective from which to understand the restructuring that has recently taken place in the environmental studies core curriculum. The curriculum restructuring has as its basis a more integrated and conscientious approach to incorporating information literacy instruction directly into the required courses.

The need for intensive information literacy instruction for environmental studies majors at the University of Vermont is influenced by the inherent nature of the major as an interdisciplinary area of study. The interdisciplinary framework of this major necessitates further information-seeking challenges not experienced by researchers and students who focus their work within a disciplinary context (Kutner, 2000; Murphy, 2003; Spanner, 2001; Westbrook, 1999). In addition, the environmental studies major at the University of Vermont is the only undergraduate major with a thesis requirement, and students are expected to produce a significant piece of their own research that can conceivably span a number of disciplines. Given this context, it has been important to understand the environmental studies curriculum as an interdisciplinary curriculum and to translate the additional information challenges presented by the curriculum into progressive, integrated information literacy instruction collaboratively taught as an integral component in the program's core courses.

Literature Review

Environmental Studies as an Interdisciplinary Area of Study

There has been significant discussion in the literature about the inherently interdisciplinary nature of environmental studies programs, the range of forms this has taken, and the curricular challenges that this represents (Braddock, Fien, and Rickson, 1994; Brough, 1994; Crawford-Brown, 2005; Maniates and Whissel, 2000). Interdisciplinary environmental programs began appearing in the early 1970s (Corcoran and Tchen, 1999) as an awareness of the complexity of environmental issues was translated into a field of academic study. The common feature in the literature on environmental studies programs is the notion of interdisciplinarity. Maniates (2000) conducted an empirical study of undergraduate U.S. environmental programs and found that although there were challenges because of their interdisciplinary nature—for example, breadth versus depth, design of core courses—most programs are thriving and are consciously dealing with these challenges by creating rigorous curricula.

It is common for environmental studies programs to have some type of capstone project requirement, which involves students synthesizing materials across disciplines to support research on complex environmental problems. Holly Brough states that "as an interdisciplinary subject, environmental studies is a process and set of skills as much as a body of knowledge." (Brough, 1994: 38) Jones, Merritt, and Palmer (1999) discuss the importance of developing critical thinking skills in students in environmental higher education, and although their work focuses on epistemological and values awareness, we can take from this discussion much broader implications of the importance of developing higher-level critical thinking skills in students focusing on researching complex environmental issues. Lattuca, Voigt, and Fath (2004) support the suggestion that interdisciplinary courses, in which students learn to think reflectively and address complex, real-world problems, enable the development of complex critical thinking skills, and because of this, Davis (1995) suggests that interdisciplinary courses may be best equipped to develop information literacy skills as an important curricular outcome.

The notion that studying and understanding environmental problems and issues in particular requires moving beyond working within single disciplines is widely discussed within the literature on interdisciplinarity. Lele and Norgaard (2005) focus their attention on embedded challenges of interdisciplinary environmental research, including working with multiple methods, within multiple theoretical frameworks, and with differing attitudes between natural and social science approaches to problems. Brewer (1999) also articulated this theme in an article that was part of an issue of the journal *Policy Sciences* devoted entirely to the interdisciplinary nature of environmental problems. The issue concludes that an interdisciplinary approach to understanding complex environmental problems is essential (Brewer and Lovgren, 1999).

Interdisciplinary Researchers and Information-Seeking Behaviors

There has been much discussion on what it means to be interdisciplinary, and it has been well established that environmental studies is an inherently interdisciplinary field of study. However, there has been relatively little discussion on how this relates to information-seeking behaviors and strategies of interdisciplinary environmental researchers, or to interdisciplinary researchers in general, and ultimately how this translates into serving the needs of these researchers at all levels. Bates (1996) observed that there has been little empirical research in this area, and she defined many potential ideas for research, suggesting that information needs may be unique in interdisciplinary fields. She additionally questioned whether students in interdisciplinary fields should have "more intensive—and different—training in library research . . . targeted to their special needs" (Bates, 1996: 162). Searing (1996) also observed that the literature on information literacy has not focused on interdisciplinary areas of study as a factor, "yet, students in interdisciplinary courses may benefit most from library instruction" (Searing, 1996: 323).

Since Bates's (1996) suggestion that interdisciplinary researchers may have different information needs than their disciplinary counterparts, there has been a small but growing body of literature that supports this assertion. Westbrook (1999, 2003) has focused her work on eliciting qualitative data from women's studies scholars to better understand the information-seeking issues and habits of these interdisciplinary researchers. She has found that they face unique challenges regarding the sheer quantity of materials needed across multiple disciplines; information that is widely dispersed; the number of databases and resources they need to use to conduct successful research; the necessity of mastering different vocabulary across disciplines; and difficulty in keeping up with everything they need to know across multiple disciplines, resulting in fear of missing important information.

Spanner (2001) also conducted empirical research, looking at information-seeking habits of interdisciplinary scholars at the University of Western Ontario. She found that most of these scholars felt they needed to know more information than scholars working within a single discipline. They reiterated difficulties with vocabularies of multiple disciplines and frustrations in searching multiple databases with multiple search interfaces. According to Spanner's research, the challenge of focusing and narrowing a topic that is interdisciplinary in nature becomes harder. Spanner also notes that as curricula become more interdisciplinary, there may be an increasing need for information literacy instruction within these curricula. By conducting in-depth interviews with faculty involved in interdisciplinary areas of study, Lattuca (2001) found these faculty members felt they had unique research challenges. They had to employ different reading strategies to keep up with the advances in their fields, they had to spend more time doing this, and they had to devote more time to understanding differing vocabulary and language use across disciplines.

What ultimately emerges is a body of empirical data that suggests additional information challenges are present for individuals involved in research in interdisciplinary fields. We are beginning to develop an understanding of what some of these challenges are, but there are many more questions that still should be addressed through future empirical research. Just as the conversations about the notion of interdisciplinarity are evolving in complexity over time (Klein, 1989, 1996, 2004), so are the approaches to understanding the information-seeking behaviors of interdisciplinary researchers. Foster (2005) conducted an empirical study of forty-five interdisciplinary researchers from the University of Sheffield by looking at their behavior in the context of the evolution of the research process, and the results of his study show a greater level of complexity in information-seeking behavior that is "cumulative, reiterative, holistic, and context-bound" and is non-linear in nature (Foster, 2005: para. 35). He feels this approach to understanding the behaviors of interdisciplinary researchers could lead to the development of new ways to work toward information literacy.

Thus far, the discussion has largely focused on additional information challenges for the interdisciplinary researcher in general. It has also been documented that researchers focusing specifically on environmental topics face information challenges that are compounded by the interdisciplinary nature of the environmental field. For example, Murphy (2003) conducted a survey of interdisciplinary environmental researchers and found that respondents reported a number of challenges when researching across disciplines. These challenges included a lack of familiarity with resources and databases not in their primary area, issues with understanding vocabulary in disciplines with limited familiarity, and information overload compounded by interdisciplinarity, all resulting in longer periods of time needed for research across disciplines. Kutner (2000) focuses specifically on a discussion of the implications the interdisciplinary environmental studies major has for the delivery of comprehensive information literacy training to this group of undergraduate students and discusses how these additional information challenges are incorporated into progressive library instruction sessions within an environmental studies curriculum. A proposal submitted by the Five Colleges of Ohio (n.d.) that focuses on improving information literacy training for their environmental studies majors stresses as a context for the proposal the additional information literacy challenges created by the interdisciplinary nature of environmental studies.

Information Literacy Instruction in Interdisciplinary Curricula

Incorporating information literacy instruction directly into interdisciplinary curricula is a subject that has not been explored in much detail in the published literature to date (Baker and Curry, 2004). Baker and Curry (2004) worked with subject faculty to incorporate information competencies with specific learning outcomes into an interdisciplinary human communications major at California State University, Monterey Bay, and note that the interdisciplinary nature of the major has certain implications for information gathering that should be addressed through instruction. Ultimately, the success of their project was predicated on the fully collaborative relationships they established with faculty over time. Kutner (2000) discusses the delivery of progressive library instruction to environmental studies majors and frames her discussion on the additional information challenges and resultant opportunities posed by the interdisciplinary nature of environmental studies.

Some of the more general seminal documents that form the basis for many discussions regarding information literacy take on an additional layer of significance when viewed from the perspective of teaching information competencies to individuals involved in interdisciplinary areas of study. For instance, the Boyer Commission report on "Reinventing Undergraduate Education" (1998) calls for a greater level of involvement for undergraduate research and more interdisciplinarity in undergraduate education, and it recommends a capstone experience as a culmination of undergraduate work. Each of these characteristics is present in the inherently interdisciplinary environmental studies major at the University of Vermont, which requires students to focus on an individually designed original interdisciplinary research project, as described later in this chapter. Therefore, the case study presented here may inform not only other interdisciplinary curricula but may apply more broadly to undergraduate education as it is reinvented for the challenges of the twenty-first century.

Institutional Context

The environmental studies major at the University of Vermont was founded in 1972 as an interdisciplinary, undergraduate major administered by the Environmental Program, an academic unit spanning four colleges—the College of Arts and Sciences, the College of Agriculture and Life Sciences, the College of Education and Social Sciences, and the Rubenstein School Environment and Natural Resources. The thirteen core faculty and staff, with the help of eight additional part-time instructors, deliver the curriculum to approximately 280 majors.

The faculty members are multi-disciplinary, both individually and collectively. Many hold degrees that are not only in different disciplines but also often in completely different academic areas, such as the humanities and natural sciences. Areas of scholarship and teaching tend to be multi-disciplinary or inherently interdisciplinary, such as religion and ecology; community forestry; sustainable communities; ecological economics; landscape and identity; natural history; and ethics. The students' interests are even more diverse than this list of fields. Their senior theses can consciously combine different fields, such as the visual arts and ecology or communications and forestry, and they often are inherently interdisciplinary, such as educational curriculum incorporating gardening or socially responsible ecotourism. By senior year, students need to be able to access and critically evaluate information that may be outside of the expertise of their professors.

To develop the breadth and depth required for engaging environmental issues, the environmental studies major is both interdisciplinary and "individually designed," though not entirely self-designed. Students work with professors to develop a rigorous academic plan that must be approved by the program director. This plan includes courses that provide exposure to a wide range of issues and disciplinary lenses as well as a focused study of a particular subfield such as environmental education, landscape conservation, environmental literature, or ecological design. Because there are other environmentally related majors on campus, including environmental science, natural resources, and others with a more prescribed discipline-oriented curriculum, the environmental studies major attracts students interested in interdisciplinary approaches to addressing pressing environmental issues. This major is designed to develop the life-long skills needed to identify and solve complex problems using data, tools, theories, and institutional frameworks that will inevitably change over time. The curriculum therefore emphasizes information literacy, critical thinking, and effective communication over delivering a given body of knowledge to all majors. Each individual student, however, must develop a strong foundation in the issues, theories, and methods of a subfield of his or her choosing.

The students have general education requirements that vary significantly by college. While each college addresses disciplinary breadth and communication skills in some way, none explicitly addresses information literacy. Given the multiple approaches among the colleges, we cannot rely on the general education requirements to address information literacy, and our students do not even have a uniform foundation on which to build such skills. Information literacy must be addressed within the major requirements.

There are four core courses in the environmental studies major. The first two, four-credit introductory courses (ENVS 001 and ENVS 002), are both taught in a large lecture format with discussion sections. They introduce students to environmental issues and central concepts in the humanities, social sciences, and natural sciences. The intermediate core course (ENVS 151) guides students in identifying and exploring a specific area within the broad field of environmental studies as the focus of further academic study and eventually their senior theses. In this course, students build skills in research, writing, and oral expression, and they develop their academic plan of courses that will constitute their major. The advanced core class (ENVS 201) is a research methods course in which students develop their thesis proposal, including an extensive literature review that will become part of the final thesis. At each step of this major, individual inquiry in multiple disciplines and interdisciplinary fields is a major focus of their academic work.

The senior thesis, the capstone experience of the environmental studies major, may be a research project, a service project, or a creative arts project. For all these, the written thesis must include an extensive literature review that situates the work in the appropriate bodies of knowledge. In almost all cases, students draw from very different disciplines and from interdisciplinary fields to research and write this review. Given the broad-ranging nature of these theses, students must find, evaluate, and integrate material from a wide range of academic disciplines as well as practitioner and advocacy literature. This task is, of course, similar to what they will experience in their professional lives after graduation. Given the rapidly changing nature of the technologies and institutions that affect the environment, as well as society's evolving understanding of those effects, environmental professionals need to know how to access and critically evaluate historical and emerging information. Our students must demonstrate that capacity in their senior projects. For all these reasons, a strong foundation in information literacy is essential by senior year.

Information Literacy in the Environmental Program at the University of Vermont

Evolution of Information Literacy in the Environmental Studies Curriculum

The relationship between the Environmental Program and the library at the University of Vermont has been shaped over the course of many years, driven essentially by the curricular needs of the environmental studies major, and has evolved purposefully over time. Since the 1980s, the library has been involved in some way in delivering instruction to environmental studies majors. In the late 1980s, single library instruction sessions were taught by the librarian as guest lectures in the intermediate- and advanced-level core courses, and in the early 1990s a library instruction session was added into the introductory-level course. By the mid-1990s a second library instruction session was added to the intermediate-level course, primarily to address the Internet and the use of the Web as a research tool, and to focus broadly on research skills and concepts within the context of the rapidly growing information environment.

In 2000, discussion began with the environmental studies faculty regarding the overwhelming information environment in which our students were now working, the additional challenges they faced as interdisciplinary researchers, and the need to provide even more information literacy training than was already incorporated into the curriculum. This discussion was possible because of the close nature of our working relationship established up to this point.

At this time, a separate one-credit environmental studies course that would focus on environmental information skills in a greater depth than was previously possible was formally proposed to the environmental studies faculty. The environmental studies faculty supported the course as a useful addition to the curriculum, and the course was developed over a summer with the support of a University Center for Teaching and Learning Grant, which was co-submitted by librarian and Environmental Studies Program chair.

In spring 2001, seven environmental studies faculty made the extraordinary decision to take the course themselves as a way to pilot the course and expand their own knowledge of information literacy, given the fast-paced changes in the Internet and library resources. Together in the classroom, through their roles as both faculty and students, the faculty and the librarian adjusted the course to be the best possible fit for the environmental studies curriculum and their students. This cooperative venture not only created a better course but also created unanimous buy-in from the faculty, which was then passed along to their student advisees, and which created a supportive atmosphere from which to launch the independent information literacy course. In fall 2001, the librarian offered the course for the first time to students, as an elective that had to be taken concurrently with either the intermediate-level or advanced-level core course.

The incorporation of this course into the environmental studies curriculum represented an important turning point in the evolution of the relationship between the library and the Environmental Program. Through the process of proposing and teaching this course, the librarian became a member of the environmental studies faculty and started attending department meetings, retreats, and other functions. These changes collectively represented another level of faculty-librarian relationship in which the librarian was starting to be considered a core faculty member in the Environmental Program. This close working relationship, in which we recognize each other's complementary and important roles, has enabled the continual evolution in providing information literacy training in the best possible manner to our students.

By fall 2003, the separate credit-bearing Environmental Information Skills course had been taught to environmental studies majors for five consecutive semesters, garnering much positive student feedback. However, it was an elective course that was limited to fifteen students per semester. We began to feel that all environmental studies majors should have equally intensive information literacy instruction. At the same time, program discussions surrounding the restructuring of the intermediate- and advanced-level core courses were beginning, which presented an opportunity to consider directly incorporating the content of the separate course more intensively into these two core courses.

Information Literacy as Part of the Core Curriculum

Throughout the spring 2004 semester, environmental studies faculty members were engaged in discussions regarding changes in the curriculum of the intermediate- and advanced-level core courses. The librarian attended these meetings as part of the faculty and at this time proposed the elimination of the separate Environmental Information Skills course in order to incorporate the course contents directly into the two core courses under discussion. This would provide all environmental studies majors with the same level of intensive information literacy training, purposefully and progressively incorporated into the curriculum. This proposed model, which garnered unanimous support from the faculty, was predicated on the partnership of the librarian and the course faculty to cooperatively create a structure in which to best deliver the course material. A subcommittee, composed of two environmental studies faculty and the librarian, was formed to focus on the curriculum restructuring. As a result, changes in the content of the intermediate-level core course (ENVS 151) included taking away one large research paper assignment, adding more skills-based small assignments, and incorporating the information literacy skills instruction in a more systematic way. The latter was achieved through cooperative planning and implementation of this section of the course by course faculty and librarian. Information literacy skills instruction in this course is now integrated with course assignments to achieve multiple goals.

Changes in the advanced-level research methods course (ENVS 201) included incorporating into the course most of the content of the separate course, Environmental Information Skills, which necessitated removing some less important elements of the course; moving the librarian into the role of co-instructor for this course, teaching six sessions of it; focusing on skills training in a workshop environment in which students use their own thesis topics as a framework for understanding concepts and resources; and incorporating information literacy assignments into the course while discontinuing some other assignments. These required workshop-type classes are taught during regular class time as a core component of the Research Methods class.

Intermediate Course (ENVS 151)

In fall 2004, we began implementing the curricular changes in the intermediate and advanced core courses. In preparation for these changes, discussion between the library and course instructors focused on indentifying information literacy outcomes expected as a result of the delivery of the librarian's content, developing a pre-test to gauge students' existing knowledge of specific information literacy concepts, developing a post-test to function as an assessment tool and to reiterate the importance of material covered, and planning follow-through by the course faculty to reinforce information literacy concepts throughout the duration of the semester. Although the librarian continued to teach two sessions in this class, the same as had previously been taught, these sessions, as a result of a different more collaborative partnership-based approach, were now part of a continuum that made more sense in the greater context of the course.

The delivery of the information literacy instruction in this course is based on a number of learning outcomes defined as important by both the librarian and the course instructors. By the end of the librarian's sessions and the resultant assessments and follow-through by the course faculty, the students are expected to

1. better understand the nature and extent of the information environment in which we are working;
2. understand research as a process;
3. know how to evaluate a source for its relevance, quality, and usefulness;
4. understand what a scholarly journal article is and its importance as a body of literature;
5. have a better understanding of the range of resources available to access different types of information;
6. know more about some basic searching rules to design effective searches;
7. develop an understanding of the additional information challenges posed by the interdisciplinary nature of environmental issues and problems; and
8. know what elements get included in a bibliographic citation.

In addition to the pre-test, instruction, and post-test, the course instructors do substantial follow-through in reiterating specific concepts during the course of the semester, teaching correct citation style in a comprehensive manner and providing much feedback to students through a career paper assignment that is done in stages to reflect the research process. The librarian is also available for individual consultations throughout the semester for students who feel they need additional assistance.

Advanced Course (ENVS 201)

ENVS 201, Research Methods, is the advanced class that comes at the point in the curriculum where students begin focusing on their senior thesis. In this class, as a culmination of the course students develop a thesis proposal that includes a substantive literature review that necessarily spans multiple disciplines. Building on the information literacy concepts and outcomes from the intermediate-level class, ENVS 151, the purpose of the information literacy component in ENVS 201 is to introduce a few new advanced research skills and concepts, such as cited-reference searching, and to methodically apply the information literacy concepts discussed in the intermediate-level course to conduct research for their thesis literature review.

In order to accommodate this in an intensive manner, the librarian has been given the title of research co-instructor for the Research Methods course and meets with the students six times during the beginning half of the semester. These sessions are framed as workshops; and through a series of guided short exercises in which students define and refine their topics, access and retrieve a wide range of resources, and critically evaluate the resources they find for relevance, quality, and usefulness, they build a growing bibliography for their literature review.

The intensive integration of this advanced level of information literacy training into the final core course in the environmental studies major has required a close collaborative partnership between the librarian and the faculty teaching this course. When ENVS 201 was restructured to include the librarian as a co-instructor with responsibilities for teaching, creating, and grading assignments, the course syllabus was collaboratively overhauled. The main course instructors and the librarian had multiple meetings, during which the syllabus was redesigned, assignment details were created, due dates were set, and details of co-teaching the course were discussed. Because of this close working relationship that builds progressively through the core courses of the major, both the students and the faculty consider the librarian a core member of the environmental studies faculty.

General Observations

As we are entering our fourth consecutive semester of this approach to the curriculum's core courses, we feel that this model has been successful. However, while we think that what we are doing makes best sense at this time, we constantly communicate about what has worked and what has not, we solicit and rely on student feedback, and we therefore never do things exactly the same from semester to semester. Because of the strong relationship between the library and the Environmental Program, there is a uniform sense that the two entities are inextricably linked, and this has served everyone well. Student comments are formally solicited through detailed evaluation forms and discussions within the context of each of the core courses, and recent student comments about the relationship between the Environmental Program and the library include these: "The classes offered through the Environmental Program have helped me tremendously in conducting research efficiently and substantially." "I honestly think that without the information sessions I would not be able to complete my thesis. I also feel it puts me at an advantage over students with other majors." (personal communication, spring 2005).

Information Literacy Assessment in the Environmental Studies Curriculum

Intermediate Course

In the intermediate-level environmental studies core course, multiple assessment tools and strategies are used, both formal and informal. First, a pre-test, which is a ten-question, open-ended short-answer test that was developed by the librarian with feedback from the subject faculty, is administered to students the week before the librarian's first meeting with them. This test is not graded, but we use the results of the pre-tests to gauge what broad concepts students feel most and least comfortable with. Based on this, the librarian determines the extent that specific concepts will be covered to make the best use of time in the information literacy instruction sessions. In addition, we have observed that a large function of the pre-test is simply as an iterative tool to get students thinking about these concepts and to recognize their importance. In this regard, the pre-test becomes an important teaching and learning tool in and of itself.

After the delivery of the information literacy content by the librarian, the students are given a post-test that is graded, in which they can demonstrate their understanding of the information literacy concepts that were discussed. Thus far, the post-test has been administered in two different forms. The first iteration of the post-test was a formal in-class exam that consisted of multiple choice questions, longer and shorter short-answer questions, and matching questions. The instructors gave students study sheets, which outlined concepts to review. Although the students generally performed well on the test, the overwhelming student feedback suggested that students were ambivalent about taking a formalized exam on information literacy concepts, removed from any other context of the course or of their research. Therefore, the post-test was entirely restructured and is now a graded "Take Home Exercise on Research Skills," and incorporates questions relevant to students' own research topics in the class. This post-test is both more productive and more satisfying to students, provides the context of their own research from which to discuss research and information concepts, and achieves the same purpose of making the point that these information skills are important and can be honed through purposeful assessment. The post-tests are graded by the course instructor and given to the librarian for review and for possible additional comments.

In addition, for the annotated bibliographies due mid-semester and students' final papers, the course instructors carefully review the variety and quality of resources that were used and examine details of students' citation style. Based on this informal and outcomes-based assessment, the course instructors are able to place immediate and sustained value on the information literacy efforts incorporated into this course.

Advanced Course

In the Research Methods course, there are multiple assignments that assess a student's information literacy skills. First, students hand in directly to the librarian an Information Plan. In this assignment, students clearly define their thesis topics and discuss in detail all the steps they will take to conduct research for their Literature Reviews. As part of this assignment, students include a preliminary bibliography of fifteen sources.

The next assignment, an Annotated Bibliography, asks the students to provide complete bibliographic citations and annotations for twenty-five sources. The annotations must not be a summary of the resource's contents, but must include a description of why each resource is relevant to the student's thesis topic, what its unique contribution is to the body of literature on this topic, and why it is deemed to be a high-quality, useful resource. Subsequent assignments include the Literature Review and ultimately the Thesis Proposal, which directly reflect the results of the time spent in the core curriculum on information literacy skills and concepts. At the end of the semester, the librarian and main course instructor discuss the overall quality of the proposals.

The ultimate outcomes-based assessment occurs at the culmination of a student's progression through the Environmental Program through the evaluation of their theses. It has been the observation of the faculty that over the years the quality of student research has increased substantially as a result of the more intensive, collaborative, uniform information literacy training that each environmental studies major receives as part of the core curriculum.

Reflections on the Library–Environmental Program Collaboration

The collaborative partnership that has led to the successful restructuring of two of the four core courses in the environmental studies curriculum, in which intensive information literacy instruction has been progressively infused, has been the result of a variety of factors. First, a strong relationship between the library and the Environmental Program already existed as a result of many years of working together in the context of including library and information literacy instruction in its core courses. The addition of the separate credit-bearing Environmental Information Skills course further solidified this relationship, as the librarian was also considered a member of the environmental studies faculty. What is perhaps most innovative about our partnership is unity of purpose and openness to experimentation among both library and Environmental Program personnel, which helped the curricular changes to be improved and adopted quickly.

Second, the environmental studies major is conducive to this level of information literacy training because of the structure of the curriculum itself. The curriculum requires a substantial piece of original interdisciplinary research from its students in the form of a senior thesis, which has led to the recognition that sophisticated research and information skills are necessary for the successful completion of this capstone requirement. Two of the four core courses, the intermediate-level and advanced-level courses addressed in this chapter, are skills-based rather than content-based courses. Because the focus of these courses is on developing certain skills, the curriculum itself presents a natural space in which to focus on developing information, research, and critical thinking skills.

Third, there has been a high level of institutional support that has enabled the success of this model of full collaborative partnership. The commitment of time that the librarian has put into working with the Environmental Program has been possible only because of the larger support of the Information and Instruction Services Department and the library administration. Building and strengthening relationships between the library and academic departments on campus has been an institutional priority.

As our model of collaborative partnership evolved, we have recognized that there have been additional benefits to our close working relationship. By introducing the librarian in the core courses, students receive a strong message that the material is important, that this is someone who can help with their research questions, that this person is considered a member of the environmental studies faculty, and that this person is readily available to them and understands their major and their topics. This has led to a strong associated program of individual consultations with the librarian as students develop their thesis and other research, and it has also led to the librarian serving as an evaluator for individual student theses. Environmental studies majors are widely known as heavy users of the library.

Conclusion

Based on our experiences, we can make some general observations. Creating successful collaborations between libraries and academic departments is the result of building strong relationships predicated on commitment to common objectives coupled with mutual respect. However, building these relationships can be extremely challenging and happens through sustained efforts over time given certain circumstances. Institutional commitment from respective administrations creates an important supportive environment from which to work. The challenge for librarians is to get to know and understand specific curricular emphases and requirements, and to create relationships with academic departments that allow for ongoing discussion. The challenge for subject faculty is to consider the broad set of skills and competencies they would like their students to graduate with and then discuss how to best address these competencies within the context of their own curriculum.

The interdisciplinary nature of the environmental studies major at the University of Vermont has lent itself very well to incorporation of information literacy skills directly into the curriculum. Interdisciplinary inquiry in higher education is on the rise, and with this interdisciplinary examination of problems and issues comes demonstrated additional information challenges. Therefore, interdisciplinary areas of study, such as environmental studies, women's and gender studies, and area and international studies, may be particularly conducive for implementation of a fully integrative collaborative model of incorporation of information literacy training into these curricula.

References

Baker, Pam, and Renee R. Curry. 2004. "Integrating Information Competence into an Interdisciplinary Major." In *Integrating Information Literacy into the Higher Education Curriculum*. Edited by Rockman and Associates. San Francisco: Jossey-Bass.

Bates, Marcia J. 1996. "Learning about the Information Seeking of Interdisciplinary Scholars and Students." *Library Trends* 45, no. 2: 155–164.

Boyer Commission on Educating Undergraduates in the Research University. 1998. "Reinventing Undergraduate Education: A Blueprint for America's Research Universities." Retrieved March 27, 2006, from naples.cc.sunysb.edu/Pres/boyer.nsf.

Braddock, R. D., J. Fien, and R. Rickson. 1994. "Environmental Studies: Managing the Disciplinary Divide. *The Environmentalist* 15, no. 6: 35–46.

Brewer, Garry D. 1999. "The Challenges of Interdisciplinarity." *Policy Sciences* 32, no. 4: 327–337.

Brewer, Garry D., and Kerstin Lovgren. 1999. "The Theory and Practice of Interdisciplinary Work." *Policy Sciences* 32, no. 4: 315–317.

Brough, Holly. 1994. "The Environment and Academia: A Fragile Accord." *Forum for Applied Research and Public Policy* 9, no. 3: 37–42.

Corcoran, Peter B., and Richard Tchen. 1999. "Assessment of the Professional Needs of Faculty in American College and University Environmental Programs. Melbourne, Victoria: The

Australian Association for Research in Education and the New Zealand Association for Research in Education. Retrieved March 27, 2006, from www.aare.edu.au/99pap/cor99497.htm.

Crawford-Brown, Douglas J. 2005. "Forging a Place for Environmental Studies." *Chronicle of Higher Education* 51 (May 20): 15.

Davis, James R. 1995. *Interdisciplinary Courses and Team Teaching: New Arrangements for Learning.* Phoenix: American Council on Education and Oryx Press.

Five Colleges of Ohio. n.d. "A Proposal for Improving Information Literacy for Environmental Studies Student Researchers." Retrieved March 27, 2006, from www.denison.edu/collaborations/ohio5/grant/development/goland.html.

Foster, Allen. 2005. "A Non-linear Model of Information Seeking Behaviour." *Information Research* 10, no. 2, paper 222. Retrieved March 27, 2006, from InformationR.net/ir/10-2/paper222.html.

Jones, Peter C., J. Quentin Merritt, and Clare Palmer. 1999. "Critical Thinking and Interdisciplinarity in Environmental Higher Education: The Case for Epistemological and Values Awareness." *Journal of Geography in Higher Education* 23, no. 3: 349–357.

Klein, Julie T. 1989. *Interdisciplinarity: History, Theory, and Practice.* Detroit: Wayne State University.

———. 1996. *Crossing Boundaries: Knowledge, Disciplinarities, and Interdisciplinarities.* Charlottesville: UP of Virginia.

———. 2004. "Prospects for Transdisciplinarity." *Futures* 36, no. 4: 515–526.

Kutner, Laurie A. 2000. "Library Instruction in an Interdisciplinary Environmental Studies Program: Challenges, Opportunities, and Reflections." *Issues in Science and Technology Librarianship* 22, no. 28 (Fall). Retrieved March 27, 2006, from www.istl.org/00-fall/article2.html.

Lattuca, Lisa R. 2001. *Creating Interdisciplinarity: Interdisciplinary Research and Teaching among College and University Faculty.* Nashville: Vanderbilt UP.

Lattuca, Lisa R., Lois J. Voigt, and Kimberly Q. Fath. 2004. "Does Interdisciplinarity Promote Learning? Theoretical Support and Researchable Questions." *Review of Higher Education* 28, no. 1: 23–48.

Lele, Sharachchandra, and Richard B. Norgaard. 2005. "Practicing Interdisciplinarity." *Bioscience* 55, no. 11: 967–975.

Maniates, Michael F., and John C. Whissel. 2000. "Environmental Studies: The Sky Is Not Falling." *Bioscience* 50, no. 6: 509–517.

Murphy, Janet. 2003. "Information-Seeking Habits of Environmental Scientists: A Study of Interdisciplinary Scientists at the Environmental Protection Agency in Research Triangle Park, North Carolina." *Issues in Science and Technology Librarianship*, no. 38 (Summer). Retrieved March 27, 2006, from www.istl.org/03-summer/refereed.html.

Searing, Susan E. 1996. "Meeting the Information Needs of Interdisciplinary Scholars: Issues for Administrators of Large University Libraries." *Library Trends* 45, no. 2: 315–342.

Spanner, Don. 2001. "Border Crossings: Understanding the Cultural and Informational Dilemmas of Interdisciplinary Scholars." *Journal of Academic Librarianship* 27, no. 5: 352–360.

Westbrook, Lynn. 1999. *Interdisciplinary Information Seeking in Women's Studies.* Jefferson, NC: McFarland.

———. 2003. "Information Needs and Experiences of Scholars in Women's Studies: Problems and Solutions." *College and Research Libraries* 64, no. 3: 192–209.

Part III
Technology and Information Literacy
Collaboration: Creating Links
through the Web, Video, Wireless,
and Blogging

Technology continues to influence teaching and learning environments in the library, the classroom, and online. Levels of access to technology resources vary across institutions, but most instructors make an effort to incorporate some aspect of computer and Web-based learning in the curriculum. Instruction librarians are faced with ongoing transformations in the physical and virtual dimensions of the library that impact how students access and understand information. Faculty members continue to see changes in the classroom through presentation media and the student use of laptops and mobile devices. Librarians and faculty have numerous choices for exploring novel teaching practices based on library Web sites and databases, course management systems (such as WebCT), and Web logs (blogs).

Problems may arise if some instructors feel more skilled with technology than others, or if they consider themselves somewhat less skilled than their students. This creates obstacles in how to effectively integrate technology instruction in an information literacy course or program. Librarians may be more knowledgeable about the latest updates to the library Web site and databases than the faculty member. At the same time, the course instructor may be well versed in software applications to facilitate assignments in digital imaging or Web development. At some institutions, the library is at the center of such activities, providing support for student explorations with the Web and multimedia, while other schools divide these resources in separate information technology units.

While technology itself presents barriers to effective communication, it also has the potential to enhance collaborative opportunities among instructors and students. In the three chapters that close this book, technology is a means for communication and learning that supports the information literacy goals of the faculty and librarian partnerships. These chapters do not simply provide insights on how to teach with technology, but rather how to incorporate technology instruction in information literacy efforts to advance critical thinking, evaluation, writing, public speaking, student-centered teamwork, and reflection.

One of the significant contributions information literacy makes to student learning is to challenge students' assumptions about the reliability of information on the Web. Lijuan Xu and Tim Silvestri from Lafayette College of Pennsylvania developed a research assignment in a first-year seminar focused on multicultural education that required students to move beyond the Web as a primary source of information. Through this process students gained insights about how to evaluate Web information effectively. They also gained practical skills in using library resources to conduct scholarly research.

Xu and Silvestri encouraged their first-year students to re-imagine the Web as a useful but limited resource through the lens of critical thinking. In the chapter that follows, Marjorie Ginsberg and Nancy J. Weiner from William Patterson University of New Jersey focus the camera on students to engage them in writing and oral presentation. This librarian-and-faculty team utilized video performance to inspire developmental learners to combine a complex set of information literacy skills. The instructors implemented an inventive approach to teaching and learning that required students to investigate meaningful topics and prepare for debates with peers that were captured by video.

In the closing chapter, we, the editors of this book, Thomas P. Mackey and Trudi E. Jacobson, collaborate with Deborah Bernnard, a colleague at the University at Albany, SUNY. We discuss our combined efforts to advance student-centered teamwork and critical reflection in an information science course that meets a university-wide general education requirement. The unique format of this class requires students to produce digital information through Web design, digital imaging, and blogging. We worked as teams to develop specialized classes that prepare students to evaluate a range of sources and to better understand the use of government documents for research.

Some key strategies to incorporate in effective technology-related collaborations, based on the chapters in this section, include these:

- Challenge student assumptions and expectations about the technologies they may be most familiar with, such as the Web.
- Incorporate opportunities for collaborative problem-solving among peer groups.
- Motivate students through fully engaged and enthusiastic collaborations between librarians and faculty.
- Utilize pop culture references to engage students in entertaining activities that promote critical thinking and collaboration.
- Think beyond the Web and consider video and interactive technology as a means to advance writing, research, and presentation skills.
- Seek out campus partnerships to effectively utilize technology resources for teaching.
- Stay current and incorporate emerging technologies in lesson plans and assignments.
- Consider the collaborative opportunities in Web design and blogging.
- Encourage students to bring laptops to class and provide opportunities for them to use wireless access to the Web in a meaningful way.

Although many of these techniques were implemented in specialized curricula, ranging from a first-year seminar, to a basic skills class, to an information science course, these approaches are scalable to different settings. These ideas will motivate librarian and faculty teams to maximize the benefits of technology instruction in support of information literacy goals and objectives.

12

Librarian and Faculty Collaborations in First-Year Programs: Re-imagining the Web in Student Research

Lijuan Xu, Library Instruction Coordinator, Skillman Library
Tim Silvestri, FYS Adjunct Faculty, Psychologist, Counseling Center
Lafayette College

First-year experience (FYE) or first-year seminar (FYS) courses are a key component for information literacy (IL) education among American colleges and universities. The FYE or FYS format of relatively small classes focused on critical thinking and writing skills makes it an ideal arena for IL enhancement. At Lafayette College, librarians work with FYS faculty each fall to teach first-year students basic IL skills. Most of our first-year students attend IL sessions through the program. But how effective are these sessions in improving students' IL skills? Are faculty pleased with the outcome? We believe that enhancing students' intrinsic motivation and librarian-faculty collaboration are central to the desirable IL outcomes and the success of any IL program. This chapter describes one approach used in a FYS course at Lafayette and several underlying principles that aided in the creation and delivery of this approach.

Information Literacy Instruction and First-Year Students

Several recent studies show that college and university faculty have high expectations for incoming students' information literacy skills, yet the faculty also demonstrate significant disappointment, estimating that two-thirds of first-year students cannot accomplish these key skills adequately (Fitzgerald, 2004). Most students "lack the critical-thinking skills and database-searching proficiency necessary for them to fine-tune their information searches" (Jacobson and Mark, 2000: 256). Such estimations and the importance placed on information literacy lead to pedagogical interventions to teach those skills. Many institutions are integrating information literacy into their first-year courses.

Jacobson and Mark suggest four common models for providing IL instruction to first-year students:

- Course-related instruction: built into courses such as English composition, it is the most popular form, but not necessarily effective, since librarians often only have one session with the students
- Web-based instruction: using online, interactive, and self-paced tutorials in the place of a library class or as a complement to the class

- Credit courses: taught by librarians as part of the general education program
- Library instruction in first-year experience (FYE) or first-year seminar (FYS) classes (2000: 258–62)

FYE or FYS classes are relatively small and often focused on critical thinking and writing skills. The format and the widespread existence of these courses in higher education make the program an ideal arena for teaching information literacy concepts (National Resource Center, 2004). Among the institutions Boff and Johnson surveyed, 315 (86%) include a library component in their FYE courses, and among those, 210 (67%) require the library component (2002: 282).

Although FYEs or FYSs are excellent venues to teach first-year students basic information literacy skills (Boff and Johnson, 2002: 277), librarians and faculty likewise have witnessed students' lack of engagement and motivation with what is presented in those classes and to learning IL skills. Several factors inhibit students' motivation to learn.

First, students' developmental level as novice academicians is a critical but overlooked issue related to undergraduate research habits. Both Jones (2002) and Thompson (2003) present a collective concern among academics regarding students' overuse of the Web when conducting academic research. We submit that the problem is not that they *start* with the Web, but that they *stop* with the Web. Faculty and librarians may promote a more reasonable use of the Web: for example, using the Web to improve basic knowledge in novel content areas, but subsequently engaging students in more sophisticated research with peer-reviewed journal articles that offer more in-depth information than the Web. This kind of approach may produce better outcomes by starting at students' current developmental level and then moving them forward.

Second, students possess inflated levels of IL self-efficacy, defined as the belief in one's ability to successfully complete a task (Bandura, 1997: 3). According to the Online Computer Library Center (OCLC) survey, although most students start with search engines to look for information for their assignment and rate themselves successful at finding information, the majority of them lack basic IL skills such as the ability to discern the effect advertising has on the information of the Web site (2002: 3–4). Geffert and Christensen's study further illustrates that among first-year students, there is "little relationship between self-confidence and knowledge of several basic library concepts" (1998: 283). Such overconfidence "creates a barrier between what they really know and what they could learn to sharpen their skills" (Macklin, 2001: 306). One such barrier is the lack of internal or intrinsic interest in developing IL skills. Seeking and conquering challenges as well as the value and importance of learning something are at the core of students' intrinsic motivation (Biggs, 1999: 56; Raffini, 1993: 65). If students think they already possess the skills that we try to teach in IL sessions, it is no wonder they are bored. Hence, students' inflated self-efficacy and low intrinsic motivation may contribute to their disengagement from library-led IL sessions that are often the foundations of IL skill development. The inflated self-efficacy of their research skills must be addressed to increase students' intrinsic interest and level of engagement in IL classes.

Third, students and faculty share a primary concern about the accuracy of the information retrieved from the Web, but only 4 percent of students believe the quality of the information is not good enough for their assignments (OCLC, 2002). It is unclear whether student misperceptions about their assignments arise from unclear faculty expectations or lack of experience on the part of the student. Either way, we believe that faculty expectations and the values they place on IL sessions bear a significant amount of the burden for poor IL outcomes. Furthermore, faculty engagement needs to extend beyond their roles in the classroom through active collaborations with librarians. Faculty can build in extrinsic factors such as grades to motivate students and to help them become engaged in IL sessions. As Jacobson and Xu point out, "When educators motivate students extrinsically, they drive students to learn, because of their desire to obtain rewards or to avoid punishment" (2004: 3). Librarians are often viewed as guest lecturers by students and typically do not have the same leverage as do faculty. Hence, overreliance on librarians and library instruction for enhancing students' IL skills may be a critical error that professors make. According to Thompson, "If college students are being seduced by the instant access to and seemingly endless supply of information on the Web, faculty need to get involved to counteract the power of the Internet" (2003: 264). Perhaps the most readily available tool faculty can use is to make some portion of the final grade dependent on the quality and relevance of sources cited in papers.

First-Year Seminar Program at Lafayette

Lafayette College is a liberal arts college with an enrollment of 2,100 full-time students. At Lafayette, all incoming first-year students are required to take a FYS course during the fall semester. Like many first-year programs, Lafayette's FYS course is writing intensive and is designed to introduce students to the college's intellectual life by

- providing students with strategies for interpretation and evaluation,
- challenging students' assumptions and biases,
- encouraging the building of informed personal perspectives,
- introducing students to the conventions of academic writing,
- encouraging intellectual communities among students and faculty, and
- developing research-oriented skills. (Lafayette College, 2005)

Initiated in 1992, the FYS program currently includes thirty-nine FYS courses on campus. Each seminar focuses on a specific topic. Limited to sixteen students each, the seminars introduce students to campus intellectual life in an intensive and engaged manner. Drawing upon expertise and resources from departments across the campus, the FYS teaching team includes full-time professors and administrative staff.

The college libraries and librarians have been actively involved in the program since its inception. To concentrate on the FYS courses and to avoid repetition, the first-year students' library orientation program was cancelled in 1993. A library liaison is assigned to each FYS course to work with the faculty instructor to teach basic information literacy skills. Generally, two sessions are held:

1. Introduction to libraries, during which students learn

    a. How to navigate the library's Web site;
    b. How to use the library catalog and a basic periodical index (*Expanded Academic ASAP*);

c. How to physically locate books and articles in the two libraries and via inter-library loan;

d. That the librarians are available for assistance.

2. Using the Web, whose objectives include

a. The nature of the Web;

b. How to evaluate Web sites for authority, accuracy, currency, and usability;

c. How to cite Web documents. (Lafayette College Libraries, 2002)

Additional sessions are available based on students' needs.

Multicultural Competence

FYS 062, Essentials for Multicultural Competence, is a course that explores issues pertaining to race and class and helps to raise students' multicultural knowledge and awareness. Tim Silvestri, a psychologist in the Counseling Center, developed the course in fall 2002. Each fall, students come to the library for two ninety-minute sessions.

Our collaboration first occurred in 2004 and again in fall 2005. In his previous FYS classes, the professor had witnessed what he considered very informative library sessions; however, he was concerned about their limited impact on his students' work: instead of library resources, students still used mostly Web materials for their research papers, including sites that were not appropriate.

Why did students ignore high-quality library resources and fall back on the Web for research? Why were they not learning as much as we hoped? What could we do to successfully connect students with the library resources and to make the library sessions more effective? These were among the many questions we discussed during our meetings in summer 2004. After a series of discussions, we decided to try something different:

- Focus the first library session on using the Web (and its limits as a research tool) before introducing students to basic library resources in a second session
- Assign homework that would provide the basis for class discussion and exercises
- Ask students to critique sources used in their peers' bibliographies
- Require students to meet with the librarian about their bibliographies in the middle of the semester
- Ask for multiple drafts of the research paper to allow critical and ongoing feedback

Research Assignment

When we first collaborated in 2004, the research paper assignment was about a historical figure who had made important multicultural contributions to his or her era. Students had to write about what message the person tried to convey, the cultural barriers that existed at that time, and how the individual might view today's society. No source requirement was specified. In their final bibliographies, we were pleased to see, students did not use many Web sites and those used were of good quality, but what was lacking from the bibliographies were journal articles. This was also evident during the librarian's meetings with individual students. When asked about their reasons, students said that finding articles was difficult and the multi-step process was simply too confusing. Our experience in 2004 prompted changes in 2005. The assignment was revised to mesh more closely with the library sessions and to teach students to distinguish types of sources and their value. The revision also represented the process of starting with the basic introductory sources such as the Web and then moving on to more substantive information for the body of the research paper:

- Section 1: provide a brief overview of the person and the sociopolitical climate he or she was seeking to create changes within. To do so you will utilize reference sources such as encyclopedias, handbooks, and online references such as online encyclopedia and handbooks.
- Section 2: define and explore in depth the person's message. To answer this question you will have to research the person with some depth. You will be expected to go beyond the generic symbolism that may be attached to this person in order to understand more fully the real complexities. To do so you will utilize books, journal articles, and scholarly Web sites.
- Section 3: using primary sources such as newspaper and other reporting media sources about an actual event your individual participated in, provide an example of how your individual sought to create change as per the message outlines in section 1.
- Section 4: using peer-reviewed journal articles, what do current scholars suggest are the best practices to address your person's original concerns highlighted in section 2?

Each section required a separate bibliography. A rubric was developed to grade students' final bibliographies, which was worth eight points toward the final grade.

Based on this assignment description, we will describe several highlights from our experience in 2005: using the first library session and peer critique exercise to challenge students' research habits and to address the limits of the Web as a research tool; using the second session to teach students more advanced research skills with regard to quality library resources and database proficiency; and building in bibliography consultations with the librarian to help students to further develop their IL skills.

Peer Critique Exercise: The Web and Its Limits as a Research Tool

At the start of the session we asked the following questions:

- If you are searching on the Internet for information on *Chief Joseph*, how will you enter your search terms?
- Is there a way to limit the search results to college and university Web sites (.edu)? How?

After the reflection, the students discussed strategies that they could employ to enhance and refine Internet search results. Students were then paired for the peer critique exercise to review Web sites their classmates had used for their draft bibliographies. We asked students to evaluate each site based on the following criteria:

- **Host:** Who is the sponsor for the page?
- **Author:** Who created it? What are their credentials? Do they have the expertise to write on the topic?
- **Purpose:** Why did the author(s) create the page?
- **Accuracy:** How accurate is the information? Can it be verified in other sources?
- **Evaluation:** Would you use this page for your paper? Why or why not?

To prepare for this exercise, we asked students to compile bibliographies of five sources on their chosen research paper topic. The bibliographies were submitted a week prior to the library session. As anticipated, students used mostly Web sites as their sources. From these sources, we selected eight representative sites for the students to evaluate during the class. They were also required to evaluate two assigned Web sites on Martin Luther King Jr. before the class.

Before students started the exercise, the professor cautioned that most of the Web sources they had used in their draft bibliographies were not acceptable and that he expected to see much better sources in their final bibliographies. His comments contradicted students' beliefs in their own research skills and made them curious about learning. In other words, the professor capitalized on both the learning and the motivational opportunities that existed. Students' inflated self-efficacy was challenged, extrinsic motivators were offered, and intrinsic motivators were supported.

Prior to their arrival at college, most students have used the Internet for school research and received endorsement from their teachers (Seamans, 2002: 115). When they enter college, they arrive with the same expectation about research and rely on the information-seeking habits formed earlier (Jones, 2002: 13). The peer critique exercise was designed to challenge students' perceptions about their own research habits. It helped them to realize that college-level work required a more sophisticated set of skills than what they were previously exposed to. The exercise captured students' attention right away, since it contradicted their past experience and their belief in their own abilities. As Raffini suggests, "Students possess a natural inquisitiveness about activities and situations that are novel or inconsistent with their experiences or expectations"; furthermore, "such events provoke their curiosity and incite students' interests in resolving inconsistencies" (1993: 70). Using sites from their own bibliographies made the exercise personally relevant to the students and therefore engaged them in meaningful thinking. Following the professor's acknowledgment of the poor performance in the assignment, students realized what they used to do was no longer appropriate for the level of work expected of them, and in order to succeed in this course, they would need to improve their current IL skills. This exercise also gave students a chance to apply the evaluation techniques discussed in class.

The professor and librarian co-teaching approach we employed made our roles in the classroom complement each other and also helped to engage students. While the librarian led the class exercises and discussions, the professor stressed important points and asked students to periodically summarize what they had learned. For the last part of the class, the professor took the lead discussing the scholarly publication process by connecting it to the Web evaluation exercises. The discussion held students' attention, since the professor, the authority figure of the course, was talking and he was describing his own personal experience. It helped to emphasize the librarian's points on Web evaluation and explain further the limits of the Web. It also confronted students' assumption that the Internet resources "have equal credibility with print resources and virtual library databases" (Fitzgerald, 2004: 22) and served as a transition to the ensuing week's class on library resources.

Advanced IL Skills: Library Resources and Database Proficiency

After the peer critique exercise, students were eager to explore resources that could help them strengthen their bibliographies. The second library session was built upon this momentum. To follow the same philosophy as the peer critique exercise as well as to make the class more effective, we surveyed students' library research skills to make them become aware of their skill deficits before introducing them to library resources and database search strategies.

Students were polled on ten multiple-choice questions (see appendix) that were related to the class content. The CPS (Classroom Performance System) or clicker technology we used for the exercise has some similarity to the popular TV show *Who Wants to Be a Millionaire*. During that show the audience members are active participants because they provide immediate responses using instant polling technology. The new CPS technology helped to create excitement in the students. Each of the students had a pad they used to respond to the questions projected on the big screen. The pre-test once again challenged students' self-efficacy. The same test was administered at the end of the class. Results from both tests were tallied and shared with the students. Seeing their own results on display introduced competition in class, and noticing the improvement they had made helped students to feel good about themselves.

After discussing how to search the catalog for books and how to locate them in the library, students were divided into four groups to explore databases pertinent to their research. Each group worked on assigned tasks and taught the rest of the class about what they had discovered. Students then worked on their own research topics. The process of learning a concept and teaching it to the others helps students to understand the topic better and retain important information. It has the effect of enhancing their intrinsic motivation and therefore encourages better learning; in addition, teaching to their needs as researchers increases the relevance of the topics and keeps students interested in learning (Jacobson and Xu, 2004). The exercises were aligned closely with the students' research paper assignment and the sources they were required to include in the bibliographies. During the class, when we went over each resource, we tied it to the research paper assignment to show students how they would be using those resources later on. As Erickson and Strommer point out, "Knowing what they will be expected to do with information presented in class influences how students listen to presentations" (1991: 98). Seeing the connection between what they are learning and what they will do with this knowledge helps to elevate the relevance of the subject to students.

To prepare students for this session, they were assigned to do preliminary database searches to find an article on inter-group bias and read it for their in-class discussion on the same topic. Throughout the session, the professor participated actively to interject his comments and to pose questions. His active involvement in class helped to keep students interested and engaged in learning. A professor's attitude toward the IL sessions has a great impact on students' motivation (Jacobson and Xu, 2004). If faculty think highly of the library sessions, students are likely to follow suit.

Bibliography Consultation Meeting

Each FYS course at Lafayette is assigned a writing associate to help students with their writings. Students meet with the writing associate to go over their drafts and then revise their writings. When the professor and the librarian met to discuss possibilities to achieve better IL outcome for the class, they decided to build in something similar to the writing revision process to help students to improve their research and their bibliographies. This process allowed students to submit multiple drafts of papers and bibliographies and required them to meet with the librarian about their bibliographies. In the middle of the semester, after students had worked on their research projects, they handed them in to the professor for feedback. After he commented on their bibliographies, they then scheduled their meetings with the librarian to discuss their bibliographies. The meetings lasted from fifteen to thirty minutes. Meeting results were shared with the professor, and two points were assigned to a student's final grade for the individual meeting.

When we first tried the bibliography consultation idea in 2004, students did not arrive at the meetings fully prepared. They were expecting the librarian to merely approve or disapprove what they had done with their bibliographies. In 2005, we decided to improve the structure of the meetings. The professor told the students ahead of time that they would be expected to discuss the sources they had used during their meetings with the librarian. During the meeting, the librarian went over the sources for each section of the paper. Students were asked to explain what they were trying to write for that section, why they used a particular source, how each source contributed to their argument, how unique it was in comparison with the other sources in that section, where they looked for sources, and how they did their searches. Problems encountered during their research process were also discussed. Based on the discussion, the librarian followed up with questions and suggestions. Oftentimes, the consultation meetings ended with students' logging into the databases they had used to discuss strategies that they could employ to improve search results and to locate new journal articles beyond those already found in their initial search. Students also learned about new resources that were pertinent to their research. For example, some students had a difficult time locating primary sources on their topic in The Historical New York Times, so during the consultation they were introduced to online digitized collections such as Accessible Archives and American Memory.

The consultation gave the librarian a chance to follow up on students' work and to monitor and critique their research process. It gave students an idea of how they were doing and what progress they were making in terms of research. Knowing this is important to students, since such "feedback about process encourages belief in future success" (Biggs, 1999: 57). Such belief in turn makes students more confident and motivated about learning (Jacobson and Xu, 2004: 8). Furthermore, for students to remember what they learn in class and to be able to apply it later on, they need to practice what they have learned through exercises such as paraphrasing, summarizing, and explaining to others (Erickson and Strommer, 1991). When students explained to the librarian what they did with their bibliographies (e.g., where they looked for information and why they used each source), they were actually reviewing the materials covered in class. The process helped them commit the information to memory.

The meeting supplemented the two library sessions and extended the role of the librarian beyond the classroom walls. Given time constraints and students' varied skills and topics, we obviously could not cover everything in class. Each bibliography meeting served as a third teaching session for the individual student, which allowed the librarian to tailor it to each individual's specific needs. Oftentimes librarians' contact with students ends as soon as the library session is over, and whatever impact the librarian has on students' IL skills is limited to those sessions. Hearn suggests that "increasing the prominence of a librarian within the context of the academic process has the effect of raising the stature of the librarian as educator to the students," thereby "enforcing to the students that the research components in the course were as important as the composition" (2005: 225). Building in the consultation session over the course of the semester raised the profile of the librarian and helped to fully integrate library research into the course. Doing so further conveyed to the students how much the professor valued library research, which in turn affected their attitude and motivation toward learning.

Outcome

Overall, we were pleased with the results of our 2005 collaboration for the FYS course Essentials for Multicultural Competence. We chose to include in the outcome our experiential reactions to participating in this intervention because of the relevance such firsthand data may have for core aspects of IL, such as students' self-efficacy as well as intrinsic and extrinsic motivation to learn IL concepts.

First, we used a rubric (see figure 12.1) to grade the bibliographies from the fifteen students of the fall 2005 class. There were originally sixteen students in the class, but one student did not complete the assignment. Each source was graded on its type as well its quality. We then compared these bibliographies with a random collection of fifteen bibliographies from the 2003 and 2004 classes. At the end of semester, students utilized more than twice as many references in 2005 ($M = 10$) than they had in previous years ($M = 4.8$). Of the references cited, students used a greater number of books (2005 $M = 4$; 2003–04 $M = 2.8$) and peer-reviewed journal articles (2005 $M = 4$; 2003–04 $M = 0$). In 2005, 7 percent of the references were Web sites, as opposed to 2003–04, where 40 percent were Web sites. Those chosen in both 2004 and 2005 were of acceptable level of scholarship, whereas many of the sites students used in 2003 prior to our collaboration effort were of questionable value. In 2005, the reference sources students used were a combination of free online encyclopedias such as *Encarta*, printed encyclopedias, library subscription reference collections such as *Oxford Reference Online*, and subject-specific reference books. Last, they also utilized *New York Times* articles and digitized collections, including Accessible Archives and American Memory.

Second, the professor held an informal feedback session about the library sessions. For the first time in the five years of the class, students voiced two prominent reactions:

Final Bibliography Grading Rubric			
Sections	Criteria		Scores and comments
	Types of sources	Quality of the sources	
Section 1 (2 points)	• Reference sources		
Section 2 (2 points)	• Books • Journal articles • Scholarly Web sites		
Section 3 (2 points)	• Primary sources		
Section 4 (2 points)	• Journal articles		

Figure 12.1   Final Bibliography Grading Rubric

their increased awareness of the pitfalls of using the Web in scholarly research and the strong connection between quality citations and rhetorical power. Most of the students expressed agreement that the use of Web sites was too tedious given the amount of background searching one had to do to judge their accuracy and appropriateness for research. In comparison with previous semesters, there was a drastic change in students' attitudes toward library sessions: they no longer viewed the sessions as a "waste of time" nor did anyone suggest that these sessions were "distractions from the course itself." Instead, they regarded the sessions as "extremely effective in teaching them how to become better researchers."

Third, it was our experience that the program we delivered was more engaging and rewarding for us, the educators. One cannot underscore enough the importance of the educators' satisfaction with the classroom experience, which in turn may help to create a more engaging environment to promote student learning. We perceived the students to be engaged and learning what we were teaching in class. This created greater satisfaction for us. In years past, the professor repeatedly felt disappointment over the students' lack of demonstrable change in IL skills and found himself repeating the same question in reference to the library sessions, "Why am I the only person learning here?" In 2005, however, the professor experienced enormous joy as students were able to demonstrate a theoretical and practical understanding of core IL concepts.

It would be interesting to determine if the students in this experience have advanced IL skills in the future. One idea that we have for future research is to collect and compare the bibliographies students develop for their subsequent introductory courses. We would ask the fifteen students in this course for their bibliographies and also randomly select another group of fifteen first-year students who take the same course. By examining the two sets of bibliographies, we hope we will have a better idea of how much students are able to retain from what they learned in this class and apply it to other research projects and how they are doing in comparison with their peers who did not share the same experience.

Conclusion

Our approach to teaching IL skills was well received by the students in the FYS class Essentials for Multicultural Competence. The primary focus of our approach was to create a learning environment conducive to enhancing students' intrinsic motivation to learn IL skills. We propose three factors that may contribute to students' disengagement in librarian-led IL sessions: students' developmental level, their inflated self-efficacy of their research skills, and faculty's expectation for students. In order for students to become interested in learning, they need to be aware that there is room for improvement as researchers and to see clearly the need for such improvement. Faculty often value the IL outcome, but simply bringing in the class and leaving instruction in the hands of the librarian will have only limited impact. More effort needs to be expended to achieve the desired outcome. Through our collaboration, we redesigned the IL classes, created assignment and exercises, and used various pedagogical interventions to address these issues to help students become engaged learners. We used methods such as the peer critique exercise to alert students of their skill deficits, and we created a multiple-section research assignment to serve as the need and basis for their learning. The professor highlighted the importance of the bibliographies by grading them and built in the librarian's presence through bibliography consultations.

Our collaboration led to a more seamless approach to IL pedagogy as well as positive results in student learning. The preliminary outcome data suggest that students' IL skills were greatly enhanced through participation in the program. We are looking forward to further refining our approach as well as collecting more data to determine the strengths and limitations of our FYS program.

References

Bandura, Albert. 1997. *Self-Efficacy: The Exercise of Control*. New York: Freeman.

Biggs, John. 1999. *Teaching for Quality Learning at University*. Buckingham, England: Society for Research into Higher Education and Open University Press.

Boff, Colleen, and Kristin Johnson. 2002. "The Library and the First-Year Experience Courses: A Nationwide Study." *Reference Services Review* 30, no. 4: 277–287.

Erickson, Bette L., and Diane W. Strommer. 1991. *Teaching College First-Year Students*. San Francisco: Jossey-Bass.

Fitzgerald, Mary A. 2004. "Making the Leap from High School to College: Three New Studies about Information Literacy Skills of First-Year College Students." *Knowledge Quest* 32, no. 4 (March/April): 19–24.

Geffert, Bryn, and Beth Christensen. 1998. "Things They Carry: Attitudes toward, Opinions about, and Knowledge of Libraries and Research among Incoming College Students." *Reference and User Services Quarterly* 37, no. 3 (Spring): 279–289.

Hearn, Michael R. 2005. "Embedding a Librarian in the Classroom: An Intensive Information Literacy Model." *Reference Services Review* 33, no. 2: 219–227.

Jacobson, Trudi E., and Beth L. Mark. 2000. "Separating Wheat from Chaff: Helping First-Year Students Become Information Savvy." *Journal of General Education* 49, no. 4: 256–278.

Jacobson, Trudi E., and Lijuan Xu. 2004. *Motivating Students in Information Literacy Classes*. New York: Neal-Schuman.

Jones, Steve. 2002. "The Internet Goes to College: How Students Are Living in the Future with Today's Technology." Pew Internet and American Life Project. Retrieved November 2, 2005, from www.pewinternet.org/pdfs/PIP_College_Report.pdf.

Lafayette College. 2005. "FYS Guidelines." Retrieved October 31, 2005, from ww2.lafayete.edu/%7Efys/fysuidelines.html.

Lafayette College Libraries. 2002. *Lafayette College Libraries Instruction Program*.

Macklin, Alexius S. 2001. "Integrating Information Literacy Using Problem-Based Learning." *Reference Services Review* 29, no. 4: 306–313.

National Resource Center for the First-Year Experience and Students in Transition. 2004. "Summary of Results from the 2003 National Survey on First-Year Seminars." Retrieved October 31, 2005, from www.sc.edu/fye/research/surveyfindings/surveys/survey03.htm.

Online Computer Library Center (OCLC). 2002. "OCLC White Paper on the Information Habits of College Students: How Academic Librarians Can Influence Students' Web-Based Information Choices." Retrieved November 2, 2005, from www.oclc.org/research/announcements/2002-06-24.htm.

Raffini, James P. 1993. *Winners without Losers: Structures and Strategies for Increasing Student Motivation to Learn*. Boston: Allyn and Bacon.

Seamans, Nancy H. 2002. "Students Perceptions of Information Literacy: Insights for Librarians." *Reference Services Review* 30, no. 2: 112–123.

Thompson, Christen. 2003. "Information Illiterate or Lazy: How College Students Use the Web for Research." *Portal: Libraries and the Academy* 3, no. 2: 259–268.

13

Writing in the Guise of a Persona: Combining Basic Reading, Library Research, and Video Performance

Marjorie Ginsberg, Associate Director of the Basic Skills Program
Nancy J. Weiner, Reference Librarian/Coordinator of User Education
William Paterson University of New Jersey

In an effort to improve the information literacy skills of students on the campus of William Paterson University of New Jersey, the Cheng Library User Education team prepared learning objectives to guide course-related library instruction. A series of library-related competencies adapted from the Association of College and Research Libraries' (ACRL) Information Literacy Competency Standards for Higher Education (2000) were developed and ideas for course-related integration were presented at the Faculty Senate Assessment Committee Forum in spring 2005. Seeking faculty partners to collaborate in the development of student information literacy skills, the Assessment Forum helped showcase the benefits of course-related library instruction while increasing faculty interest in collaboration. However, none of the initial library competencies were specifically geared toward developmental learners, providing, in part, the impetus for collaboration. Marge Ginsberg, associate director of the Basic Skills Program, was one of the first to express an interest in collaborating and met with Nancy Weiner, Cheng Library's coordinator of user education, to create competencies for developmental learners and plan a pilot project with one Basic Reading class.

The pilot project was designed to expose students to the fundamentals of research while helping to improve their reading, writing, and oral presentation skills. What made the pilot project unique was that the student presentations were videotaped, and this was used as a motivating factor for many of the students. The pilot was launched in a very short period of time, primarily because of the inclusion of just one class. Plans for expanding the program to include additional class sections were discussed, and a decision was made to include four Basic Reading classes in the project during the fall 2005 semester.

The topic of stem-cell research was selected by Ginsberg and Weiner, the project coordinators, to expose students to an issue that was somewhat unfamiliar, challenging in terms of vocabulary, and controversial enough to spark debate. Each class was divided into two groups, pro and con, and within each group students took on different personae that would help guide them during the project. Students came to the library for a series of instructional lessons that focused on basic information literacy tasks such as accessing information through library databases, evaluating information, utilizing an online dictionary, and preparing bibliographic citations. The library instruction sessions helped students navigate databases and locate two relevant sources of information. After summarizing the selected articles, students were asked to prepare vocabulary lists utilizing an online dictionary. Finally, students were provided with an overview of the Modern Language Association (MLA) citation style they would follow to prepare their final papers.

Students used their information to prepare short (two-page) presentations in the guise of their personae that ranged from clergy members and politicians to scientists and individuals afflicted with diseases, each of whom had a pro or con stance toward stem-cell research. The capstone project consisted of a debate between the opposing sides in each class, using a modified presidential debate format that included students in the role of moderators who were well versed on the topic. The debate was filmed by members of the Instruction and Research Technology (IRT) Department in the campus's state-of-the-art facility, providing students with the opportunity to be videotaped in an actual television studio. The project was completed over a six-week period and the final, edited versions of the segments were burned on DVDs and distributed to all the participating students by the end of the semester.

Related Literature

There is an abundance of literature that discusses the importance of developing information literate students, and research indicates a correlation between student success in college and the ability to use library resources (Bordonaro and Richardson, 2004; Grimes and Charters, 2000; Kuh and Gonyea, 2003). However, there is a lack of attention given to information literacy programs implemented for developmental learners such as those enrolled in Basic Reading and Writing. Only a few discuss collaborative instruction programs that address the needs of undergraduate developmental learners at four-year universities and colleges (D'Angelo, 2001; McDermott, 2005). While only a few articles addressed the needs in terms of library instruction for high-risk developmental learners, a few instruction methods, such as having students work in groups, engaging students through hands-on activities, and focusing more on the facilitation of learning, were identified as successful methods of teaching developmental students (McDermott, 2005).

A number of practical ideas about college reading and learning strategies are discussed by Simpson, Stahl, and Francis (2004), and many of the effective teaching strategies described correlate to the student learning outcomes that were developed for this project. While the majority of the recommendations focus on extant theory and research, ways to apply the techniques within the framework of evolving educational technologies while remaining focused on teaching the fundamental concepts of reading comprehension are discussed throughout. Of particular interest were the recommendations to teach students how to not only read but *think* about multiple sources to foster critical evaluation skills. Another critical component essential to reading comprehension is vocabulary building. The importance of providing students with contextually meaningful approaches to vocabulary building, as opposed to presenting students with word lists to define, is the suggested approach to make this activity more productive and engaging (Simpson, Stahl, and Francis, 2004). Although there is no literature supporting the use of videotaping in the classroom in relation to information literacy instruction, there is support for use of videotaping as an instructional tool, particularly in relation to public speaking (Bourhis and Allen, 1998). There is also evidence to suggest that students learn when they are motivated (DeJong and Eckard, 2005), and we propose that many of the students considered the videotaping to be a motivating factor during the project.

Our School and Our Students

William Paterson University of New Jersey is a comprehensive public institution of higher learning, committed to promoting student success, academic excellence, diversity, and community outreach. Primarily a commuter campus, it draws students from both urban and suburban areas. Many of our students are immigrants, first-generation college students, and minorities. Similar to national trends, some students arrive underprepared for college-level work and are therefore placed in basic skills classes in reading, writing, and mathematics. Approximately 20 percent of incoming students are enrolled in Basic Reading classes in which reading passages from across the curriculum help students identify main ideas and patterns of organization, learn new vocabulary, and develop study and test-taking skills.

Cheng Library has a strong and active User Education Program and provides library-related instruction for about 300 classes during the academic year. While most classes are course- or assignment-related in nature, the difficulty in providing meaningful instruction to first-year students remains a challenge, as does finding ways of introducing library resources to underserved populations. Members of Cheng Library's User Education Committee developed a series of library competencies they deemed appropriate for each class level—first-year through graduation—that incorporated the ACRL's Information Literacy Competency Standards for Higher Education (2000).

As a Middle States institution, William Paterson University is required to show the integration of information literacy into the curriculum by providing evidence such as collaboration between librarians and teaching faculty (Thompson, 2002). Weiner, having worked with many of the first-year seminar classes, felt if students could learn library skills at the outset of their college career, it would help them as they move on to upper-level coursework. Ginsberg, along with the reading instructors, felt the project would be a great motivating factor for reluctant readers. A scaled-down pilot project was carried out in spring 2005 with one of the Basic Reading classes to assess the feasibility of incorporating library instruction within Basic Reading.

For the pilot, students were provided with one library instruction session that focused on accessing and locating information relevant to the topic of stem-cell research that had been selected by Weiner and Ginsberg. The final project would culminate with students participating in a panel discussion that would be videotaped. Students were randomly assigned to a pro or con persona (i.e., clergy member, scientist, or politician) and were required to prepare a short commentary on stem-cell research from the perspective of their persona. Based upon the student presentations and the written assignments submitted by the students, the pilot project was deemed successful. All the stakeholders were pleasantly surprised by the effort and preparation put forth by the students that culminated in the taping of their presentations. The success of the pilot spurred Weiner and Ginsberg to consider expanding the program to include more sections during the fall 2005 semester.

In preparation for expansion, information related to having the presentations taped by professionals on campus (as opposed to Weiner and Ginsberg handling this aspect) was investigated. The costs associated with having the taping handled by professionals on campus (studio set up and take down, camera work, editing, and burning of DVDs) prompted Weiner and Ginsberg to apply for a Provost Incentive Grant. These one-year grants are competitively awarded to new, experimental projects that are intended to have a positive impact on student success and retention. The collaborative project between the library and the Basic Skills Program fit the criteria of the grant. Once it was awarded, planning for the expanded project began in earnest during the summer.

Why Basic Skills Students Need the Library

The reading instructors were very excited about the collaborative library project. The basic skills classes had recently switched from a skill-and-drill text to a reading-across-the-curriculum textbook, and the instructors felt the project would augment the learning occurring in the classroom. Developmental readers often have a limited vocabulary, and this becomes an obstacle for their understanding and retention of material. Requiring the students to create vocabulary lists while reading difficult, unfamiliar scientific material was an important component of the project, and students were introduced to online dictionaries that would facilitate the defining of unfamiliar terms. The instructors also felt this aspect of the project would help students develop a skill that would carry over into their other courses and increase independent word learning.

During the pilot project, students often lifted whole portions from the articles they had found and inserted them into their presentation papers. In addition, many students incorporated words into their presentations that they could not pronounce and probably did not understand. This issue was addressed by now requiring students to summarize, in their own words, the articles they would be using for their presentation papers. Instructors supported this requirement, which would be an essential component of the project protocol. In addition, students would also be required to define and learn the correct pronunciation for unfamiliar terms. Since many of the instructors had students write summaries of the their text's chapters as a way of making sure the students comprehended and integrated the material, requiring the students to perform similar tasks during the project helped reinforce many learning strategies introduced in the classroom.

Two of the reading courses selected were linked with Basic Writing, which required the same students to attend both classes. The writing instructors were eager to work with the project and help the students through various drafts of the papers, for this was a persuasive writing assignment not usually required of the Basic Writing classes. Requiring students to follow specific guidelines added another dimension to the assignments.

Basic skills students often arrive at the university with poor oral skills as well as content-area deficiencies. Requiring students to "speak" their roles provided them with the opportunity to overcome their fears about public speaking early in their academic careers and allow them to experience the anxiety and satisfaction often associated with oral presentations. The instructors recognized the value of including a public speaking component, especially since many of their students were reluctant to speak up in class. The instructors stressed that preparation was key to projecting a confident persona, and many of the students spent much time and energy on this aspect of the project.

Planning and Preparation

Weiner and Ginsberg met several times to discuss the details of the project and what the topic should be. The general idea for the project came from a National Association of Developmental Educators (NADE) presentation at the 2005 conference in Albuquerque, New Mexico (Eisenhaur and Dossett, 2005). We wanted to select a topic that was current, important, somewhat controversial, and new to the students that would stretch their capabilities in terms of learning about the unknown. We did not want to use topics such as abortion or drugs or violence, as these issues are usually explored in high school and would be familiar to the students. While we discussed a few potential topics we eventually decided on stem-cell research, since its value was proven by the pilot project. We also decided to have all four sections use the same topic, since this would help streamline the preparation process and allow for comparisons among the four sections.

Meetings were held with the six instructors who would be working on the project—four Basic Reading and two Basic Writing instructors—to solicit input and to establish a timeline for the project that could be incorporated into their syllabi. We brainstormed what library skills would be appropriate for students at this level and discussed possible suggestions as to what were the most important for basic skills students. Although collaboration between librarians and teaching faculty is not unknown to the university, having a librarian move from a tangential role to a more active role represented a new way to work as a team. This collaborative effort was instrumental to the overall success of the project, for it allowed library skills to be more fully integrated into the project. The librarian described library skills appropriate for this level, and together they discussed what research skills the students would need to know and when to teach them.

As a group, it was decided that one of the most important college-level library skills was having students learn how to use library databases for research. Based upon survey responses received from students in first-year seminar classes, many of our students consider themselves experts when searching the Internet using Google, and we wanted to show them there was so much more valuable information available. We wanted the students to become familiar with specialized databases and to be introduced to the concept of scholarly resources. We also wanted them to become familiar with newspapers and basic reference sources that are available in various library databases.

In these preliminary meetings between the librarian and the instructors, it was decided which pieces of student work would be required at the end of the semester. Each student had to submit a project folder that included a vocabulary list and summaries of what they were reading. The instructors valued this approach, since it would provide evidence that students spent time identifying and defining unfamiliar terms. The summaries were developed as a way to build comprehension skills, to help students with paraphrasing, and to help them avoid plagiarism by requiring them to provide their own analysis of the articles. Also included in the folders were the drafts and the final version of the presentation papers written by the students.

We thought it important to ascertain a baseline of student knowledge on the subject of stem-cell research and library skills, so during one meeting with the instructors, we decided to draft a questionnaire on the topic of stem-cell research. Students were required to submit their responses before the project began and again at the conclusion of the project. In this way, we could assess whether knowledge and skills had been learned and integrated.

The questionnaire included the following questions:

1. Do you have any prior knowledge about stem-cell research?
2. List three things you know about stem-cell research.
3. Why do you think stem-cell research is controversial?
4. Do you believe stem-cell research is a

    Personal Issue
    Religious Issue
    Political Issue
    Medical Issue

5. Do you know of anyone famous involved in the area of stem-cell research?
6. If you were looking for additional information, where would you go? Be specific.
7. What is your opinion of stem-cell research?

When we reviewed the pre-project responses, our opinions regarding prior knowledge and research resources were confirmed by the following: 76 percent of the students indicated they had no prior knowledge about the topic of stem-cell research, with 67 percent indicating they had no opinion on the topic. More interesting, but not surprising, is that 70 percent of the students indicated that the Internet, specifically Google and Yahoo! search engines, would be the place to go to find information on the topic. The pre-project questionnaire did establish a baseline of knowledge on the topic that would be used for comparative purposes at the end of the semester.

Before the semester was underway, we scheduled sessions to be held in the library's instruction classroom that is equipped with computers and would allow the students hands-on research time. Each class was scheduled for two sessions, which were scheduled two weeks apart. The students were required to search for material based upon their assigned persona. During the first instruction session, students were provided with an introduction to the university library's Web site and information pertaining to the numerous databases that provided access to full-text material from a variety of sources.

Since most of the students were not familiar with the issue of stem-cell research, it was decided first to introduce students to a source that would provide a basic overview of the topic. Students were shown how to access the Congressional Quarterly Researcher (CQ) database from the library Web site and were introduced to an information source that provided a concise, easily understood overview of stem-cell research. The topical reports that are found in CQ were also helpful in illustrating the pro and con aspects of the assignment. While the students could not substitute CQ for one of their sources, they were encouraged to use this often under-utilized reference source as a way of familiarizing themselves with the topic. In addition, students were encouraged to draw upon the information found in CQ to help them come up with keywords or phrases to use when searching additional databases for information relevant to their topic.

Stressing the importance of using broad, keyword searching when embarking on a research project, students were given the opportunity to explore additional resources and were directed to search in the Lexis/Nexis Academic Universe database. This resource, which was selected specifically for its scope of coverage, provides students with access to more than 5,000 full-text publications and includes many national and regional news sources. The mechanics of searching within a database are different than searching the Internet, which required students to spend time developing search strategies and learning how to navigate this particular database. Students were also briefly instructed in the use of the Academic Search Premier database. Most students were able to locate two sources relevant to their position, and they were able to print them out while in the library. Before the end of the initial library session, the students were reminded to identify any term or word they did not understand.

Instructors then worked on summaries with the students in the following class sessions in an attempt to keep them on schedule and prepared for their next visit to the library. The second library session instructed the students in the use of online dictionaries and included the online versions of the *American Heritage Dictionary of the English Language* and the *Merriam-Webster Dictionary*, as well as the *MedTerms Medical Dictionary*, and students were encouraged to utilize these freely available Web sites. In addition, time was spent discussing the implications of relying on Web sites for information. While Web site evaluation was not the focal point of the project, it became a component during the second library instruction sessions, since many of the students had continued their research outside the classroom and identified organization Web sites that would be useful to their presentations. Providing the students with an introduction to the concept of critically evaluating Web sites was beneficial, and so they were allowed to incorporate information into their presentations, although the Web sites would be an additional source of information and not a substitute for the two required sources.

The remainder of the second library instruction sessions focused on the MLA style of citation that also fostered discussion of issues related to plagiarism and the importance of properly citing information. While the majority of the students were well on their way to completing their assignments, some instructors scheduled subsequent library time in the computer lab without formal instruction to ensure that all the students had ample time to gather their resources.

Back in the Classroom

The instructors now had their work cut out for them. The students needed to go over their summaries, check for new words, and discuss any problems they might be having understanding the material. Class discussions were lively as students argued the pros and cons of the subject. One instructor had her students access Amazon.com and read the excerpt from *My Sister's Keeper*, a novel by Jodi Picoult (2005) about a girl born as a genetic match for her older sister, who had leukemia. The younger sister's umbilical cord was frozen to be used as her sibling needed cells and medical attention. Since the decision to include this book as a point of discussion for students was made after the project was underway, the instructor's decision to direct students to the freely available excerpt was made to expedite their access to the material. It was also felt the novel would be too long to read in class; the chapter was read to introduce students to the moral dimensions of the issue. Instructors also brought in articles from the *New York Times* and New Jersey–based newspapers to illustrate how stem-cell research was very much in the news.

The students then wrote rough drafts of their presentation papers. The sections of Basic Reading that were linked to a Basic Writing class had an advantage here, for the writing instructors had both the time and skills to help students work on the drafts. Once the papers were in their final versions, class time was set aside for rehearsal, and students practiced presenting their papers. Along the way, some of the students decided to come in costume and we had many hospital scrubs, as well as shirts and ties, in evidence. As required by university policy, waivers were signed by each student, giving permission for the institution to film them and use the edited film for conferences and in-house presentations. We wanted the students to look up, take off the baseball caps, and stand tall. While many of the students were up to the challenge, it was not an easy task, and this is evident when viewing their performances.

Lights, Camera, Action!

Before we knew it, the first day of filming was upon us, with each class scheduled to arrive during their regular class meeting times over a two-day period. The filming was held in the Martini Conference Room, a broadcast and teleconference studio that is housed on campus. On the stage, facing the audience, were two podiums. Facing the students on stage was a moderator's desk. It was meant to be a replica of the format for presidential debates. Lights and cameras were everywhere, and the reality of being taped set in for many of the students when it was their turn to approach the podium and have a microphone attached to their clothes. Students came up in pairs—scientists, pro and con; religious leaders, pro and con; politician, pro and con, and so on. They were very nervous, and many of the students seemed overwhelmed by the professional atmosphere they had been thrust into. Producer-Director Patrick Ryan of the IRT Department joked with many of the students and succeeded in easing many of their fears and concerns. As the students relaxed, he told them which camera to look at and what to expect once the cameras started rolling. He practiced the countdown with them, told them not to worry if they made mistakes, and reminded them to look up at the camera during their segments.

Five . . . four . . . three . . . and you are live! The students introduced themselves in their persona and then read their prepared speeches. It was wonderful to see some of the shy students or those who told us they would rather die than go in front of a camera blossom, hold their own, and get into their parts. The intimidation factor in the studio was initially overwhelming (even to those of us in the audience), but the majority of the students seized the moment and successfully defended their assigned stance during the stem-cell research debate.

One of the highlights for each segment occurred when the moderator asked questions of the debaters at the end of their speeches. The speakers had no foreknowledge of the questions, and the responses indicated how well prepared they were. In answering, the students had to exhibit their range of knowledge and understanding of the topic and how their personae would respond to such a question, demonstrating comprehension, synthesis, and critical thinking, a much desired goal. The students did quite well with this portion of the project and spoke with authority. Some of them spoke at great length, showing off their expertise, and everyone in attendance during the taping was impressed.

We also taped short interviews with the students at the end of their segments to allow them to express their opinions about their participation in the project. Their reactions, for the most part, were quite positive and enlightening. Most of the students felt that having a persona to guide their research was beneficial, for it allowed them to draw upon the experiences of others to craft their presentations. Some of the instructors were interviewed and taped as well, and Weiner and Ginsberg did some voice-overs that provided background information about the project. Although the videotaping segment was complete, each student still had to turn in a folder with all the work, including the summaries, vocabulary lists, rough drafts, and the final presentation papers. These would be considered part of the semester's work and graded by the instructors.

Campus Collaboration

While the major collaboration was between the coordinator of the Library User Education Program and the basic skills associate director, the participation of the course instructors for the four classes was essential to the project, as was the involvement of the IRT production staff. Providing the students with the opportunity to experience the workings of a production facility was another benefit, exposing students to an aspect of the university that many were unaware existed.

Selecting the dates for videotaping was challenging, since we soon discovered it would be impossible to tape all four classes in one day. The input of the IRT production team was essential to the project, and working out the logistics of how and when the taping would take place was a priority. Meetings were mutually beneficial; as it turns out, the production team was as excited as we were about the project and offered many creative ideas. It was they who decided on the presidential debate format that proved so very effective. Any questions or concerns we had about the process were answered and explained, and all members of the IRT production team went out of their way to make the students (and us) feel as comfortable as possible during the entire process. What started out as a collaborative project between the library and the Basic Skills Program grew to include the willing, capable members of the IRT production staff that resulted in a professional final product.

Upon Further Review

Our curriculum does not dictate that a research paper is required in the introductory writing course, so students are often first confronted with this challenge in their upper-level major coursework, which presents some problems. Some professors assume that students know how to do sophisticated research (i.e., database, non-Internet research) by the time they have reached upper-level classes, but many students have no idea how to start or where to get help. Thus the inevitable question, "Where can I find journal articles?" is heard often at the reference desk. The majority of library instruction requests on our campus emanate from the College of Humanities and Social Sciences and the College of Education, and whereas many introductory courses are provided with at least one library instruction session, the number of upper-level courses that schedule instruction continues to decline.

Anecdotal evidence indicates that professors do not want to give up class time for library instruction. They seem to think that library instruction and research is being covered in another course. The number of adjuncts, who may not be sophisticated library users themselves, is an area of concern, While we attempt to promote library services and resources to adjunct faculty, many do not take advantage of the full range of services that are available. Without a mandate from departments that would require students to have some type of library instruction, we do not have a systematic method in place that fills this need. The students who do seek assistance from reference librarians are the ones that we know about who allude to the fact that professors expect them to know how to conduct research at this stage of their college career or be able to figure it out on their own. It was such a situation that gave impetus to promoting library literacy initiatives. Now the library's User Education Committee is actively seeking collaborative partnerships from the greater campus community.

Basic Reading students are at an even larger disadvantage, for although they have passed Basic Reading and moved on to upper-level coursework, they often still struggle with the reading material in the course and find the added burden of library work overwhelming. We hope that by acclimating students to research while they are in a Basic Reading class, we will help them become comfortable and confidant library users. Instructors and librarians walked the students through this project, held their hands, and made sure the students were going to be able to do the work on their own in the future.

Weiner noted that she saw students from the project and from the pilot project in the library after the filming, and they continue to be "regulars" in the library. While most of the students Weiner spoke with afterward had initially been reluctant participants, they all seemed grateful for the experience and are no longer terrified of speaking in front of a group. Instilling this sense of accomplishment at this early stage can certainly benefit students in basic skills classes. Based upon feedback, participation in the project seemed to have a positive impact on most of the students.

The writing instructors were pleased with the outcomes as well. It is often difficult to get basic writers to develop a persuasive, argumentative piece because the students would rather write narrative at this stage of their college learning. This assignment offered students a useful structure for research and writing. Students were provided with a defined research focus, a persona from which to write, and the knowledge that their participation in a debate would be videotaped. More important, though, the reading instructors were able to use the stem-cell research project as a way to reinforce the skills they were teaching in their classrooms.

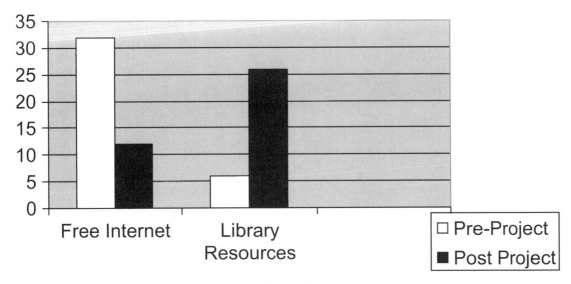

Figure 13.1   Preferred Source to Locate Information

Perspectives and Assessment

Fifty-eight students in four Basic Reading classes were involved in the project. The same questionnaire was administered to all students pre- and post-project, and it was a helpful tool for assessment purposes. When asked pre-project where they would go to find information about stem-cell research, 70 percent of the students said they would go to the Internet.

Many mentioned Google as their search engine. There was a dramatic turnaround on the post-questionnaire. Now 63 percent said they would use the university library and the specialized databases (see figure 13.1). Instead of Google, Lexis/Nexis was frequently mentioned. Students now indicated that the library Web site and databases would be the first place they would check to find information on a topic. One student's comments seem to sum up the overarching sentiments of the classes: "I feel that this project definitely enhanced my college experience because I learned how to research a topic and use citations." If these searching skills are incorporated into the students' learning habits, then they are well on their way to becoming successful college learners.

Eighty-three percent of the students felt they had a good working knowledge of the topic after the project and were able to see the complexities inherent in the debate on stem-cell research. The pre-questionnaire showed that 40 percent of the students felt this was a one-issue subject: medical. By the end of the project, 40 percent saw that the issues were inextricably interwoven and that three or four of the issues on the list (personal, political, religious, and medical) were involved. A student wrote, "I feel that stem-cell research is covered by all of these categories. Personal, because most people have their own opinion about stem cells; political, because politics will either support or deny stem-cell research in order to be elected; religious, because most religions oppose stem-cell research; and medical, because obviously stem cells have to do with the medical

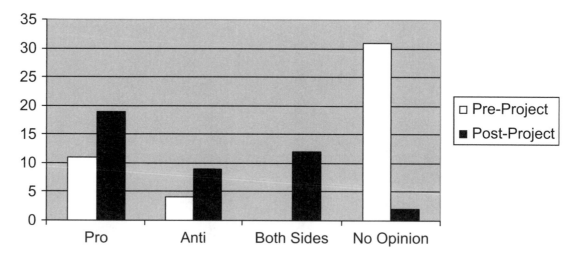

Figure 13.2   Opinion of Stem-Cell Research

field." This response, and the 40 percent who agree with it, is an indication of good critical thinking. Students were able to see that there were many sides to the debate, and the post-questionnaire responses indicate the majority of students had developed opinions on the topic of stem-cell research (see figure 13.2).

The presentation papers, along with the other assignments, were graded by the instructors and became part of the semester assessment. The linked reading and writing instructors were able to do more with the process—rough draft through final version—and so it weighed more heavily for their classes. We were pleased to see that the pass rate in these sections was similar to that of the classes not involved in the project.

The instructors gathered for a post-project debriefing. Ginsberg had prepared a list of questions to start the discussion:

1. Was the project worthwhile?
2. Should we do it again?
3. Are there other ways to prepare the students?
4. Are there other library skills that should be taught?
5. Did the students rely too much on Web-based resources as opposed to library resources?
6. What problems did you encounter?

The instructors were enthusiastic about the project's results. All agreed a similar assignment should become part of the Basic Reading syllabus and repeated every year. The project fostered development of basic information literacy tasks, such as accessing and using information for a specific purpose, and introduced students to essential library resources that would benefit them throughout their academic careers. Structuring the project in incremental steps was helpful for the students. One of the instructors noted that the various deadlines throughout the project helped teach students writing as process. For example, gathering sources, writing summaries that could then be incorporated into the paper, dealing with unfamiliar vocabulary, and submitting multiple drafts at specific times helped the students stay focused. The taping lent a "now or never" sense of urgency to the project that many students need.

The integration of the library instruction within the framework of the classes benefited students, for they could spend time in the library to explore resources with a specific goal in mind and help near at hand. Students used both library resources such as Lexis/Nexis and the Internet and were more discriminating in their Web site selections. One instructor noted that the project made the students use all the skills she was teaching (identifying main ideas, building vocabulary, summarizing, etc.) in a practical, relevant way. The students had a goal and were able to explore and apply the basic reading skills to achieve this goal.

One result that we did not anticipate was the feeling of camaraderie that developed in each of the classes. The students became more comfortable with groupwork, which the instructors found carried over into other parts of the course. Groupwork and team projects are an important part of upper-level college coursework and even after graduation in the workplace, so we were quite pleased that this was one of the outcomes.

While the overall project was successful, it was not without its problems. A few students did not adequately summarize the articles used for preparing their presentations and final papers. This lack of analysis and synthesis resulted in final papers that relied more on direct quotations, rather than on the summation of the information. A few students were absent from class at different critical points, which set them back in terms of research, although only two students did not appear at the taping. The biggest limitation that the reading instructors faced was time. Although we thought the advance planning would circumvent the issue, some of the students had difficulty with the initial writing assignments. One instructor felt she could not adequately work on the writing part or see it through multiple drafts because it would take too much time away from reading instruction.

Our assessment of the project consisted of many activities that encompassed both statistical and anecdotal analyses. We compared the pass rates of the Basic Reading classes involved in the project with the pass rates of the sections that were not involved. They were both 81 percent. We used a pre- and post-questionnaire to measure changes in knowledge, attitude, library usage, and critical thinking. The responses, from both faculty and students, indicate support for this type of project. The DVD became a great tool for stimulating in-house interest and excitement about library collaborative projects and can be used to motivate students and faculty alike.

Conclusion

Technology has made our lives easier, but it has also overwhelmed our students by the sheer amount of information readily available. The structure of information retrieved online is too often taken out of context, and it remains a challenge for students to reconcile what they access online on the free Web as opposed to what is provided by utilizing library subscription resources. Helping students navigate a growing body of resources, while stressing the importance of selection and evaluation of sources, remains a priority, and this project addressed these issues. Even without funding, we plan to incorporate this type of collaborative project into the Basic Reading syllabus. There was so much gained—in reading, writing, and oral presentation skills as well as library skills—that discussions about topics for future collaborations are already underway.

As demonstrated in the presentations and in the final papers, the students succeeded in locating information relevant to their persona's perspective on stem-cell research and were able to incorporate this information into their work. The pro and con aspect of the project also helped develop reading skills because the students had read with their persona's bias in mind. Students found the oral presentation and taping part, though daunting and nerve-racking, good preparation for their other classes. After the project was concluded, some felt they would never be scared or intimidated by talking in front of a group again.

The students' comments about the overall project indicated that the videotaping, the debate-style format, and adopting a persona were critical to the project's success; all can be viewed as helping to motivate the students. In addition to the academic progress and library familiarity, the experience of being taped by professionals was beneficial to student self-esteem. Many of the students were apprehensive and reluctant participants at the outset of the project, but we were pleased to have the initial comments of "I can't" become "I did it!"

Developmental learners, such as those enrolled in Basic Reading classes, represent a segment of undergraduate populations that, as we have discovered, benefit from integrated library instruction. We found that engaging students in research and writing for videotaped debate performances can have a positive impact on the learning outcomes of developmental learners.

References

Association of College and Research Libraries (ACRL). 2000. *Information Literacy Competency Standards for Higher Education*. Chicago: Association of College and Research Libraries. Retrieved January 4, 2006, from www.ala.org/acrl/ilcomstan.html.

Bordonaro, Karen, and Gillian Richardson. 2004. "Scaffolding and Reflection in Course-Integrated Instruction." *Journal of Academic Librarianship* 30, no. 5 (September): 391–401.

Bourhis, John, and Allen, Mike. 1998. "The Role of Videotaped Feedback in the Instruction of Public Speaking: A Quantitative Synthesis of Published Empirical Research." *Communication Research Reports* 15, no. 3 (Summer): 256–261.

D'Angelo, Barbara J. 2001. "Integrating and Assessing Information Competencies in a Gateway Course." *Reference Services Review* 24, no. 4: 282–293.

DeJong, Mark, and Sandra Eckard. 2005. "Faculty and Librarian Cooperation in Designing Course Projects for At-Risk Freshman." *NADE Digest* 1, no. 2 (Fall): 8–13.

Eisenhauer, Beth, and Racann Dossett. 2005. "Beyond the Classroom: Library Research in a Reading Course." Presented at the National Association for Developmental Education 29th Annual Conference, Albuquerque, NM, March 9–13.

Grimes, Paul W., and MaryBeth F. Charters. 2000. "Library Use and the Undergraduate Economics Student." *College Student Journal* 34, no. 4 (December): 557–572.

Kuh, George D., and Robert M. Gonyea. 2003. "The Role of the Academic Library in Promoting Student Engagement in Learning." *College & Research Libraries* 64, no. 4 (July): 256–282.

McDermott, Dona. 2005. "Library Instruction for High-Risk Freshman: Evaluating and Enrichment Program." *Reference Services Review* 33, no. 4: 418–437.

Simpson, Michele L., Norman A. Stahl, and Michelle Anderson Francis. 2004. "Reading and Learning Strategies: Recommendations for the 21st Century." *Journal of Developmental Education* 28, no. 2 (Winter): 2–15.

Thompson, Gary B. (2002). "Information Literacy Accreditation Mandates: What They Mean for Faculty and Librarians." *Library Trends* 51, no. 2 (Fall): 218–241.

14

Promoting Teamwork and Critical Reflection: Collaborative Information Literacy and Technology Instruction

*Thomas P. Mackey, PhD, Assistant Professor, Department of Information
    Studies, College of Computing and Information*
*Trudi E. Jacobson, MLS., Coordinator of User Education Programs,
    University Libraries*
*Deborah Bernnard, MLS., User Education Librarian and Information Science
    Bibliographer*
The University at Albany, State University of New York

This chapter will examine the role of faculty and librarian collaboration in the development of an undergraduate course that integrates information literacy and technology. IST301X, The Information Environment, is a discipline-specific course that combines student-centered Web design with information literacy instruction. Students gain technical skills in how to produce Web information, through Web pages and Web logs (blogs); they also gain critical thinking skills in analyzing and evaluating information from a range of sources in the library and online. This course is offered by the Department of Information Studies in the College of Computing and Information at the University at Albany, SUNY. Although IST301X is taught primarily by a faculty member from Information Studies, ongoing collaboration with teaching librarians at the University Libraries has informed several key aspects of the course. For example, this partnership has led to in-class co-teaching among faculty and librarian teams, student-centered group assignments, the use of wireless laptops during class, the integration of online tutorials, shared plagiarism prevention efforts, and an evolving research paper requirement.

We will examine the planning and implementation of two specific in-class co-teaching opportunities that have changed over time through our collaboration. First, we will describe our efforts to teach students to differentiate between scholarly, popular, and trade sources of information and to apply this knowledge to effectively access and retrieve articles from information science academic journals. This prepares students to conduct academic research for their formal information science research paper requirement and also provides them with the skills to critically evaluate sites for their research-oriented pages. We will describe how we designed this session through dialogue and team teaching and why we believe this particular topic is essential to this course. Second, we will describe another in-class collaboration that introduces students to the theory and practice of government documents. This session also prepares students for their research paper and provides them with a new perspective on the dissemination of government information through specialized databases and the Web. It also prepares students to critically evaluate

Web resources and to think about Web information beyond the limited parameters of search engines and commercial Web sites. This session in particular transformed dramatically through faculty-librarian collaboration. We will describe how we changed this lesson to make it more interactive and student-centered through an in-class experiment with wireless laptops. This approach was modified further based on our own assessment and feedback from students (through their weekly blog postings). It also provided the instructors with a valuable lesson on both the promises and limits of teaching with technology.

Frameworks for Combining Information Literacy and Technology

Information literacy and technology have always been intertwined in the literature. At first there was a particular emphasis on the ways technology is used to deal with a seemingly unmanageable amount of information. For example, the American Library Association's (ALA) "Presidential Committee on Information Literacy: Final Report" (1989), states, "Information is expanding at an unprecedented rate, and enormously rapid strides are being made in the technology for storing, organizing, and accessing the ever growing tidal wave of information." Technology is often discussed as a necessary tool for controlling the flow of information or accessing information through databases, sites, and search engines. For example, in *The Information Literacy Competency Standards for Higher Education* (2000) the Association of College and Research Libraries (ACRL) explored the relationship between information literacy and technology by arguing that "information literacy initiates, sustains, and extends lifelong learning through abilities which may use technologies but are ultimately independent of them." Information literacy is often described as the essential skills needed to understand the content of and contexts for information, regardless of a particular technology format.

Information literacy has had some influence on the development of *information fluency*, although the emphasis of each approach is somewhat different. In *Being Fluent with Information Technology* (1999) the Committee on Information Technology Literacy argued that "information literacy focuses on content and communication: it encompasses authoring, information finding and organization, research, and information analysis, assessment, and evaluation." At the same time, the committee defined information fluency as "a set of intellectual capabilities, conceptual knowledge, and contemporary skills associated with information technology." Central to both terms is the focus on critical thinking and the adaptation to changing technologies, but information fluency emphasizes technology as a key factor in how information is accessed, organized, and produced. For example, information fluency "involves an understanding of information resources and how they are mapped into technological and economic structures, and how these resources interrelate." In today's information environment, the differences between information literacy and information fluency are not as important as the similarities. Technology is a vital dimension to information literacy courses and programs, and some instructors even use the terms interchangeably.

Accrediting agencies such as the Middle States Commission on Higher Education (MSCHE) recognize the inter-relationship among a set of diverse information skills. In

Characteristics of Excellence in Higher Education: Eligibility Requirements and Standards for Accreditation, MSCHE defines the key proficiencies a student should possess after completing the general education requirements of an accredited institution, including "oral and written communication, scientific and quantitative reasoning, technological capabilities appropriate to the discipline, and information literacy, which includes critical analysis and reasoning" (2002: 38). In a separate guidebook for integrating information literacy in the curriculum, MSCHE further emphasizes the need for an integrated approach for students to apply these skills and proposes a number of creative ways for students to actively produce information. As such, information literacy can be a catalyst for "active learning assignments in research, writing, oral presentation, constructions for engineering or the visual arts, performances, service learning, and digital media" (35). This work supports the larger goals of information literacy to prepare students to analyze, evaluate, and synthesize information in a meaningful way.

The focus on specific technologies such as networked computers, multimedia, and the Web has influenced the development of a variety of frameworks for defining literacy in a digital age. For example, Gilster (1997) defines *digital literacy* as "the ability to access networked computer resources and use them" (1). He also defines it as "the ability to understand and use information in multiple formats from a wide range of sources when it is presented via computers" (Gilster, 1997: 1). Gurak (2001) addresses the unique aspects of the Web as a medium for interactivity and communication and argues that *cyberliteracy* "is about taking a critical perspective on a technology that is radically transforming the world" (16). Selber (2004) critiques a basic computer literacy model that focuses on computing skills only and argues for "multiliteracies" based on "three literacy categories" including "functional, critical, rhetorical" (24). Selber (2004) argues that through this framework "teachers should emphasize different kinds of computer literacies and help students become skilled at moving among them in strategic ways" (24). Further, the Center for Media Literacy asserts that *media literacy* "expands the basic concept of literacy (i.e. 'reading' and 'writing') to *all forms of communication*—from television to T-shirts, from billboards to multi-media environments."

Changes in technology are inevitable and have the potential to impact how students apply information literacy competencies. According to Marcum (2002), information literacy has not fully addressed the importance of "technological literacy" (16). He argues that in an effort to separate information literacy from a rudimentary computer literacy, it "has shifted too far and often pays too little heed to the technological factors" (2002: 16). Marcum (2002) calls our attention to the impact of emerging technologies on our understanding of information literacy. He argues that students need to acquire a complex set of skills to communicate effectively in a new media environment that may include "constructing a Web page, navigating the Web, and participating in an online chat group" (2002: 13–14). This suggests that as a practice of lifelong learning, information literacy should prepare students to understand information in a variety of media contexts and that technology is used to access, produce, and communicate information.

As we will see in this case study, Web design is combined with information literacy instruction along with other technologies that reflect a changing information environment such as blogs and wireless laptops. In many ways IST301X is a course that consistently explores the relationship between information literacy and technology and provides an ideal setting for faculty-librarian collaboration. This shared effort among faculty and librarian teams benefits from ongoing dialogue about how to advance teamwork and critical reflection among students.

Information Literacy Collaboration at the University at Albany

In 2000, the University at Albany instituted a new general education requirement. Information literacy was a new required category in this substantive revision to the general education program. Within this structure students have a selection of courses to choose from, including one-credit generic and science information literacy courses offered by librarians and three-credit courses offered by departmental faculty members in a number of disciplines. The range of participating departments is varied and includes Communication, Women's Studies, East Asian Studies, Linguistics, Information Studies, and the first-year experience program Project Renaissance. After years of working toward a broad implementation of information literacy skills instruction, librarians, working with other campus partners (including faculty and administrators), were finally successful in making a significant change to the undergraduate curriculum. Besides teaching credit courses themselves, user education librarians pledged their support to professors teaching information literacy courses in the departments. Through this wide support structure that extends beyond the library, several creative and productive collaborations between faculty and librarian teams emerged, including the partnerships that contribute to IST301X.

Librarians provide the following support options for information literacy course instructors:

1. Information literacy Web site
2. Web-based tutorials on research methods
3. Development of Information Literacy course components
4. Course-related instructional sessions
5. Instructional guides (in print and online)

Librarians produce and maintain an information literacy Web site for faculty members that provides instructional resources for information literacy in general and on campus. It also includes an online form for faculty to register for several information literacy tutorials. These Web-based tutorials (http://library.albany.edu/usered/tut.html) teach students the basics of doing research, including using the online catalog and article databases, evaluating information found on the Internet, and understanding plagiarism. There is also a virtual tour of the University Library. At the end of each of these tutorials, students are able to complete a form, which is recorded in a database. Reports are returned to information literacy course professors who have registered to receive these data (http://library.albany.edu/usered/cours.html).

Librarians also work with faculty members as they develop the information literacy components of their courses. The Information Literacy Subcommittee approves courses that must adhere to a number of criteria, including classroom activities; assignments, coursework, or tutorials; and a research project that requires students to find, evaluate, cite, and use information in a variety of formats. User-education librarians and bibliographers teach course-related sessions to students in discipline-specific departmental courses and provide a number of online and print guides and bibliographies to support student learning.

Faculty-librarian collaboration varies greatly for the different information literacy courses. In one case, for example, the coordinator of User Education Programs reviewed the syllabus for a new course and worked closely with the professor at this early stage. However, the professor is adept at providing the actual instruction and meeting all the required criteria now that the course is being taught and no longer needs assistance from librarians. In another case, the coordinator consulted with a professor during a trial run of the course, when it was found that the information literacy assignments needed much revision. It was only after the glitches were smoothed out that the professor even requested that the Information Literacy Subcommittee review his proposal. Some professors make heavy use of the interactive tutorials and may or may not call on librarians to teach their students key information literacy skills. Course-related instruction sessions, when requested, may be taught by librarians in the User Education Unit or by bibliographers with specializations in the appropriate discipline. Different professors need varying levels of assistance, which can be accommodated by the current model.

While information literacy instruction at the University at Albany is decentralized and highly variable, the structure does make it possible for all students to meet this requirement. Without the availability of these courses in some departments, it would be impossible for librarians to meet the general education information literacy needs of students. There is currently no option for students to test out of this requirement, nor is doing so seen as desirable.

The intent of this approach was to require all students to take their information literacy general education course in either their freshman or sophomore year. However, the system that tracks students' courses is unable to chart compliance this closely, so students in these courses run the gamut from those in their first semester to seniors to the occasional graduate student. Faculty and librarians assess where students are in terms of their information literacy skills and then build on their current level of competency, regardless of their academic status (from first year to senior). The courses themselves, however, are generally lower-level undergraduate ones.

Information Literacy Collaboration in IST301X

IST301X, The Information Environment, is distinctive because it is taught as an upper-level course, and many students who register for it have already completed a lower-level information literacy course in the same major. This presents a unique challenge for the faculty and librarians because they must approach the instruction at a higher level to avoid repetition of the lower-level course and to motivate students in a unique way. Since students in this course may have a range of skills based on prior experience and academic status, a pre- and post-survey is used to measure their familiarity with the information literacy and technology terms explored in the class. This survey helps to determine where the students are at the start of the class and also how they have improved as a class at the end of the semester.

The course instructor for IST301X utilizes most of the available resources offered by the library and works closely with teaching librarians to develop in-class research sessions. Students in this class are required to complete all three Web-based tutorials, including *Researching 101*, *Evaluating Internet Sites 101*, and *Plagiarism 101: How to Write Term Papers without Being Sucked into the Black Hole*. Students receive participation points for completing each tutorial (participation encompasses both in-class and online activities and accounts for 20% of a student's final grade for the course). Students also receive extra credit for completing the University Libraries' Web-based Virtual Tour. The tutorials are extremely useful in supporting instruction for the required research paper, but the tutorial for evaluating Internet sites also supports in-class discussions about evaluating Web sites. It also informs a Web assignment in the course that requires students to produce their own page that critiques a Web site genre (such as news sites, search engines, blogs, or college and university sites). The plagiarism prevention tutorial is critical to the research paper and Web page assignments and supports the larger goals of the course to encourage the ethical use of information and technology.

Disciplinary Framework: Information Science

The undergraduate degree program offered by the Department of Information Studies in the College of Computing and Information provides the ideal context for an information literacy course that also involves Web design and information theory. Students in this program pursue a faculty-initiated BA in interdisciplinary studies with a concentration in information science. This provides an inherently interdisciplinary context for explorations in information literacy, information theory, and information technology. Students complete core requirements in information science, as well as programming, linguistics, statistics, logic, and psychology. Courses offered by the Department of Information Studies include such areas as information access, Web development, Web database programming, information storage and retrieval, networking, hardware, and a senior seminar focused on professional development. Students are also encouraged to take electives offered by the *IT Commons*, which is a listing of courses related to information technology that are available throughout the university. For example, the *IT Commons Course Catalog* features several classes in digital imaging offered by the Art Department, an electronic music course offered by the Music Department, and a film course offered by the Communication Department.

The interdisciplinary nature of the undergraduate degree program is also reflected in the MSIS Program in Information Studies, as well as the PhD Program in Information Science. This larger context is now supported through a recent reorganization that further promotes collaboration among the disciplines. In 2005, the School of Information Science & Policy (SISP) worked with the Department of Computer Science and the PhD Program in Information Science to form the College of Computing and Information (CCI). Faculty from the School of Information Science & Policy (SISP) created the Department of Information Studies within this new framework, transforming the previous format of a professional school to a departmental one (within a larger college). The purpose of this structure is to enable closer alliances among information and computer

Module 1: Web Design and W3C Standards	Module 2 Academic Research and Writing	Module 3: Topics in Information Science and Technology
UNIX HTML	Accessing and Retrieving Information Science Journals	Social Software Human-Computer Interaction
XHMTL Cascading Style Sheets (CSS) File Transfer Protocol (FTP) Mark-up Validation Digital Imaging	Research Paper Planning Developing a Topic Outlining Writing a Thesis Statement Supporting an Argument Plagiarism Prevention Government Documents	Web Usability Web Accessibility Copyright, Fair Use, Intellectual Property Personal Computing, Security Practices Internet Access and the Digital Divide

Figure 14.1   IST301X Course Modules

science that may lead to the further development of the undergraduate and graduate degree programs, as well as potential research opportunities. This process of transformation and reconfiguration illustrates for students ongoing changes in the field and emphasizes the importance of collaborative partnerships among the disciplines.

Case Study: Collaboration through Co-Teaching

This case study will discuss two specific research sessions developed for IST301X in collaboration with teaching librarians and departmental faculty in the Department of Information Studies. In IST301X, The Information Environment, information technology is understood as a means for access, retrieval, and the production of digital information (through text, image, hypertext links, and code). Information literacy provides a context for students to raise critical questions about information sources and to gain critical thinking skills that prepare them to conduct effective academic research in the library and online. Students combine information literacy and information technology to access and produce information in a range of documents, including a formal research paper, weekly blog postings, three individual Web pages (coded in XHTML, CSS, and XML), digital images, and a final collaborative Web site.

As an introduction to the field of information science, this course also explores a range of current topics, including Web usability, Web accessibility, copyright and intellectual property, Internet security, the Digital Divide, human-computer interaction (HCI), and social software (blogging and wikis). The course is organized into three interconnected modules (see figure 14.1).

Accessing and Retrieving Information Science Journals

The session on accessing and retrieving information science journals, which is generally taught about a third of the way through the course during the Academic Research and Writing module, supports the goals of the course to teach students how to conduct academic research for an information science research paper. It also provides students with a critical perspective for evaluating Internet sources and for understanding the importance of content development for the Web.

The class session was planned in advance through discussions between two of the authors—Thomas Mackey, the course instructor, and Trudi Jacobson, the coordinator of User Education Programs. The original meetings took place before the syllabus was created, but it has been portable to every semester with slight modification as discussed through phone conversations and e-mail correspondence. A critical consideration during the initial discussions was the need for student involvement in the session. Because the class is fairly large, ranging from 60 to100 students every semester, and the lecture hall setting is not automatically conducive to student engagement, with fixed seating in rows and the large size of the hall, we began with the premise that students must play an active role. We also wanted to show that we valued students' knowledge, as this is a 300-level course and we sought to involve as well as challenge students. We also knew that students would arrive to class with varying understanding of the topics to be covered in this particular session, and it would be important for those with more sophisticated understanding to be able to contribute their knowledge to the conversation.

Before students actually arrive in class on the day journals are to be discussed, they have been assigned Researching 101, one of the interactive tutorials mentioned earlier. This tutorial teaches students basic concepts related to research methods, such as determining the information needed for a project and searching the online catalog and a research database. We saw this as a valuable supplemental resource for this activity and wanted to build on the basics with a more advanced active-learning approach.

The first part of this class session focuses on types of information sources: magazines, trade publications, and scholarly journals. Rather than a traditional lecture format in which the librarian simply explains the differences, we decided to build upon what students already knew. We developed a worksheet that would elicit student knowledge about this topic and about how to find appropriate articles effectively, which is taught later in the class period (see appendix 14.1).

At the start of class, it is clear that this will be a team-taught session. The librarian is introduced by the faculty member and asks the students to form groups of approximately six people. The two instructors (faculty and librarian) and the teaching assistants give each group a worksheet and copies of two periodicals connected to the field of information science: *Journal of the American Society for Information Science and Technology (JASIST)* and *American Libraries*. The student groups must consider and record on their sheets specific characteristics of these two types of periodicals as well as a popular magazine of their choice. Once they have finished discussing these characteristics and writing a group response, the students are then asked to indicate which of the features they have identified do not apply to full-text articles (such as clues given by use of color, graphics, or advertising). The librarian calls the class back together and asks for volunteers to provide characteristics, first for magazines, then for trade journals, then for scholarly journals. She creates an on-the-spot electronic document based on student responses by recording key concepts in an outline format and projecting this information so that all students can see the list that begins to develop. This is an effective and visual way for teams to report back to the class and to observe a collaborative and critical thinking process taking place. Generally, among the contributions of the various student groups are most of the characteristics that the librarian would have mentioned in a traditional lecture-only format. She fills in any other important features missing from this student-generated list. At the appropriate point, the professor takes a few minutes to discuss the peer review process used by scholarly journals, which might turn into an interactive exchange of ideas between the professor, librarian, and students.

Once the characteristics are gathered and a brief discussion is held to further highlight those that remain pertinent to online journals and full-text articles, students return to their groups. They are then asked to critically evaluate the research process itself based on their prior experience. We ask them to identify one strategy in particular that they considered a failure when trying to find scholarly articles and to contrast this negative experience with one approach that worked extremely well for them. This provides another opportunity for students in each group to learn from one another, at the same time punctuating the class with some comic relief as students relate horror stories about the research process. We have found that this activity keeps students' energy from diminishing at this point in the class and seems to increase their motivation for critically evaluating academic research methods. The librarian asks one member from each group to write his or her responses on the chalkboard. Once this is done, she gives an overview of recurring themes to the whole class and then launches into instruction on how to find and use appropriate databases for the assignment. Whenever possible, she incorporates the students' comments from the board. The class finishes with a demonstration of Ulrich's International Periodicals Directory, so students will have a back-up resource to determine periodical types.

We have facilitated this session every semester since this course was first offered in 2000 and have found it effective every time. Rather than present lecture-based instruction in a large lecture hall, we have managed to transform the space into an active learning environment through a co-teaching strategy that fully involves students in the process.

Introducing Students to Government Documents

The session on government documents also takes place in the second course module, Academic Research and Writing, and involves collaboration between the course instructor and Deborah Bernnard, the information science bibliographer for the University Libraries. We will discuss the rationale for including this instruction in the course and how it transformed from a short lecture-based research session to a co-teaching opportunity that incorporated group work and wireless technology in a full-length class.

Conducting research using government information from primary sources is a component of research with which undergraduate students are often unfamiliar. In undergraduate research and writing students tend to use secondary material that cites government information, but they do not always examine the sources from which that information is obtained. A great deal of government information is now easily accessible on the Internet. This makes government information a preferred resource for students who tend to gravitate toward information that is available full-text online.

The research paper assignment in IST301X requires students to develop a topic that relates in a substantive way to an issue in information science. They are required to use seven different sources, including at least one government document. They are also required to refer to the following: two information science scholarly journal articles, one newspaper article, one professional or academic site, one trade or one popular magazine article, and one chapter from a book. Government sources lend themselves well to information science research because many government entities are currently grappling with issues brought about by technological advances. For example, Congress has introduced bills that seek to address file sharing, censorship, and Internet security. The commerce and defense departments can also be effective sources for information on how government is responding to changes in technology, and the courts are hearing arguments that involve copyright and censorship.

Although this information is readily available, Deborah Bernnard recognized that undergraduates may be mystified about what a government document is and where and how to locate such a document. To address this, she put together a brief PowerPoint presentation to highlight the three branches of the federal government, their unique roles in creating law, and the type of information that each branch generates. She also demonstrates the use of databases, such as LexisNexis Congressional, GPO Monthly catalog, Westlaw Campus, and LexisNexis Academic. Web sites such as GPO Access and Thomas are also covered. Students are given a list of these information resources so that they can later access the resources on their own.

The lecture approach worked up to a point. We knew that students who were interested in the material would be able obtain an overview of what types of government documents are available for their research. However, the original lecture only lasted twenty minutes and students did not have an opportunity for guided practice. It was likely that they would have some difficulty recalling the type of information available from each of the many sources that had been discussed.

After lecturing to students in this fashion for several semesters we decided to devise active learning exercises for fall 2005 that would reinforce the material on locating and evaluating government information. We knew that this aspect of the course could be expanded beyond the brief twenty-minute session and we wanted to model a revision to this instruction based on the success of the active-learning techniques developed for accessing and retrieving information science journals.

Concurrently, the faculty member had been experimenting with how to effectively utilize laptops and wireless access in the lecture hall. Although we do not have an official university policy that requires students to purchase laptops, and the access to a wireless signal on campus is still somewhat limited, the number of students who bring their laptops to class continues to increase. This is especially evident during the first module on Web design, but it also continues throughout the semester. Of course, such easy access to the Web from the lecture hall does raise questions about what students are doing with their laptops, and we have had problems with students using instant messaging software during class or surfing the Web for sites that have no relevance to the course. Rather than prohibit students from using laptops in the lecture hall, however, it seemed that students' willingness to bring their laptops to class presented an opportunity to integrate this technology into the course instruction. It provided a new context for thinking about all the class sessions, beyond those that involved Web design instruction. As we started to talk about revisions to the government documents lecture, we both agreed that the students needed an opportunity to do some hands-on research. This particular class seemed like the ideal opportunity to incorporate wireless access and the students' own laptops into the day's lesson plan.

We first began our revision of this lecture through e-mail, but the substantive redesign of our session took shape during a face-to-face meeting. During this discussion we were able to create a lesson plan that incorporated our desire for a more active classroom as well as our wish for the students to have some practice searching for information. We designed a worksheet for students to complete in groups using one laptop per group (see appendix 14.2). The questions on the worksheet were intended to help students focus on a research topic and select a government information resource and an information science database in which to conduct research on the topic. Students were also asked to use Google and to compare the results from all three search strategies.

The PowerPoint lecture on conducting research using government information was retained to provide students with the necessary background information they needed in the group activity. After the lecture we divided students into groups based on their proximity to a laptop. Although some students brought their laptops to class every day, we made an effort to encourage them to do so for this particular class session. We knew that we would have to share a limited number of laptops among several groups, but we also wanted to have access to as many as possible to decrease the number of students per team. Although several students brought their laptops to class that day, each student group contained approximately seven students, which was a large team for this kind of research activity.

At first we were impressed with the novel revision to our session, but we found that in practice the lesson plan contained several barriers to a successful learning experience. A major obstacle was that the groups were too large for students to work together effectively. We observed many students sitting around confused about what they were supposed to do. Three students per computer would have ensured that each student was fully involved with the exercise, but seven per team did not work. Another barrier was that the worksheet asked too much of the students within the available time. They had to decide upon topics, categorize their topics, create a search strategy, select relevant resources, and run their search through three online resources. This placed too much of a demand on seven people trying to work together in a busy lecture hall. It was clear that our worksheet assignment was too ambitious and would need to be pared down in the future. Several students even wrote about the experience in their weekly blog and obviously shared our disappointment with this experiment. Several commented on the lack of computers for such a large class and others expressed confusion over what they were asked to do.

Although this session did not work as well as we had hoped, the experience did provide us with several useful insights. For example, we observed that students with full access to computers were actively engaged in the exercise. They took on leadership roles to apply the material introduced in the brief lecture and did so during class time. Some of the groups were more effective than others and worked through the difficulties as a team. This provided an opportunity for students to address the technical and content problems and to work together on a solution. In addition, we were not concerned about whether or not students were instant messaging or surfing the Web during class because they were focused on the assignment (even if it was a bit complicated and confusing). Given some of our positive observations about this experiment with wireless technology, we did not give up on the idea completely.

In spring 2006 we revised this session again to clarify the assignment requirements and to include more reasonable expectations for the use of wireless than we did in fall 2005. Rather than center the entire activity on the laptops we offered it as an option for students who happened to have laptops with them that day. We restructured the entire class session. Before the brief lecture that introduces students to government documents, we had students think through the research process by filling out a worksheet that asked them to define their topic, pose a research question, and develop a tentative thesis (see appendix 14.3). This exercise was modeled after one of the assigned readings for the day, a chapter entitled "Planning and Drafting the Paper" from Diana Hacker's *The Bedford Handbook* (1998). In this reading, Hacker (1998) explains that a "thesis will answer the central research question," which is a key concept that we reinforced in class through this active-learning assignment (p. 563). At this point Deborah Bernnard conducted the formal lecture using PowerPoint. After the lecture we asked students to organize themselves into teams based on their research topics. This was an interesting moment in class because it encouraged everyone to engage actively with other students and to seek out teammates based on common research areas. In some ways it also illustrated the research process itself, at first somewhat wide in scope, but through questioning, searching, categorization, and dialogue it became focused and provided a direction for further investigation. Once the teams were identified we asked them to complete a second worksheet, which was a modified version of the assignment from the previous semester (see appendix 14.4).

This worksheet asked students to identify and search only one online resource. Some teams still experienced hands-on searching using wireless laptops but were not required to search multiple resources in order to compare the databases. The assignment itself was much more focused than our first revision. We also provided time for students to demonstrate their search strategies in front of the entire class using the dedicated computer and projection in the lecture hall. This provided everyone with the opportunity to see the search process, regardless of whether or not their team had wireless access.

This approach diminished the exclusive emphasis on the technology and refocused the exercise on the deeper issues related to how students would conceptualize a search based on government information and how they would incorporate these resources in a research paper. The revision also allowed us to organize students into smaller teams, which enhanced their ability to interact and problem-solve. Students who were able to execute a successful search gained confidence in their ability to retrieve relevant information. We also provided an opportunity for critical reflection because the worksheet included a question asking students to analyze their search.

Overall, this most recent revision to the assignment was the most successful because it carefully balanced the application of information literacy and technology in the classroom. It also enabled us to reshape the delivery of library instruction in a large lecture hall, allowing us to move beyond a traditional lecture format. Because laptop computers are becoming ubiquitous among students, we believe it is essential to think about ways to incorporate this technology in the classroom rather than prevent students from utilizing it as an educational resource. This collaborative teaching experience provided us with an opportunity to expand and enhance this session on government document research and to apply technology in a meaningful way.

Assessment as an Ongoing Process

In IST301X, assessment includes both institutional and instructor-based assessment strategies. Each method offers valuable insights about the effectiveness of information literacy instruction in this course. As part of the general education program, this course was involved in a mandated institutional assessment in fall 2004. This procedure provided the instructor with a great deal of input in defining the appropriate assessment tools to measure how this course met the learning objectives of both general education and information literacy. This required an overall assessment of the course as well as an evaluation based on the specific learning outcomes of information literacy. The institutional assessment was a structured process that required the faculty member to complete written reflections before and after the course. For this course, there were many instruments that could have been used, but an analysis of the research paper most clearly addressed the learning objectives for information literacy, which demonstrated the ability of students to

1. locate, evaluate, synthesize, and use information from a variety of sources;
2. understand and use basic research techniques appropriate to the course discipline;
3. understand the various ways in which information is organized and structured;
4. understand the ethical issues involved in accessing and using information. (http://www.albany.edu/gened/cr_infolit.shtml)

The instructor's written reflection argued that all four learning objectives were applied by students in the development of their research papers. For example, students learned how to research a variety of sources and then integrate this information in a cohesive essay. They applied these skills to learn about a discipline-specific topic in the field of information science. In addition, students learned how to organize information through a writing process that involved outlining, drafting, and revising. Further, they learned about information ethics through several plagiarism prevention efforts that included online tutorials, in-class discussions, and a requirement to properly document all their sources using the American Psychological Association (APA)–style guidelines.

The mandated institutional assessment reinforced the importance of the research paper assignment, although it did not fully reflect the intersections between information literacy and technology in this course. For example, in addition to information literacy skills students also gained a critical perspective on how to find and evaluate Web sites and how to locate government information through the Web and library databases. They learned about information organization through the development of several Web pages that required them to learn XHTML, XML, and Cascading Style Sheets (CSS). They also explored the organization of visual information through the juxtaposition of digital images in a Photoshop assignment. Issues related to information ethics were further emphasized during in-class discussions about copyright and through assignments that required students to properly cite sources used for their research-oriented Web pages.

The course-specific assessment allowed us to expand the scope of the mandated procedure to include student response to information technology competencies. This is an instructor-based strategy that takes place every semester and has a more immediate impact on the development of the course than the mandated assessment. The most effective course-specific strategy developed for IST301X is a pre- and post-survey facilitated in WebCT that measures student familiarity with both information literacy and technology terminology. Students respond to questions that address their familiarity with such key technology terms as XHTML, UNIX, and XML. They are also asked to define their familiarity with information literacy terms such as EBSCO, information science scholarly journals, and academic research methods. The multiple-choice responses are based on a five-point Likert scale (ranging from somewhat familiar to extremely familiar). The survey data provide the course instructor with a snapshot of how students define their own awareness of essential information literacy and technology concepts at the start and end of the class. This measure has consistently demonstrated an increase in student familiarity with this terminology, suggesting that this course is effective in enhancing student knowledge of these concepts.

Conclusion

In today's information environment the relationship between information literacy and technology continues to overlap and the two areas affect each other. It would be difficult to imagine an information literacy initiative that did not engage with technology in some way, or an information technology course that did not emphasize the importance of critical thinking, analysis, and evaluation of online information. In IST301X, The Information Environment, the association between information literacy and technology is emphasized through student-centered active-learning assignments that involve research, writing, and Web design. Faculty-librarian collaboration has been instrumental in developing and facilitating teaching that promotes teamwork and critical reflection. This shared effort has taken place within an institutional context that recognizes information literacy in general education and values collaboration among campus partners.

References

American Library Association. 1989. "Presidential Committee on Information Literacy: Final Report." Retrieved April 12, 2006, from http://www.ala.org/ala/acrl/acrlpubs/white papers/presidential.htm.

Association of College and Research Libraries (ACRL). 2000. "Information Literacy Competency Standards for Higher Education." American Library Association Retrieved April 12, 2006, from http://www.ala.org/ala/acrl/acrlstandards/informationliteracycompetency.htm.

Center for Media Literacy. FAQ: Best Practices. *There are several terms—digital literacy, information literacy, technology literacy—which seem related to media literacy. Are there differences?* Retrieved April 12, 2006, from http://www.medialit.org/faq_best.html#terms.

Gilster, Paul. 1997. *Digital Literacy*. New York: Wiley Computer Publishing.

Gurak, Laura J. 2001. *Cyberliteracy: Navigating the Internet with Awareness*. New Haven: Yale University Press.

Hacker, Diana. 1998. *The Bedford Reader*. 5th ed. Boston: Bedford Books.

Marcum, James W. 2002. "Rethinking Information Literacy." *Library Quarterly* 72, no. 1 (January): 1–26.

Middle States Commission on Higher Education (MSCHE). 2002. *Characteristics of Excellence in Higher Education: Eligibility Requirements and Standards for Accreditation*. Philadelphia: MSCHE.

———. 2003. *Developing Research & Communication Skills: Guidelines for Information Literacy in the Curriculum*. Philadelphia: MSCHE.

National Research Council. Committee on Information Technology Literacy. 1999. Being Fluent with Information Technology. Retrieved April 12, 2006, from http://newton.nap.edu/html/beingfluent/index.html.

Selber, Stuart A. 2004. *Multiliteracies for a Digital Age*. Carbondale: Southern Illinois UP.

Appendix 14.1: Research Methods Worksheet: Fall 2005

IST301X: The Information Environment
Prof. Jacobson / Prof. Mackey
Fall 2005
Module 2: Research Methods
20 Participation Points

Part I. Periodical Comparisons

1. As a small group of four students, examine your copy of a scholarly and a trade journal, and think about a popular magazine that you read for fun. Then list several key characteristics for each

Scholarly: ASIST	Trade: American Libraries	Popular:

2. Your review of these materials has been based on the print format. If you access these same articles in an electronic format (for example, through the EBSCO database), what characteristics do you lose?

Part II: Effective Searching for Scholarly Articles (before filling out table, please wait for instructions):

Worst	BEST

After writing several responses in each category, write one of each on the board. After doing so, select one student representative to stay at the front of the room to report your findings.

Participation Credit (up to 20 points)—Please print clearly!!!!

Student Name	E-mail Address

Appendix 14.2: Government Documents and Information Science Journals Worksheet: Fall 2006

IST301X: The Information Environment
Prof. Bernnard / Prof. Mackey
Fall 2005
Government documents and information science journals
20 Participation Points

Divide into research groups

Defining the Topic

1. As a team, create a list that includes each student's research paper topic. Then, categorize this list into several topic areas (based on similar concepts). Highlight two or three topic areas that you want to research.

Choose sources

2. Based on the topic areas you have highlighted in the previous question, identify government document sources to research (refer to the list handed out in class). Also, identify an information science database to find journal articles on the same topic.

Creating Search Strategy

3. Identify one research question you have about each of your selected topics. From that question, identify key search terms.

Conduct Search

4. Using the wireless laptop search your terms using the government document source you identified in question 2. Locate at least one specific government document and write down the name of the source in the table below. Then, locate at least one specific journal article via the information science database you have chosen. Write down the title of the article, title of the journal, and author's name in the second column below. Using the same search terms, conduct a Google search and write down the first three sources of information that appear in the results list.

Government Document Source	Information Science Database	Google

Be prepared to report on the similarities and differences of your search results.
Participation Credit (up to 20 points)—Please print clearly!!!!

Student Name	E-mail address

Appendix 14.3: Government Documents and Information Science Journals Worksheet: Spring 2006

IST301X: The Information Environment
Prof. Bernnard / Prof. Mackey
Spring 2006
Government documents and information science journals
10 Participation Points

1. What is your topic?

2. What is your research question?

3. What is your tentative thesis statement?

Appendix 14.4: Government Documents and Information Science Journals Worksheet: 10 Participation Points

IST301X: The Information Environment
Prof. Bernnard / Prof. Mackey
Spring 2006
Government documents and information science journals
10 Participation Points

1. As a team, compare your preliminary thesis statements and identify keywords for a government documents search:

2. Review the hand-out and identify the resource in which you will search for a government document on your topic. What is the name of this resource?

3. Identify one student from your team to conduct the search for the class (if someone from your team has a wireless laptop, try the search before demonstrating to the class).

4. How does your team reflect on these searches? What went well? What could be improved? Would you repeat this searc\h for your own research paper? If not, what would you change?

Index

About the Editors

Trudi E. Jacobson is Head of User Education Programs at the State University of New York (SUNY) at Albany, and an adjunct faculty member at the School of Information Science and Policy at the same institution. She coordinates and teaches in the undergraduate Information Literacy course program. Her professional interests include the use of critical thinking and active learning activities in the classroom. She is the co-author, with Lijuan Xu, of *Motivating Students in Information Literacy Classes* (Neal-Schuman, 2004), co-editor of *Teaching the New Library to Today's Users* (Neal-Schuman, 2000) and *Teaching Information Literacy Concepts: Activities and Frameworks from the Field* (Library Instruction Publications, 2001), and editor of *Critical Thinking and the Web: Teaching Users to Evaluate Internet Resources* (Library Instruction Publications, 2000). She has published articles in a number of journals, including *The Journal of General Education, College & Research Libraries, portal, Journal of Academic Librarianship, Research Strategies, College Teaching,* and *The Teaching Professor*. She is the editor of *Public Services Quarterly*. She may be contacted by e-mail at tjacobson@uamail.albany.edu.

Thomas P. Mackey, PhD, is Assistant Professor in the Department of Information Studies in the College of Computing and Information at the State University of New York (SUNY) at Albany. He has been teaching information literacy since 2000 and has co-authored several articles on this topic. In 2003 he worked with the Middle States

Commission on Higher Education (MSCHE) as a member of the Advisory Panel on Information Literacy to publish a guidebook on integrating information literacy in the curriculum. His teaching and research interests also include Web-based multimedia, Web usability, Web accessibility, social informatics, and social software (blogging, wikis, and RSS). He may be contacted by e-mail at mackey@albany.edu.

About the Contributors

Deborah Bernnard is Associate Librarian at the Thomas E. Dewey Graduate Library, University at Albany, SUNY. Her primary responsibilities are as User Education Librarian and Information Science bibliographer. Deborah holds an MLS from the University at Albany and a BA in political science from Fairfield University. Her research interests include user interaction with library systems and information literacy. Deborah is the 2005–2006 recipient of the University at Albany Award for Excellence in Librarianship and President of the Eastern New York Chapter of the Association of College and Research Libraries (ENY/ACRL) for the 2006–2007 year. She may be contacted by e-mail at dbernnard@uamail.albany.edu.

Joel Burkholder is currently Instruction Librarian and coordinator the information literacy program at York College of Pennsylvania. His primary research interests include the information-seeking behavior of students and their perceptions of information literacy. He may be contacted by e-mail at jburkhol@ycp.edu.

Patricia J. Campbell is Professor of Political Science at the University of West Georgia. She has numerous publications, including the edited work *Democratization and the Protection for Human Rights: Challenges and Contradictions*, and articles in various journals, including *International Journal of Feminist Politics, Africa Studies Quarterly, Third World*

Quarterly, College Teaching, and *Politics & Policy.* She is currently working with Christy Stevens to integrate information literacy into her courses. She may be contacted by e-mail at pcampbel@westga.edu.

Susan Campbell has been Library Director at York College of Pennsylvania for twenty-one years. She directed the development of the College's Information Literacy core course and was its coordinator for seven years. Other research interests include library design and renovation, library staff reorganization, and library-community partnerships. She may be contacted by e-mail at scampbel@ycp.edu.

Alice Crosetto, MA, MEd, MLS, is currently Acquisitions Librarian for the University of Toledo, Toledo, Ohio. She was Head of Instructional Media and Technical Services at the Ralph M. Besse Library of Ursuline College, Pepper Pike, Ohio, for seven years. She has taught at both the high school and the university level and has spent many years as a librarian in college and school libraries in the Cleveland and Youngstown, Ohio, areas. She may be contacted at alice.crosetto@utoledo.edu.

Cecilia Danks is Assistant Professor at the University of Vermont. She teaches environmental studies, community forestry, and forest certification. Her scholarship there focuses on institutional issues in community-based approaches to sustainable forestry and collaborative processes in natural resource management. Cecilia received her PhD from the University of California, Berkeley, in wildland resource science and her BA from Williams College, where she majored in biology and did a coordinate major in environmental studies. She may be contacted by e-mail at cecilia.danks@uvm.edu.

Grace Peña Delgado graduated from the University of California, Los Angeles, in 2000, earning a doctorate degree in American history. She is currently working on a book, *Making the Chinese Mexican: Race and Transnationalism at the U.S.-Mexico Border, 1882–1943* (under active review at Stanford University Press), and has published several articles in borderlands studies. Dr. Delgado was an Assistant Professor in the Chicano and Latin Studies department at California State University, Long Beach until spring 2006. She taught courses on the Chicano and Latino experience, U.S. social history, U.S.-Mexico border history, Asian and Latino immigration, and women's studies. Her courses combine traditional face-to-face instruction with multimedia and e-learning environments. Dr. Delgado is currently an Assistant Professor of History and Religious Studies at Pennsylvania State University. She may be contacted by e-mail at gdelgado@ psu.edu.

Dominic DelliCarpini is Writing Program Administrator of York College of Pennsylvania. His research interests, grounded in the work of John Dewey, focus on the ways that rhetoric and writing can develop more informed workers and citizens. His book on this topic, *Composing a Life's Work: Writing, Citizenship, and Your Occupation,* 2005, was published by Longman's Press. He is the co-editor, with Jack Selzer, of *Conversations: Readings for Writing* and an Executive Board member of the Council of Writing Program

Administrators. His article "Composition, Literary Studies and the End(s) of Civic Education" recently appeared in *Composition and/or Literature: The End(s) of Education* (NCTE Press, 2006). He may be contacted by e-mail at dcarpini@ycp.edu.

Elizabeth A. Dupuis is Associate University Librarian for Educational Initiatives and Director of Doe/Moffitt Libraries at the University of California, Berkeley. She received her BA. in English and MS in library and information science from the University of Illinois at Urbana, Champaign. Prior to this position, she was Head of Instructional Services at University of California, Berkeley, Head of the Digital Information Literacy Office at the University of Texas at Austin, and project manager for the award-winning educational site TILT. She has served on committees for organizations such as the Association of College and Research Libraries and the Institute for Information Literacy and was recognized as a 2004–2006 Research Library Leadership Fellow by the Association of Research Libraries. She is currently Project Director for the Mellon Library/Faculty Fellowship for Undergraduate Research at Berkeley. She may be contacted by e-mail at edupuis@library.berkeley.edu.

Margaret Fain is Head of Public Services at Kimbel Library, Coastal Carolina University, and also serves as Information Literacy Coordinator. She has published articles and chapters on plagiarism, freshman English research assignments, and cross-department training. Co-presentations with Sara Sanders include sessions at the Southeastern Linguistics Association on politically correct language and the Inquiry-based Word Study. She may be contacted by e-mail at margaret@coastal.edu.

Marjorie Ginsberg heads the Basic Skills Program at William Paterson University of New Jersey and is Acting Reading Coordinator. She has been a member of the English Department faculty for ten years and received her PhD in English from the University of Iowa. She may be contacted by e-mail at ginsbergm@wpunj.edu.

Dorothy F. Glew, MLS, PhD, has been Reference/Public Services Librarian in Reeves Library, Moravian College, and Moravian Theological Seminary for ten years. Three years ago she became Coordinator of Instruction, and in that capacity she heads the library's information literacy initiative. To supplement and enhance the librarians' formal teaching of information literacy competencies, she created an online research tutorial. She has a chapter in the most recent publication of the Active Learning Series, *Empowering Students 11; Teaching Information Literacy Concepts with Hands-on and Minds-on Activities.* She is a contributor to *Renaissance Women Online*, a subset of the Brown University *Women Writers Online Project.* As Chairperson of the Lehigh Valley Chapter of the Pennsylvania Library Association she oversaw the planning of the chapter's annual conference. She was a recipient of the American Library Association's 1999 EBSCO Conference Scholarship, which funded her attendance at the American Library Association Annual Conference in New Orleans. In 2004 she was awarded a grant to underwrite a program at Moravian in commemoration of the centennial of Isaac Bashevis Singer. She may be contacted by e-mail at medfg01@moravian.edu.

Shonah A. Hunter is Professor in the Department of Biological Sciences at Lock Haven University of Pennsylvania. She earned her BS in zoology at University of Arkansas, Fayetteville, and her MA and PhD in zoology at Southern Illinois University, Carbondale. Since 1989, she has been at Lock Haven University teaching the introductory biology courses for science majors, as well as upper-level ecology courses. Over the years she has participated in several workshops and grants that emphasize hands-on and inquiry-based learning in the sciences. She has also collaborated for many years with library faculty to integrate information literacy activities and assignments into her courses. She believes that teaching students information-seeking strategies is another example of inquiry-based learning and is necessary for them to develop as scientists. She may be contacted by e-mail at shunter@lhup.edu.

Sara K. Kearns is currently Assistant Professor and Instruction Coordinator for Kansas State University Libraries. The author of "Marketing Library Service Assessment," (published in *Technical Services Quarterly, 2004*) she received her MLS from Catholic University of America. She may be contacted by email at skearns@ksu.edu.

Laurie A. Kutner, Library Associate Professor at the University of Vermont, has been working in the Information and Instruction Department there since 1991, performing general reference and instruction duties. She specializes in environmental information and works closely with the Environmental Program at the University of Vermont to incorporate information literacy instruction directly into their curriculum. Her research interests include a focus on information literacy training for students involved in interdisciplinary areas of study, and understanding the research needs of interdisciplinary scholars. Kutner received her MLS from Syracuse University in 1998, an MA in Anthropology from Syracuse University in 1985, and a BA in Anthropology from SUNY Oneonta in 1980. She may be contacted by e-mail at laurie.kutner@uvm.edu.

Susan C. Luévano is Librarian in athropology, Spanish, and ethnic and women's studies at California State University, Long Beach (CSULB). A graduate of the University of Oregon, School of Library Science, she has worked in academic libraries in California and Texas for over thirty years. A tenured full-librarian, she regularly conducts information competency classes for students and faculty at CSULB. She participated on the Curriculum Team, which developed the CSULB Information Literacy Minimum Standards in 1997. She was awarded a California State University information competence grant in 2001 to work with the CSULB black studies faculty and in 2004 to work with the Chicano and Latino studies faculty. Luévano has presented at local, state and national conferences on the project's outcomes. She is the editor and author of *Immigrant Politics and the Public Library* (Greenwood, 2001). She may be contacted by e-mail at sluevano@csulb.edu.

Linda Martin is Adjunct Instructor in the English Department at Coastal Carolina University. She received her BA and MAT degrees from Coastal and has been a co-presenter during the South Carolina Teachers of English conference. She is currently involved in creating an English 101 syllabus combining civic engagement and popular culture. She may be contacted by e-mail at lmartin1@coastal.edu.

Christina Maslach is Vice Provost for Undergraduate Education and Professor of Psychology at the University of California, Berkeley. She received her AB, magna cum laude, in social relations from Harvard–Radcliffe College and her PhD in psychology from Stanford University. She has conducted research in a number of areas within social and health psychology and is best known as one of the pioneering researchers on job burnout and the author of the Maslach Burnout Inventory (MBI), the most widely used research measure in the burnout field. Among her many honors, Maslach received national recognition in 1997 as "Professor of the Year," an award made by the Carnegie Foundation and the Council for the Advancement and Support of Education (CASE). In addition, she has served as President of the Western Psychological Association, is a recipient of the Distinguished Teaching Award and the Social Sciences Service Award from the University of California, Berkeley, and was selected as a Fellow of the American Association for the Advancement of Science (which cited her "for groundbreaking work on the applications of social psychology to contemporary problems"). She is co-Principal Investigator of the Mellon Library/Faculty Fellowship for Undergraduate Research at Berkeley. She may be contacted by e-mail at maslach@berkeley.edu.

Sarah McDaniel is Instructional Design and Assessment Librarian in the Doe/Moffitt Libraries at the University of California, Berkeley. She received her BA from the University of Wisconsin, Madison, and her MA and MLIS from the University of Wisconsin, Milwaukee. Before coming to UC Berkeley she worked as Instructional Services Coordinator for the Information Services Division at the University of Southern California. Her past publications and presentations have addressed topics such as working with graduate student instructors to facilitate undergraduate research, research assignment design, and student-centered instruction. As Assessment Consultant for the Mellon Library/Faculty Fellowship for Undergraduate Research at Berkeley, she works with faculty to embed assessment of student learning into research assignments. She may be contacted by e-mail at smcdanie@library.berkeley.edu.

Steve McKinzie is currently Library Director at Catawba College. Originally from Texas, he did graduate work in history at both East Carolina and Vanderbilt, where he also received his MLS in 1988. Shortly afterward, he began working as a librarian at Dickinson College, where he labored respectively as the documents librarian, head of serials, head of reference, and chair or director of the library, before moving to North Carolina in 2006 to assume the directorship of the library at Catawba College. His research interests include virtual reference, information literacy, collection development, library management, and librarianship as a profession. He may be contacted by e-mail at smckinzi@catawba.edu.

Dianne Runnestrand, PhD, is Education Unit Leader for graduate and undergraduate programs and Director of the Master Apprenticeship Program (MAP) at Ursuline College, Pepper Pike, Ohio. Throughout Dr. Runnestrand's professional career she has been an active supporter of libraries and librarians. She received a $100,000 National Library of Medicine Rural Library Coordination Grant to develop mobile medical rural libraries in New Mexico and a $300,000 Health Care Financing Grant, Information Sharing: The

Key to Survival in a Frontier State, to develop information sharing strategies among several Montana health agencies. She served on the governor of Montana's Distribution of Health Information Task Force. She may be contacted by e-mail at DRunnestrand@ursuline.edu.

Sara Sanders is Chair of the Department of English, Communication, and Journalism at Coastal Carolina University. Her PhD is in linguistics, and she has published research on language variety, listening comprehension, communicative language teaching, and the effect of political correctness on language change. She may be contacted by e-mail at sara@coastal.edu.

Cynthia D. Schrager received her BA in English from Wesleyan University and her PhD in English from the University of California, Berkeley. She taught as a lecturer in the literature Board at the University of California, Santa Cruz. In 1997, she returned to Berkeley as a staff member in the Office of Undergraduate Research to serve as the first program coordinator for the Robert and Colleen Haas Scholars Program, an interdisciplinary undergraduate research program. Since 2001, she has served as Special Assistant to the Vice Provost for Undergraduate Education working on a wide variety of undergraduate education program and policy issues. She is a member of the Steering Committee of the Mellon Library/Faculty Fellowship for Undergraduate Research at Berkeley. She may be contacted by e-mail at schrager@berkeley.edu.

Tim Silvestri is Assistant Director of the Lafayette College Counseling Center and Adjunct Faculty. He received a BA from Muhlenberg College and his PhD in counseling psychology from Lehigh University. His areas of expertise include multicultural issues, addictions, and performance concerns. His research has been published in the *Journal of Counseling & Development* and in *Racial and Ethnic Identity in School Practices*. He may be contacted by e-mail at silvestt@lafayette.edu.

Christy R. Stevens is currently Humanities Librarian at California State University, Sacramento. Previously, she was an assistant professor and instructional servises librarian at the University of West Georgia (UWG), where she worked with Dr. Patricia Campbell to integrate information literacy into the political science and global studies curricula. Prior to earning her MA in library science from the University of Iowa, she earned MA degrees in woman studies and English from San Diego State University and the University of California at Irvine, respectively. She has taught numerous writing and literature courses over the years in addition to a for-credit information literacy course. Her current research interests include information literacy instruction; faculty-librarian collaborations; and the connections among lifelong learning, social capital, global citizenship, and information literacy. She may be contacted by e-mail at stevensc@library.csus.edu.

Marcia G. Stockham (MA in library science, University of Missouri, Columbia) is Associate Professor and Education Librarian for Kansas State University Libraries. She has co-authored publications on the topics of virtual reference and distance learning library services. She may be contacted by e-mail at stockham@ksu.edu.

Lori J. Toedter, PhD, is Professor of Psychology and former Department Chair at Moravian College in Bethlehem, PA. She is a licensed clinical psychologist specializing in health psychology and for the past twenty-four years has regularly taught courses for the department in the clinical\counseling track, including Abnormal Psychology, Tests & Measurement, and Personality. For the past fifteen years she has also served as research curriculum consultant to the medicine and surgery residency programs at Easton Hospital in Easton, Pennsylvania. It is in that capacity that Dr. Toedter began to teach and conduct research on evidence-based practice in medicine. With colleague Lora Thompson, MSLIS, AHIP, she has conducted workshops for and presented papers to residency program directors in both medicine and surgery on how to integrate evidence-based medicine into daily teaching and practice. Most recently she published the lead article in the evidence-based surgery section of the *Journal of the American College of Surgeons*, entitled "Training Surgeons to *Do* Evidence-Based Surgery: A Collaborative Approach," with co-authors Thompson and attending surgeon Dr. Chand Rohatgi. Integrating evidence-based decision-making principles into undergraduate education through her collaborative pseudoscience course is the logical extension of this work. She may be contacted by e-mail at meljt01@moravian.edu.

James B. Tuttle II, PhD, received his BA in English (with distinction) and French, and his MA in English literature, from James Madison University; he earned his PhD in education curriculum and instruction from the University of Virginia. He has won several awards as a public school teacher, including the Richmond *Times-Dispatch* Journalism Teacher of the Year award. He taught at Dickinson College prior to joining the faculty at Shepherd University, where he is currently a member of the Department of Education and principal investigator for the West Virginia Professional Development School Initiative. Dr. Tuttle has published research in educational fields ranging from systems engineering to school renovation. He may be contacted by e-mail at jtuttle@shepherd.edu.

Nancy J. Weiner is Reference Librarian at Cheng Library and serves as Coordinator of Library's User Education Program at William Paterson University of New Jersey. She holds an MLS from Rutgers University and an MA in media studies from William Paterson University. She may be contacted by e-mail at weinern@wpunj.edu.

Karin E. Westman (PhD, Vanderbilt University) is Associate Professor of English at Kansas State University, where she teaches courses on modern and contemporary British literature and women's literature. She has published essays on Virginia Woolf, A. S. Byatt, J. K. Rowling, Georgette Heyer, and information literacy, as well as *Pat Barker's Regeneration: A Reader's Guide* (Continuum, 2001). She is currently completing her second book, *The New Realism: British Women Novelists since 1950*. She may be contacted by e-mail at westmank@ksu.edu.

Polly Wilkenfeld, MLS, is Head of Reference and Instruction Services at the Ralph M. Besse Library of Ursuline College, Pepper Pike, Ohio, where she coordinates all information literacy sessions. She has taught credit and non-credit courses on information skills and is currently working on a graduate initiative in information literacy for Ursuline College. She has spent many years as a librarian in college and school libraries in both the Cleveland and New York City areas. She may be contacted by e-mail at pwilkenfeld @ursuline.edu.

Elsa E. Winch is Assistant Professor in Stevenson Library at Lock Haven University of Pennsylvania. She is also Instruction Coordinator and Biology Liaison Librarian She earned her BA in humanities at Oklahoma State University and her MA in library and information science and MA in art history at Indiana University, Bloomington. Since 1991, she has taught and coordinated information literacy instruction throughout the campus. She has been active in developing information literacy general education requirements and has served as the chair of the General Education Committee for many years. She believes integrating information literacy into the curriculum is necessary to develop lifelong learners. She may be contacted by e-mail at ewinch@lhup.edu.

Lijuan Xu is Library Instruction Coordinator at Lafayette College. Prior to her work at Lafayette, she was User Education/Reference Librarian at the University at Albany, SUNY. In 2005, her co-authored book with Trudi E. Jacobson *Motivating Students in Information Literacy Classes* (Neal-Schuman, 2004) received the ACRL Instruction Section's publication award. She holds a MLS from Clarion University of Pennsylvania and a BA in library science from Wuhan University, China. She may be contacted by e-mail at xul@lafayette.edu.